All Things New
God's plan to renew our world

MICK POPE

a. Acorn
Press

Published by Acorn Press

An imprint of Bible Society AustraliaACN 148 058 306

Charity licence 19 000 528

GPO Box 4161

Sydney NSW 2001

Australia

www.acornpress.net.au | www.biblesociety.org.au

ISBN 978-0-647-53341-3

First published by Morning Star Publishing in 2018,
ISBN 978-0-648-37658-3

NATIONAL LIBRARY OF AUSTRALIA

A catalogue record for this work is available from the National Library of Australia

Design and typesetting: John Healy

Contents

Contents

AUTHOR'S INTRODUCTION

Some readers may know of the late John Chapman. John was an evangelist and gifted communicator with a passion for training preachers. When I first started to learn to preach, I attended his preaching workshops three years running just to hear him speak. One of his standard jokes was that eschatology was a great name for a cat but not a word to use in a sermon. However, I'm going to use the word eschatology quite a bit in this book because I think it is an important word for us to understand.

I was very blessed to launch *A Climate of Justice: Loving Your Neighbour in a Warming World* at the 2017 Justice Conference in Melbourne. In it, I argued that to love God means to love our neighbour, and to love our neighbour means to care about justice issues like poverty, aid and development, slavery, refugees and asylum seekers, and the gap between Aboriginal and Torres Strait Islander peoples and non-indigenous Australians in important social measures. Moreover, to care about those issues means to care about climate change. When I heard that the theme for the 2018 conference would be 'all things new', taken from Revelation 21:5, I knew that I had another book to write. Because of that word: eschatology.

Eschatology is the branch of theology that studies the end times or last things. In the Old Testament, it is represented by the phrase 'the Day of the Lord.' In the New Testament, it is associated with the return of Christ, the resurrection of the dead, and judgement of all people.

I've found over the years that my theological education can be a curse. I sing in church, and often choke on words. You see, for me, heaven has become something of a dirty word. Not because I don't believe in heaven, but because I believe we misunderstand the word, misuse the word, and misapply the word. Christians often think of heaven as a disembodied place, our final destination, and our ultimate hope. The first idea is plain wrong, the other two, confused. How, for example, can we really engage in acts of justice if we think that this world will pass away, discarded as no longer necessary? Don't we undercut ourselves and our compassion for this world? Aren't we being inconsistent, hypocritical even?

But what if 'all things new' really meant that all things will be renewed? We know in our hearts that all things need to be made new but often times think that means being scrapped and starting over, like that sketch we tear off the art pad and throw in the bin. So, the aim of this book is quite straightforward: to show that all things need making new, to show that 'all things' really does mean all things, to show that being made new means being renewed rather than thrown away, and to show that this work of making all things new has already begun. God's plan to renew our world is our mission.

In more fancy terms, what I want to do is to understand the world theologically, so that we might speak and act prophetically, and live proleptically. To understand the world theologically means to understand it as in need of renewal by God, and indeed that this work has begun. Secondly, to speak and act prophetically doesn't necessarily mean foretelling the future, although it's clear sometimes it does (see for example Deut 18:22). In the case of climate change and our other devastating ecological impacts, we are called to be ecoprophets, studying seriously and supporting what scientists tell us. However, prophets were usually more interested in forth-telling about God's character, human sin, and divine judgement. This means that that we need to point towards both the need for repentance and renewal and to affirm that this renewal is occurring.

Finally, to live proleptically is to live hopefully in anticipation of the completion of this renewal, to live as if this renewal were already happening, and to make God's plan to renew our world our mission.

I think this point is well illustrated by British intellectual, Terry Eagleton

> the kingdom of God brings to fruition a pattern of transfigurative moments immanent within it, a fractured narrative of justice and comradeship which runs against the grain of what one might call its central plot.[1]

---

1 Terry Eagleton, *Hope Without Optimism* (New Haven: Yale University Press, 2015), 28.

Notice how he links the return of Christ to make 'all things new' as the kingdom of God summing up all of the moments before it. Acts of justice, beauty, and evangelism are, as Tom Wright states, all parts of the mission of the church as we image the future world in the present.[2] They are 'transfigurative moments' because the glory of God that is sometimes hidden by the brokenness of the world is revealed in them. The other aspect of Eagleton's imagery is the 'fractured narrative of justice and comradeship.' This idea of fracture reminds me of the cover to this book, of kintsugi, the method of repairing broken pottery with gold. The eschaton is that gold, bringing together the pieces of what we have been doing to make something new and more beautiful than before, just like the resurrected and transformed Christ still bears the wounds of his crucifixion.

There's much ground to cover, and just a few words in which to do it, but hopefully this book will help open your eyes to just how big God's plan for this world really is!

---

2 Tom Wright, *Surprised by Hope* (London: SPCK, 2007).

Acknowledgements

The bulk of this book was written sitting on a sofa in my lounge room in Melbourne. My house sits on stolen land, belonging to the people of the Kulin nation. Their sovereignty was never ceded and I pay my respects to their elders past, present, and emerging. As for the writing of the book, it is more than the work of my hands. My thanks go to Paul and the amazing Zara of The Justice Conference for allowing me to once more contribute to the conference in my own small way. Thanks to John and Amanda from Morning Star for their amazing work. Thanks to Claire for her reading and editing as well as her ongoing inspiration, and to Dom for looking over the study questions. Thanks to Jo for comments and additions from the Renew Our World perspective. Thanks to Kuki for passing on information about food banks in India. Viv has written a wonderful introduction for which I am very grateful, and Ruth and Mark wrote some kind words of endorsement. Thanks too for Joel, Luke, and Dawn for their creative work contributions and permission to reuse their work.

My last thanks are somewhat ironic. Anna Jane was going to write a foreword to the book, but events in the US with a very hectic hurricane season overtook her. Sea level rise and increased rainfall potential, both due to rising temperatures, have made these phenomena all the more dangerous. Not only do our thoughts and prayers go to those affected in the US and Philippines as I write, it makes the task of advocating for action on climate change all the more urgent.

INTRODUCTION

By Viv Benjamin

We live in a world that is broken, on a planet in crisis. But at the end of the world, just when we fear destruction, God reveals, *"Behold, I am making all things new!"*

In this important and timely book, Dr Mick Pope artfully depicts *kintsugi*, the practice of repairing broken pottery with gold, to illustrate how God will not discard our broken world but is restoring everything to be even more beautiful than before. God is making all things new.

In the face of crisis, we have a choice: will we give up hope, or will we join in God's mission to renew our world?

I remember a moment when this choice hit home for me.

It was November, 2013. I will never forget watching in horror as headlines broke news that Super Typhoon Haiyan was about to hit the Philippines, where my mum's family live. It was described as the strongest tropical cyclone to strike land in the course of human history.

As the hell storm hit, I can't really express the agony of waiting to find out if my loved ones were okay. I messaged my cousins frantically, without response. I knew they would have lost all power and phone lines. But it felt like an eternity. All I could do was watch the news, as the death toll continued to mount. I remember a news report that the typhoon had dislodged a boulder the size of a blue whale. It was the deadliest Philippine typhoon on record, with 11 million people affected and at least 6,300 people killed.

At the same time as the typhoon wreaked death and destruction in the Philippines, the world's leaders gathered at the UN climate summit in Poland to negotiate global climate action.

Yeb Sano, the Philippines' delegate, made the opening address. With eyes brimming and voice breaking, he said, "To anyone who continues to deny the reality that is climate change, I dare you to get off your ivory tower and away from the comfort of your armchair. What my country is going through as a result of this extreme climate event is madness. The climate crisis is madness. We can stop this madness."

As communications returned, I heard how the typhoon had ripped the roof off our family home, how my cousins were in hospital, how there was no safe drinking water, and how diseases were spreading like wildfire. But we were lucky. My family survived, unlike thousands of our neighbours who perished. My family rebuilt, unlike millions of our neighbours left homeless.

The experience left me shaken, but with a new determination to act.

Two years later, I found myself campaigning internationally on climate change in the lead up to the historic Paris Climate Summit. For the first time in history, the world committed to a landmark global agreement to tackle climate change and help the poorest people adapt. Now it is up to us to uphold the promise to protect people and planet.

The challenge is real. Our poorest neighbours are hit hardest by climate change, despite having contributed the least to the problem. The changing climate is already producing more frequent and more fatal floods, fires, famine, hurricanes, heatwaves and humanitarian disasters. For millions of precious people made in the image of God, particularly the poorest people, this is a matter of survival. This is a matter of justice.

Right now, we stand at a unique and urgent moment. We are perhaps the first generation to witness the dangerous consequences of climate change, but we're also the last generation with the chance to prevent the worst impacts. We have a choice to make. Will we sit back and give up hope, or will we act?

God has given us everything we need, if we choose to accept it. We can change our ways and choose clean renewable energy, if we harness the unending power provided by God in the sun and wind and waves. We can build a more just and restorative economy for all, if we have the will to change.

The good news is that God is already on the move.

God is at work to make all things new, and we're called to be part of it.

This is who we are as Christians. This is our purpose. To follow Jesus means to love our neighbours. To bear good news in a world of bad news. To care for the good creation that God has made. To bring justice and restoration. This is our mission. To help make all things new.

This beautiful book invites us to join God's grand plan to renew our world.

Chapter 1 — Houston, We Have a Problem

Where were you when ...?

They say that a generation can be identified by those events where you ask your friends 'where were you when ...?' The events that people identify with tell you a lot about what is important to them. Where were you when JFK was shot? When Neil Armstrong stepped onto the moon? When the Spice Girls broke up? The title for this chapter is a misquote from one of those kinds of events. On 13 April 1970, the lunar bound Apollo 13 crew ran into problems. It is a testament to human hubris that we could conceive of flinging ourselves into the inky void of space in the hope of conquering the moon. In another sense, it is a testament to human ingenuity that it was accomplished, and that on this occasion, a disaster was averted and three lives saved. The real quote was not 'Houston, we have a problem.' Instead, astronauts Jack Swigert and James Lovell said 'Houston, we've had a problem.'[1]

Regardless of its lack of historical precision, 'Houston, we have a problem' makes a good title for the first chapter in a book that looks at the idea that God is making all things new. This is because that statement begs the question of why God needs to make all things new in the first place. You probably have a few ideas already from a casual look at the news, or maybe even in the mirror. Perhaps we could say, 'Heaven, we have a problem' instead. I think this problem is well illustrated by a similarly memorable event from my own lifetime, an event now referred to by the date on which it happened: September 11, 2001, or simply 9/11.

9/11 is understood by many as a landmark event in history, when the world changed permanently. Nineteen men hijacked four commercial airplanes and crashed them into the World Trade Centre in New York,

---

[1] Michael S. Rosenwald, "'Houston, we have a problem': The amazing history of the iconic Apollo 13 misquote," *The Washington Post*, 13 April, 2017, accessed 17 January, 2018, https://www.washingtonpost.com/news/retropolis/wp/2017/04/13/houston-we-have-a-problem-the-amazing-history-of-the-iconic-apollo-13-misquote/?utm_term=.d091d33d9314.

the Pentagon in Washington, and into the ground near Shanksville, Pennsylvania. In the Pennsylvania crash, it is believed that passengers and crew attempted to retake control of the plane. A total of 2,977 people lost their lives that day.[2] The images of commercial airliners crashing into buildings, and the eventual collapse of the twin towers, will forever haunt the minds of people all over the world.

What is even more haunting for me is the imagery of the 'Falling Man.'[3] People were faced with a stark choice: either be burnt alive or suffocate due to the smoke, or fall to their deaths. The iconic image of the Falling Man is of someone who took control of their fate. We don't know for certain who the Falling Man was; he may have been Jonathan Briley. Briley was a preacher's son. He had siblings. A wife. He worked for Windows on the World, a restaurant on the 106th and 107th floors of the World Trade Centre. All of this he left behind, jumping into the void. Photographer Richard Drew has recorded for all time the tragedy of a choice between Scylla and Charybdis, what sculptor Eric Fischl called the 'extremity of choice,' which he captured in his bronze sculpture, the 'Tumbling Woman.' Yet Drew's photo was soon covered up and dismissed as 'disaster porn.' Ultimately, any comment on the disaster, in words or pictures, fails to fully do it justice. It seems as if we can't face the depth of the evil involved. And evil is a word that was quickly invoked following the events of 9/11.

The evil that men do[4]

The day after 9/11, US President George W. Bush addressed the nation.[5] In this short address, he used the word evil four times. Lives

---

2 CNN Library, "September 11th Terror Attacks Fast Facts," *CNN International Edition*, Updated August 24, 2017, accessed 21 March, 2018, https://edition.cnn.com/2013/07/27/us/september-11-anniversary-fast-facts/index.html.

3 Tom Junod, "The Falling Man: An unforgettable story," *Esquire*, 9 September, 2016, accessed 21 March, 2018, https://www.esquire.com/news-politics/a4803l/the-falling-man-tom-junod/.

4 This section title is taken from a song by the heavy metal band Iron Maiden. I'm not suggesting women do no evil, but 11 September and the following military response were all due to the decisions of men. So, if the shoe fits....

5 George W. Bush, "Bush addresses nation: Full text," *BBC News*, 12 September, 2001, accessed 21 March, 2018, http://news.bbc.co.uk/2/hi/americas/1539328.stm.

were ended by 'evil, despicable acts of terror', 'evil acts,' and exhibited 'evil, the very worst of human nature.' Bush invoked Psalm 23, saying that the nation should not fear evil but be comforted (by God). The terrorist acts were an attack on freedom and the American way of life, an attack on a nation that is 'the brightest beacon for freedom and opportunity in the world.' Bush asserted that the military was ready for action and that the nation was still open for business. The 9/11 attacks had been aimed at the Pentagon, a symbol of American military might, and the World Trade Centre, symbolic of economic power. Bush's resolve was for 'justice and peace.' It is, however, questionable that the events that followed were just or that they resulted in peace.

George W. Bush was not the only one to use the language of evil. The Canadian Prime Minister Jean Chrétien claimed that every day practices and places were distorted by evil.[6] Likewise, British Prime Minister, Tony Blair, declared that 'mass terrorism is the new evil in our world today,' and that nations would 'have to come together to fight it together and eradicate this evil completely from our world.'[7] Apparently, evil was now something you can simply bomb into non-existence. British foreign secretary, Jack Straw, claimed that 'What we have witnessed on the TV screens from America are acts of evil and horror beyond the imagination of us.' This captures a sense of what evil is, something beyond rational thought (and bombs). The political use of the language of evil continues to this day. President Donald Trump recently declared that 'our eyes were opened to the depths of the evil we faced.'[8] He stated that the US was committed to 'destroying the enemies of all civilized people' and that nowhere was beyond their military grasp. Typically, less prosaic than his predecessors, Trump is at

---

6 Mark Kennedy, "Canada's 9/11, Part 1: Chretien urged calm amid chaos," *Postmedia News*, 3 September, 2001, accessed 21 March, 2018, http://www.canada.com/Canada+Part +Chretien+urged+calm+amid+chaos/5347551/story.html.

7 Michael White, and Patrick Wintour, "Blair calls for world fight against terror," *The Guardian*, 13 September, 2001, accessed 21 March, 2018, https://www.theguardian.com/ politics/2001/sep/12/uk.september11.

8 Glenn Thrush, "Trump Commemorates Sept. 11 Attacks With Vow to Conquer 'Evil'," *The New York Times,* 11 September, 2017, accessed 21 March, 2018, https://www.nytimes. com/2017/09/11/us/trump-commemorates-sept-11-attacks-with-vow-to-conquer-evil.html.

least bluntly honest. Dealing with evil, from his political point of view, means destroying your enemies.

Not all public discourse has followed this narrative. Prominent atheist and evolutionary biologist, Richard Dawkins, has repeatedly attacked the idea of religion, and it is arguable that 9/11 was religiously motivated and helped kick started the new atheism in response.[9] Dawkins controversially claimed that

> They might not be horrible people, they may be righteous people who believe they're doing right. I think the 9/11 hijackers all sincerely believed that they were doing the right and proper moral, religious thing. They were not in themselves evil. They were following their faith. And faith is pernicious because it can do that to people. It can do that to otherwise decent people.

In other words, the problem is not evil per se, but faith, in particular in this case, the Islamic faith of Osama bin Laden's Al-Qaeda, who claimed responsibility.[10] Evil ceases to be a person but an idea or, as Dawkins has written about on a number of occasions, a meme. He was accused of downplaying the evil of those involved in an attempt to smear religion. He seems to think that a solution to 'evil' is then the eradication of faith. In response to an interview question, 'Can religion be eradicated?' Dawkins responds

> Yes, because individuals clearly get rid of it, and they can be educated into realising the truth. Faith is the lack of evidence, and it shouldn't be that difficult to convince people that the right reason to believe something is that there is evidence for it.[11]

So, while Dawkins would use evidence and reason against the evil of faith, Blair was happy to use violence to combat violence. Notwithstanding Dawkins' anti-religious agenda, fellow new atheist,

---

9 Kashmira Gander, "Richard Dawkins says 9/11 hijackers weren't evil, prompts angry response from religious right," *The Independent,* 25 October, 2015, accessed 21 March, 2018, https://www.independent.co.uk/news/people/richard-dawkins-says-911-hijackers-werent-evil-prompts-angry-response-from-religious-right-a6708171.html."

10 CNN Library, *September 11th Terror Attacks Fast Facts.*

11 Isaac Chotiner, "Interview: Richard Dawkins Keeps Making New Enemies," *The New Republic,* 29 October, 2015, accessed 21 March, 2018, https://newrepublic.com/article/115339/richard-dawkins-interview-archbishop-atheism.

Christopher Hitchens, maintained that 'simply evil' was still the best description of what occurred.[12] Hitchens denies that there is any oppression of Islamic people, which is a very blinkered take on US foreign policy and ignores the claims of bin Laden himself. Likewise, he lampoons TV evangelists Jerry Falwell and Pat Robertson who claimed that the attacks were a punishment from heaven for American sinfulness. Typically, this will be whatever raises their political ire, not issues like the environment, or US foreign policy. To Hitchens, evil becomes an explanation that needs no explanation.

There are multiple issues with use of the language of evil in public discourse. Firstly, it quickly polarises the discussion of how to respond. While President Bush allowed that not all nations would provide troops, the choice was a stark: 'You're either with us or against us in the fight against terror.'[13] As if terror were something you could fight against any more than evil! Theologian, Tom Wright, affirms that the terror attacks were indeed evil but believes that the response was 'knee-jerk, unthinking, immature lashing out, which gets us nowhere.'[14] The bombing of Iraq and Afghanistan were the practical counterpart of philosophical theories that claim they solve the problem of evil. In other words, if you think you've solved evil either as a pure intellectual exercise or by violence, you're kidding yourself. This military response also trades on the myth that Hitchens supported: that the US was a 'pure, innocent victim' and the world can be neatly divided into good people (the US in particular) and evil people (in this case, Arabs). It is this kind of thinking that gave rise to the initial name for the military response, 'Operation Infinite Justice.'[15] Now, don't misunderstand me; it makes perfect sense to divide the 9/11 attacks into those carrying out evil acts versus their innocent and undeserving victims. That's not what

---

12 Christopher Hitchens, "Simply Evil: A decade after 9/11, it remains the best description and most essential fact about al-Qaida," *Slate*, 5 September, 2011, accessed 21 March, 2018, http://www.slate.com/news-and-politics/2018/03/fifteen-years-after-the-start-of-the-iraq-war-the-u-s-is-at-war-in-at-least-seven-countries.html.

13 CNN, "Bush says it is time for action," *CNN*, 6 November, 2001, accessed 21 March, 2018, http://edition.cnn.com/2001/US/11/06/ret.bush.coalition/index.html.

14 N. T. Wright, *Evil and the Justice of God* (London: SPCK, 2006), 11.

15 BBC News, "Infinite Justice, out - Enduring Freedom, in," *BBC News*, 25 September, 2001, accessed 21 March, 2018, http://news.bbc.co.uk/2/hi/americas/1563722.stm.

I'm arguing against. However, as Christians, what we need is not simply the ability to identify evil with others, our enemies real or imagined. We also need a robust understanding of evil that can be applied inward to ourselves and our own in-group.

Aleksandr Solzhenitsyn was a Russian novelist and historian, who was jailed for dissent and exiled to a gulag or labour camp. His dissent was to criticise Stalin in personal letters after observing the way in which the war was conducted on the Eastern Front. He wrote *The Gulag Archipelago*, a three–volume work on his experience in the gulag system. In this work, Solzhenitsyn recalls a long march on the way to the gulag with other Russian soldiers and German prisoners of war. As a former Russian officer, he was able to make other soldiers carry his suitcase. Solzhenitsyn reflects on how, during the war, he was prepared to do anything to serve the state, to become an executioner, and had held aspirations to enter Internal Affairs and join the secret police. Understanding the irony of his situation, Solzhenitsyn did not write a political expose, for he knew his own heart. This is articulated in a now famous quote:

If only there were evil people somewhere insidiously committing evil deeds, and it were necessary only to separate them from the rest of us and destroy them. But the line dividing good and evil cuts through the heart of every human being. And who is willing to destroy a piece of his own heart?[16]

Solzhenitsyn understood that it was hard for him to critique the regime that had imprisoned him, when he had been a part of it. This is not to say that we can't engage in a prophetic critique of the evil systems in which we are embedded, indeed it is a fundamental claim of this book that we must do so. But we first need to recognise where we stand in such networks of evil, that we are, in fact, complicit. We are not the 'good guys' collectively or individually in the way in which we like to think. Jesus said that we need to deal with our logs before dealing with the specs of others (Matt 7:1–5). While the Soviet system in its

---

16 Aleksandr I. Solzhenitsyn, Thomas P. Whitney (trans), The Gulag Archipelago 1918-1956: An Experiment in Literary Investigation, I-II (New York: Harper and Row Publishers, 1973), 168.

day, and many aspects of our current day, are more like a boreal forest than a log, should we want to speak prophetically, we need first to have our lips cleansed (Is 6).

So, when governments make pronouncements that 'they are evil' while 'we are the good guys,' we are right to be somewhat suspicious. This might seem like a typical leftie critique of the US and its allies. There is of no getting around the evil of Al-Qaeda, ISIS, the former Soviet regime, insert-your-favourite-bad-guy-here. But we need to hold our own governments to account as well. In the Hebrew scriptures, the strongest and most sustained prophetic critiques were reserved for Israel and Judah, not their neighbours. If our countries proclaim to be the good guys on the world stage, then the claim should hold up to scrutiny. But does it?

In the case of the response to 9/11, political scientist, Louise Richardson, has suggested that the US overreacted.[17] By this, Richardson doesn't mean the outpouring of public grief, particularly that of families of the victims. Instead, the unfolding military strategy was little more than the enacting of a doctrine of regime change in the region, aimed at getting rid of one-time ally Saddam Hussein. At its heart, the invasion of Iraq was a conflict over oil.[18] Furthermore, the Islamophobia, restrictions on civil liberties, and the re-emergence of the language of 'un-American' for those who oppose violence, demonstrates how ugly patriotism can become when it is united against a common enemy. Similar things were observed, albeit not to the same extent, in the other countries that formed part of the 'coalition of the willing,' (or as peace activists would have it, 'the coalition of the killing'). Our Australian Prime Minister claimed at the time that anti-war protesters, like myself who marched against the invasion, were giving 'comfort to Saddam Hussein.'[19] As I write, icasualties.org claims that 4,864 coalition lives

---

17 Thomas Mills, "Did the US overreact to 9/11?," *The Conversation*, 5 June, 2015, accessed 6 May, 2018, https://theconversation.com/did-the-us-overreact-to-9-11-42840.

18 Mick Pope, 'Oil and Blood on the Bayonet': Empire, Oil, War and Ecology in Anne Elvey, Deborah Guess, and Keith Dyer (eds), *Ecological Aspects of War: Religious and Theological Perspectives* (Adelaide: ATF, 2016).

19 Mark Riley, "PM denounces protesters for aiding Saddam," *Sydney Morning Herald*, 21 February, 2003, accessed 6 May, 1018, https://www.smh.com.au/articl

have been lost in Iraq, and 3,549 in Afghanistan, since 2003.[20] That's over twice the number of lives lost in the twin towers on 9/11. And what of civilians? The Watson Institute documents 31,149 deaths in Afghanistan, 22,100 in Pakistan, and estimates 137,000 to 165,000 deaths in Iraq.[21]

Philosopher, social critic, and activist, Noam Chomsky, asks whether there was an alternative to this prolonged military campaign.[22] If Osama bin Laden was responsible for masterminding the attacks, he was guilty of a 'crime against humanity.' So, surely a law abiding state would capture and try him?[23] While the Bush administration captured and interrogated (read tortured) suspected militants, it was the darling of the left, Barak Obama, who had bin Laden assassinated. Former West German Chancellor, Helmut Schmidt, described bin Laden's death as 'a violation of international law.'[24] When the good guys feel free to place themselves above the law, wherein does good lie? What value does law have?

Chomsky comments on the name of the operation to assassinate bin Laden, Operation Geronimo. Geronimo was the name of the Apache chief who led a resistance against the invaders, you know, the ones who 'won the west.' John Quincy Adams was the sixth president of the United States. Chomsky identifies him as the grand architect of the doctrine of 'manifest destiny' that resulted in the stealing of territory from Mexico and which has underpinned expansionist ideologies since then. Adams described the fate of the first nations under occupation as 'among the heinous sins of this nation.'[25] The choice of Geronimo as the name for an illegal operation carried out in a sovereign country that was

es/2003/02/20/1045638427837.html.

20 Iraq Coalition Casualty Count, accessed 6 May, 2018, http://icasualties.org/,

21 Watson Institute, "Costs of War," 2018, accessed 6 May, 2018, http://watson. brown.edu/costsofwar/figures/2016/direct-war-death-toll-iraq-afghanistan-and-pakistan-2001-370000.

22 Noam Chomsky, *9-11: Was there an Alternative?* (Crawley, Western Australia: UWA Publishing, 2011).

23 Chomsky, *9-11*, 22.

24 Chomsky, *9-11*, 27.

25 Chomsky, *9-11*, 36.

supposed to be an American ally – Pakistan – is historically tone deaf and reflective of an ongoing imperialism.

So why, in a book ostensibly about climate change, have we spent so long talking about the response to the evil of 9/11? Because this book also examines the New Testament book of Revelation, where evil, empire, and violence are front and centre. We need to start thinking about our place in things. For example, were you for or against the invasion of Iraq? Did the events of 9/11 make you more fearful of Muslim people? Did you feel united with others in fear and patriotism, or did you unite in love and prayer that violence would not win? Do you think that war achieves positive ends, or does the message of the Prince of Peace tell us that we need to find other ways to resolve our problems? And even if you didn't cheer the war, did you vote for the government who declared it? Did you march against it? If war is evil, what role do we ourselves play in that evil? Are we always to be plagued by war, or is the world slowly marching towards peace?

Are things getting any better?

Things can only get better

Physicist and TV personality, Brian Cox, was in a band before he became a scientist. The band, D:Ream, had a number one hit in the UK after which the title of the section is named. The phrase is something you might use to comfort someone going through a hard time. It's an aphorism, sometimes true in the short term, but the problem with life is that no one gets out alive. But does the idea apply to humanity as a whole? Is the world getting better? Or are people so evil that we expect that things can only get 'worser'? Under some theologies, humans are totally depraved and all we can expect is to see things get progressively worse before God comes down to destroy it all. Such is the understanding of much premillennialism, where the elect are raptured to heaven while those left behind suffer an increasingly decaying world. We examine this understanding briefly in chapter six. Yet, for thinkers like cognitive psychologist, Steven Pinker, the world is getting better.

Pinker is not on his own. I once attended a public lecture by futurist, Michio Kaku, the sort of talk where you hear about cancer killing nanobots, uploading our consciousness into computers, and other sci fi presented as our very real future. When it came time for questions from the floor, Kaku was typically dismissive of a question about environmental degradation. It is simply part of the price we must pay, he claimed, and we will move on. His response was illustrative of how he and his ilk live in a technological bubble, and how such considerations of the physical world fade in the bright lights of a techno utopia where we transcend our physical limitations. This is not to say that I want to baptise pessimism as the gospel, but a clear eyed realism takes the problems we are presented with at face value, rather than wishing them away.

Pinker seems to have shown that the world has gotten less violent over time in his 2012 book, *The Better Angels of our Nature*.[26] Rates of homicide have fallen by a factor of 50 and death in war by a factor of more than 20.[27] In his most recent book, *Enlightenment Now: The Case for Reason, Science, Humanism, and Progress*, Pinker claims that the world is a better place because of the Enlightenment and he takes on religious fundamentalism, postmodernism, and the extreme left and right for their denial of this fact.[28] Taking on the environmental movement, Pinker demurs from what he sees as moralistic fist shaking, preferring that that technology will solve all. Bring on nuclear power and genetically modified crops to power and feed our future. Progress is sustainable, so full steam ahead. After all, development is what is bringing wealth and movement out of poverty in countries like China and India, so how can we disapprove of capitalism and its many blessings?

However, Pinker is not without his critics. In a review of his book, Ian Goldin takes issue not with Pinker's claims for optimism, but with his fundamental premise.[29] Many of the Enlightenment's breakthroughs

---

26 Steven Pinker, *The Better Angels of Our Nature: Why Violence Has Declined* (London: Penguin Books, 2012).

27 Quoted in Andrew Anthony, "Steven Pinker: 'The way to deal with pollution is not to rail against consumption'," *The Guardian*, 11 February, 2018, accessed 6 May, 2018, https://www.theguardian.com/science/2018/feb/11/steven-pinker-enlightenment-now-interview-inequality-consumption-environment.

28 Steven Pinker, *Enlightenment Now: The Case for Reason, Science, Humanism, and Progress* (New York: Viking, 2018).

29 Ian Goldin, "The limitations of Steven Pinker's optimism," *Nature*, 16 February, 2018, accessed 6 May, 2018, https://www.nature.com/articles/d41586-018-02148-1.

(1715–1789) actually pre-date it, going back to the Renaissance (14th – 17th centuries). Likewise, both Renaissance and Enlightenment were tied to expansionism and empire building at the expense of indigenous cultures in the so-called 'new worlds', accompanied by wars, slavery, and genocide. Goldin notes that globalisation has bought both benefits and risks, particularly in the form of risks to ecosystems, which we will discuss in the next chapter. There has been a 'wider failure of global commons management' in the form of climate change. Goldin is also critical of Pinker's dismissal of inequality, as Pinker's statistics 'do not reflect recent sharp economic reversals in many places.' Goldin also highlights how complex and interconnected society has become with greater risks of 'pandemics, cascading financial crises and cyberattacks.' Ultimately, he sees Pinker's book as a welcome antidote for pessimism, something some Christians should embrace at one level. And at the same time, Pinker presents an unbalanced account of the past, present and future.

Optimism, however, can be problematic. Terry Eagleton sees optimism as banal and shallow, an outlook that is self-sustaining and illuminates facts from a particular angle in a way that is 'resistant to being refuted by them.' In other words, it is a view of the world that looks through that cliché of 'rose-tinted spectacles.'[30] Further, he sees optimism as essentially a conservative, ruling-class ideology that tells us things are basically ok and assures us that the future will be a benign version of the present. A form of fatalism, if you will.[31] Indeed, some forms of optimism can be critiqued on the grounds that they present a theodicy that makes evil necessary and understandable, rather than something to be defeated and that will probably always remain a mystery.[32] In this vein, Eagleton savages the book *The Rational Optimist* by Matt Ridley in the same way in which others have skewered Steven Pinker's works, as we saw earlier on. Ridley blithely ignores problems like poverty and climate change and, as a former banker, gives capitalism a free indulgence for its 2008 Global Financial Crisis sins.[33]

---

30 Terry Eagleton, *Hope Without Optimism* (New Haven: Yale University Press, 2015), 2.

31 Eagleton, *Hope Without Optimism*, 4.

32 Eagleton, *Hope Without Optimism*, 8.

33 Eagleton, *Hope Without Optimism*, 18.

Finally, historian, Peter Harrison, takes Pinker to task for his use of the concept of reason.[34] Most of the early figures of the Enlightenment were somewhat sceptical of reason. Philosopher, statesman and scientist, Francis Bacon, saw knowledge as a way of controlling nature for our own ends. He also said that 'the human intellect left to its own course is not to be trusted.' Philosopher, Immanuel Kant, who wrote a book entitled *Critique of Pure Reason*, said that 'reason alone can never produce any action ... Reason is, and ought only to be, the slave of the passions.' Philosopher, John Locke, believed that our knowledge is limited by 'the weakness of our faculties in this state of mediocrity.' Harrison further points out that, although many Enlightenment thinkers thought some arguments for God were invalid, they assumed rather than dismissed the idea of God. This is ironic. A Christian view of history is teleological, that is, history has a point and a direction. Harrison critiques Pinker for his secular teleology, a providential view of history that envisages that things have and 'can only get better.' But will technology save us from our climate disaster? What disaster?

Where were you when we broke 400?

Do you know where you were and what you were doing in September 2016? Not any particular day, but just anytime during that month. Where were you living? What were your concerns then? Something very important happened in September 2016, apart from my 47th birthday. A major milestone was reached. Due to the seasonal cycle of snow and ice over the northern hemisphere forests, the lowest value of carbon dioxide in the atmosphere occurs in September. In September of 2016, the value failed to fall below 400 parts per million. It won't return below this value in our lifetime, indeed in the lifetime of any human, for a very long time to come.[35]

Carbon dioxide is a greenhouse gas and is released when we burn fossil fuels, clear forests for agricultural land, or produce cement. Back

---

34 Peter Harrison, "The Enlightenment of Steven Pinker," *ABC Religion & Ethics*, 4 April, 2018, accessed 6 May, 2018, http://www.abc.net.au/religion/articles/2018/02/20/4806696.htm.
35 Brian Kahn, "The World Passes 400 PPM Threshold. Permanently," *Climate Central,* 27 September, 2016, accessed 4 May, 2018, http://www.climatecentral.org/news/world-passes-400-ppm-threshold-permanently-20738.

in 1824, French scientist, Joseph Fourier, discovered that the earth was warmer than it should be given its distance from the sun. In the 1860s, Englishman, John Tyndall, showed that gases including carbon dioxide, methane and water vapour act like blankets on a bed, trapping some of the heat. Before the start of the Industrial Revolution, when we started burning fossil fuels in large amounts, the amount of carbon dioxide in the atmosphere was 280 parts per million. That's about 700 litres of water in an Olympic sized swimming pool of 2,500,000 litres. While small in proportion, this concentration is powerful in effect. And the fifth assessment of the Intergovernmental Panel on Climate Change states with very high confidence that greenhouse gas concentrations are larger than they have been for the past 800,000 years!

The net result is that we have already enough greenhouse gases in the atmosphere to break the 1.5° C limit that Pacific Island nations sought at the Paris Conference of the Parties in December of 2015.[36] I've written a few times about the Pacific Island nations' plight because their fate is a damning indictment of our indifference.[37] As the atmosphere warms, so does sea water, which expands in volume. This effect, known as thermal expansion, together with the melting of glaciers and ice sheets, contributes to sea level rise.

This book is about 'the end of the world,' whatever that means. But did you know that sea level rise is slowly ending people's worlds right now? Take, for example, the Pacific Island nation of Tonga. I've had the pleasure of teaching Tongan students over the years. The Kingdom of Tonga is a group of 170 islands with a population of about 107,000. Like many Pacific Island nations, their islands are only a few metres above sea level. Every centimetre of sea level rise takes away more land, leaving what is left vulnerable to erosion. It is threatening fresh water supplies by polluting the water table and poisoning crops. Hotel manager, Vincent Morrish, tells of having to move the restaurant and

---

[36] John Upton, "UN Climate Pact Moves Closer to Taking Effect," *Climate Central,* 21 September, 2016, accessed 4 May, 2018, http://www.climatecentral.org/news/un-climate-pact-closer-to-taking-effect-20721.
[37] Mick Pope, *A Climate of Justice: Loving Your Neighbour in a Warming World* (Reservoir: Morningstar Publishing, 2017), 78-81. Mick Pope, "The Sea Is Eating the Ground: A Theology of Sea Level Rise," *Anglican Theological Review* 100:1 (2018): 79-92.

bar of his resort 5 to 10 metres inland. He knows he is 'fighting the inevitable' and that his island won't exist in 100 years. Morrish's world and that of his compatriots is coming to an end before their eyes. Tonga's senior climate finance analyst, Sione Fulivai, compares the fate of Tonga with the developed world

> A lot of countries and governments are in Paris negotiating their economies – we're just asking for survival. We don't want to become another extinct culture.[38]

So, where is history headed? For some of us, it feels like it's headed in the right direction. Disciples of Pinker think that the world is just getting better, and Dawkins would add that the decline of religion will help. Yet, Christian Tonga faces its own climate apocalypse. In the next chapter, I look at the unfolding future of climate change, and the larger framework in which it sits, the Anthropocene. What role will we play in it, individually and as the church? Indeed, given our discussion about evil, what role do we play in it right now?

---

38 Sarah Treanor, and Katy Watson, "Tonga facing up to rising sea levels," *BBC News*, 1 December, 2015, accessed 6 May, 2018, http://www.bbc.com/news/business-34738408.

CHAPTER 2 — APOCALYPSE NOW

Darkness before the dawn

They say that fear is not much of a motivator. That it paralyses us. Hope is a more powerful message. This is a book of hope. But I think that now is not the time to bury our heads in the sand: we need to understand that we are headed towards an apocalypse now of environmental destruction. Forewarned is forearmed. And no, I don't like the smell of climate change in the morning.[1] How the idea of environmental destruction links to what the bible says about the 'end times' is something for us to examine in a later chapter. For now, let me say that the damage we have done to God's world is not 'part of a divine plan', but is the result of God handing us over to our sin. The direct corollary is that if we repent and work with God in renewing our world, we should see changes. It's not too late to turn things around, and while the world won't be the same, the future is not set in stone.

For now, we need to get our heads around the science of what has come to be known as the Anthropocene, the period of human influence on all aspects of the Earth System.[2] Climate change, as we will see, forms a part of the Anthropocene, but there are a number of other ways in which we are messing up the world. Yes, this is the science chapter, but any big words I use I'll explain for the non-geeks. And yes, it's also the doom and gloom chapter. But they say that it's always darkest before the dawn, and I just happen to believe in the dawn.

The Great Acceleration

Geologists deal with huge periods of time. I know for some Christians the idea of an old Earth is problematic, but nothing of what I say ultimately hinges on it. Geologists work with rocks that they

---

1 The title of this chapter is taken from the movie *Apocalypse Now* about the Vietnam War. The line I'm echoing is 'I love the smell of napalm in the morning.' There are more resonances here between the movie and the issue at hand than I care to think about.
2 Paul Crutzen, "Geology of mankind," *Nature* 415 (2002): 23.

date both absolutely, using radioactive material, and relatively, given that layers are laid down sequentially one on top of the other. In order for geologists to count a period of time as a distinct geological era, there has to be a representative site that is datable with some measure of precision, and there needs to be something distinguishable about them. Take, for example, the boundary between the Cretaceous and the Paleogene. In the former, there are dinosaur fossils, in the latter, there are not. In between lies a thin layer that bears evidence of a massive meteorite impact. All of this adds up to two distinct geological periods. It is easy to look back and do the science. The problem with deciding on if and when we entered the Anthropocene is the fact that we are living in it. But, consensus is being reached.

One of the things that characterises the 20th and 21st centuries is economic development. Things began apace with the Industrial Revolution, marked as it was by industrialisation and an increased dependence on fossil fuels. However, the last 50 years or so has been dubbed 'The Great Acceleration.' The Great Acceleration is illustrated by a series of plots that were constructed for the International Geosphere-Biosphere Programme, which was carried out between 1999 and 2003. These plots showed the accelerating growth of the human economy and its resulting impacts on the planet. A key concept in all of this is the Earth System science, which looks at the earth in its entirety, and how each of the individual components interact with each other.[3]

There are five spheres or components of the Earth System. The atmosphere is the very air that we breathe, including the oxygen that our bodies burn, the carbon dioxide that absorbs heat and keeps our planet above freezing, water vapour that forms clouds and rain and also absorbs heat, and ozone that keeps out harmful ultraviolet radiation. The hydrosphere is the water cycle, not only the water vapour, clouds, and rain, but the rivers, lakes, oceans, surface run-off, ground water, and underground aquifers. Water brings life, something the biblical writers knew all too well (e.g. Ps 104:10–13). The cryosphere represents snow and ice. It deserves a special mention apart from the hydrosphere

---

3 Will Steffen, Wendy Broadgate, Lisa Deutsch, Owen Gaffney, and Cornelia Ludwig, "The trajectory of the Anthropocene: The Great Acceleration," *The Anthropocene Review* 2 (2015): 1-18.

because snow and ice reflect back sunlight into space. Our planet is cooler with ice than without it, which is a concern since we continue to lose it via global warming related melting. The geosphere is the solid earth. It holds down everything by gravity. Over time, the earth recycles carbon from the air by burying it in rock and belching it out in volcanoes. Tectonic plates move slowly, at about the rate at which your fingernails grow. But their movement causes volcanoes to erupt, mountain ranges to grow, and earthquakes to shake the earth's foundations. The Himalayas, for example, are the result of India colliding with Eurasia. Continents are built and grow over time. The solid earth can be a force for both destruction and creation.

The biosphere represents the sum total of life, which interacts with the other spheres. Plants consume carbon dioxide and produce the oxygen that we breathe. They form the bottom of the food chain. Plants help break up rock for soil, then store carbon in that soil. They are, in turn, dependent on the hydrosphere for water, and on animals to help pollinate them or spread seeds. Plants change how much sunlight is reflected off the earth's surface and help recycle water for rain. In addition to the biosphere is humans. Some scholars these days don't like to separate humanity from other creatures and it's true that we have tended to focus on ourselves to the exclusion of our non-human neighbours. But we represent what Teilhard de Chardin called the noosphere; the human sphere of thought. At times we are ignorant, wilful or otherwise, but we can make conscious decisions about our actions. Human beings are an essential consideration of the Earth System because we run our economies totally dependent on this system for our raw materials and, in turn, impact the Earth System through our activities. The concept of the Great Acceleration then is an attempt to capture the holistic, comprehensive and interlinked nature of the post-1950 changes simultaneously sweeping across the socio-economic and biophysical spheres of the Earth System.[4]

Since the 1950s, the human population has boomed (hence the phrase baby boomers). Relative peace, improved health, and the so-called green revolution and increase in yields due to the use of fertilisers, means that a larger population can be supported. As I write,

---

4 Steffen et al., *The trajectory of the Anthropocene.*

a web-based population counter tells me that the world currently has over 7.6 billion people.[5] Recent United Nations estimates put the global population at 8.6 billion in 2030, 9.8 billion in 2050, and 11.2 billion in 2100, for the median projection.[6] A plot showing the possible and most likely scenario is shown below. With an increased population has come a marked increase in primary energy use, an increase in real Gross Domestic Product (GDP), foreign investment, transportation, telecommunications, and international tourism. This has meant also an increase in the consumption and control of resources, such as water use and the construction of large dams, fertiliser use, and paper production. As agriculture becomes automated, so societies are becoming more urban, and by 2030 it is expected that about 61% of the world's population will live in cities.[7]

World: Total Population

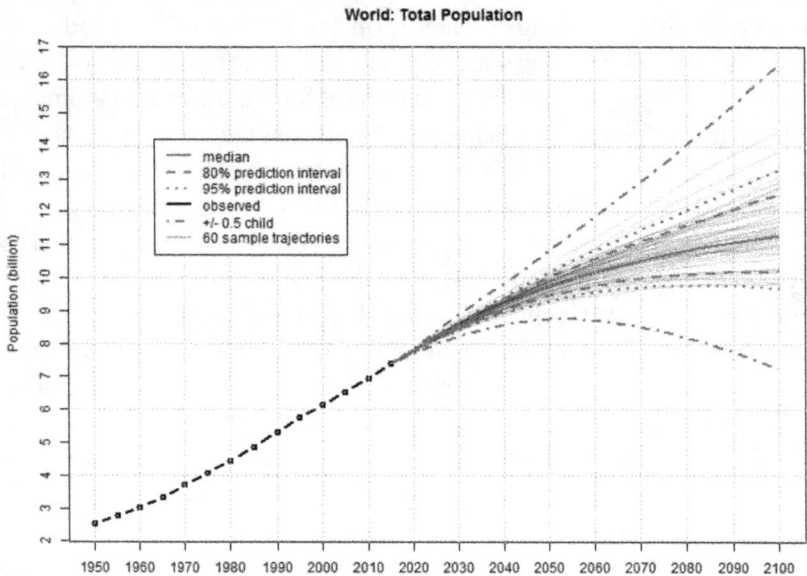

Source: United Nations, Department of Economic and Social Affairs, Population Division (2017).
World Population Prospects: The 2017 Revision. http://esa.un.org/unpd/wpp/

---

5 http://www.worldometers.info/world-population/.

6 United Nations, "World population projected to reach 9.8 billion in 2050, and 11.2 billion in 2100," *United Nations Department of Economic and Social Affairs*, 21 June, 2017, accessed 8 May, 2018, https://www.un.org/development/desa/en/news/population/world-population-prospects-2017.html.

7 UNESCO, "Global Trend Towards Urbanisation," Unesco.org, accessed 8 May, 2018, http://www.unesco.org/education/tlsf/mods/theme_c/popups/mod13t01s009.html.

A s the global economy has grown there have been gains in education, health, a rise in the standard of living, and the alleviation of poverty. It is clear that the benefits of development have not been evenly shared, both internationally, and domestically. In Australia, there is a real gap between Aboriginal and Torres Strait Islanders, and non-indigenous Australians.[8] In Brazil, favelas sit right next to affluent gated communities. However, there have been gains. According to the World Bank, in 2013, 767 million people lived on less than $1.90 a day. This is down from 1.85 billion in 1990.[9] So, some steps have been made, but the reality is that, where economic growth is concerned, there is always a cost involved. This is where the planetary boundaries come in.

Pushing the Boundaries

The disruption of the various aspects of the Earth System can be quantified in nine planetary boundaries, which represent a safe operating space for human society to flourish. While anthropocentric (i.e. focused on humans) it also implies maintaining essential parts of the Earth system for their own wellbeing. It is estimated that we are pushing seven of these boundaries and threatening our own existence in doing so.[10] So, let's look at each of the nine planetary boundaries in a little detail.

Climate change

We've already seen that the concentration of carbon dioxide in the atmosphere has permanently passed 400 parts per million (ppm).[11]

---

8 See Mick Pope, *A Climate of Justice: Loving you Neigbour in a Warming* World (Reservoir: Morningstar Publishing, 2017), chapter 5.

9 World Bank, "Poverty Overview, updated 11 April, 2018, accessed 16 May, 2018, http://www.worldbank.org/en/topic/poverty/overview.

10 Will Steffen, Katherine Richardson, Johan Rockström, Sarah E. Cornell, Ingo Fetzer, Elena M. Bennett, Reinette Biggs, Stephen R. Carpenter, Wim de Vries, Cynthia A. de Wit, Carl Folke, Dieter Gerten, Jens Heinke, Georgina M. Mace, Linn M. Persson, Veerabhadran Ramanathan, Belinda Reyers, and Sverker Sörlin, "Planetary Boundaries: Guiding Human Development on a Changing Planet," *Science* 347 (2015): 1-17, accessed January 15, 2015, *DOI: 10.1126/science.1259855.*

11 Brian Kahn, "The World Passes 400 PPM Threshold. Permanently," *Climate Central,* 27 September, 2016, accessed 4 May, 2018, http://www.climatecentral.org/news/world-passes-400-ppm-threshold-permanently-20738.

Indeed, at the time I am writing this, it has exceeded 410 ppm.[12] At the start of the Industrial Revolution, atmospheric concentrations were at 280 ppm. The plot shown is from US National Oceanic and Atmospheric Administration, showing monthly and annual carbon dioxide concentrations. The effects of the seasons in the Northern Hemisphere is evident in the rise in carbon dioxide while snow and ice cover Northern Hemisphere forests, and its decline when photosynthesis is in full swing. The steady rise in annual concentrations is obvious.

Atmospheric CO_2 at Mauna Loa Observatory

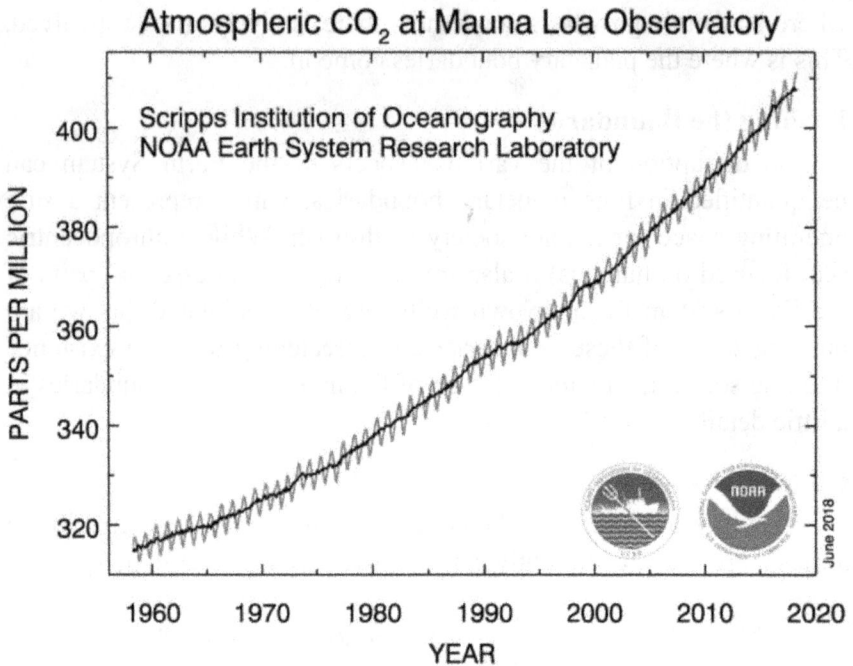

A suggested safe threshold for carbon dioxide is 350 ppm, which is the key idea behind Bill McKibben's organisation, 350.org.[13] To

---

12 Chloe Farand, "Carbon dioxide levels in Earth's atmosphere reach 'highest level in 800,000 years'," *The Independent,* 5 May, 2018, accessed 6 May, 2018, https://www.independent.co.uk/environment/carbon-dioxide-concentration-atmosphere-highest-level-800000-years-mauna-loa-observatory-hawaii-a8337921.html.

13 Bill McKibben, "Remember This: 350 Parts Per Million," *Washington Post,* 28 December, 2007, accessed 6 May, 2018, http://www.washingtonpost.com/wp-dyn/content/article/2007/12/27/AR2007122701942.html. See also 350.org.

get back down to 350 ppm means stopping our carbon emissions by switching to renewable energy sources, and there are plenty of technologies to fill the gap in the generation of electricity like solar, wind, hydro-electric, and geothermal power. However, we will also need to draw down carbon dioxide from the atmosphere. This requires a mixture of old technologies like zero till farming and reforestation, and newer technologies like artificial photosynthesis. A whole suite of approaches already exists.[14]

We've already looked at sea level rise in Tonga as an impact of climate change. Spare a thought also for the people of Pakistan. On Monday 30 April 2018, the highest ever recorded temperature for April was set in Nawabshah, a city of 1.1 million people in southern Pakistan: 122.4° F or 50.2° C! For a period of a week, nowhere in the surrounding region had a maximum temperature less than 113° F or 45° C.[15] Events like this are now five times more likely to occur as Pakistan's annual average temperature has increased by about 0.5°C.[16]

Ocean acidification

To live in the Pacific Ocean, or in Oceania, is to live with the ocean. This means that fish forms a large part of the diet. In New Caledonia, many coastal communities depend on fish for 50 to 90 per cent of their animal protein.[17] Fisheries face numerous threats from warming ocean temperatures, pollution, and ocean acidification. As industry pumps out more and more carbon dioxide, about 40 per cent of it ends up absorbed in the oceans like a giant can of soft drink (or soda, or pop, depending on your country).[18] Carbon dioxide forms a weak acid when

---

14 Paul Hawken, *Drawdown: The Most Comprehensive Plan Ever Proposed to Roll Back Global Warming* (London: Penguin Books, 2018). See also www.drawdown.org.

15 Maggie Astor, "Hottest April Day Ever Was Probably Monday in Pakistan: a Record 122.4°F," *The New York Times*, 4 May, 2018, accessed 6 May, 2018, https://www.nytimes.com/2018/05/04/world/asia/pakistan-heat-record.html.

16 Staff Report, "Pakistan's annual average temperature increasing by 0.5°C," *Pakistan Today*, 19 March, 2018, accessed 6 May, 2018, https://www.pakistantoday.com.pk/2018/03/19/pakistans-annual-average-temperature-increasing-by-0-5c/.

17 Lisbeth Fog, "Rising ocean acidity worst for Caribbean and Pacific," *Sci Dev Net*, 2 July, 2012, accessed 6 May, 2018, https://www.scidev.net/global/fisheries/news/rising-ocean-acidity-worst-for-caribbean-and-pacific.html.

18 Tim DeVries, Mark Holzer, and Francois Primeau, "Recent increase in oceanic carbon

it mixes with water, and the oceans have become slowly more acidic (technically, less alkaline) over time. A 2012 study showed a 30-fold increase in the natural variation in ocean acidity in the Pacific and the Caribbean, associated with a decline in coral growth rates of 15 per cent. In general, the concentration of hydrogen ions, which make the oceans more acidic, has increased by about 30 per cent over the past 200 years.[19]

Elizabeth McLeod, co-author of the 2012 study, noted that

Coral reefs provide economic and environmental services to nearly 500 million people, and decreases in coral calcification would reduce the benefits that they provide to coastal communities, including tourism revenues, food security, and shoreline protection, from waves and storms.[20]

This is set to exacerbate the shortfall by 2030 in demand versus supply of fish due to population growth in Oceania nations.[21] While many resources have been locally overexploited, various management strategies, including customary means and traditional systems, are being employed. Warming and acidifying oceans will further impact fish populations, both directly ands via loss of coral reefs.

Ocean acidification is not just a problem for those living on islands. Diani Taylor of Shelton, Washington, and her cousin, Brittany, are fifth-generation oyster farmers, but the oceans in which they work are very different from their ancestors.[22] Diani observes that, 'The ocean is so acidic that it is dissolving the shells of our baby oysters.' Over 100 years ago, the family business, which is a large employer in the area,

uptake driven by weaker upper-ocean overturning," *Nature* 542 (2017): 215-218.

19 Will Steffen, Katherine Richardson, Johan Rockström, Sarah E. Cornell, Ingo Fetzer, Elena M. Bennett, R. Biggs, Stephen R. Carpenter, Wim de Vries, Cynthia A. de Wit, Carl Folke, Dieter Gerten, Jens Heinke, Georgina M. Mace, Linn M. Persson, Veerabhadran Ramanathan, B. Reyers, Sverker Sörlin, "Planetary boundaries: Guiding human development on a changing planet," *Science Express* 15 January 2015, 1 0.1126/science.1259855.

20 Fog, *Rising ocean acidity worst for Caribbean and Pacific*.

21 Quentin Hanich, Colette C.C. Wabnitz, Yoshitaka Ota, Moses Amos, Connie Donato-Hunt, and Andrew Hunt, "Small-scale fisheries under climate change in the Pacific Islands region," *Marine Policy* 88 (2018): 279-284.

22 *The Story Group*, "Oyster farmers and Ocean acidification," accessed 6 May, 2018, http://thestorygroup.org/oyster-farmers-and-ocean-acidification/.

relied upon the natural reproduction of oysters to provide their harvest. They now cultivate their own baby oysters before planting them on the beaches. Diani and Brittany discovered that the shellfish had difficulty in growing their shells, resulting in them dying in the first few weeks of life. In due course, a multi-generation business could disappear, along with the oysters.

Stopping ocean acidification will be a slow business, but like global warming, the technology exists to stop emitting carbon dioxide.

Changes in biosphere integrity

Extinction is final. The loss of unique plants and animals is something to be lamented. Christians especially who recognise that God has created the multitude of life on this planet (Ps 104) should be concerned. Steffen and co-authors attempt to define boundaries on extinction rates in two ways. The first is the 'role of genetically unique material as the "information bank" that ultimately determines the potential for life to continue' as it, along with the non-living part of the world, change. The second focuses on the functional traits that species have and the role they play in ecosystems.[23] The idea of measurable boundaries for such things is not without critique.[24] Notwithstanding the concerns that the boundaries themselves are hard to define, the loss of species is greatly troubling.

Estimates of extinction rates can vary wildly due to our incomplete knowledge of what is out there, especially our ignorance of invertebrates.[25] Taxonomy is not always a perfect science, and one species of sea snail has been counted 113 times under different names. While the clearing of tropical rainforests has yet to result in significant extinctions to our knowledge, this may simply be a stay of execution. Extinctions can be caused by overhunting, climate change, ocean acidification, habitat loss, and pollution, to name a few. But I realise for some, focusing on the cute and cuddly is a distraction from more important issues like

23 Stefen et al., *Planetary boundaries*.
24 José M. Montoya, Ian Donohue, and Stuart L. Pimm, "Why a Planetary Boundary, If It Is Not Planetary, and the Boundary Is Undefined? A Reply to Rockström et al.," *Trends in Ecology & Evolution* 33:4(2018): 234.
25 Fred Pearce, "Global Extinction Rates: Why Do Estimates Vary So Wildly?," *Yale Environment 360*, 17 August, 2015, accessed 6 May, 2018, https://e360.yale.edu/features/global_extinction_rates_why_do_estimates_vary_so_wildly.

poverty and feeding starving millions. So, if polar bears or sea snails are not your thing, I can guarantee you that you should care about bees.

In a recent landmark decision, the European Union will ban the world's most widely used insecticides, neonicotinoids, from all fields by the end of 2018, due to the danger they pose to bees.[26] Bees and other insects pollinate three-quarters of all crops, and hence are essential for global food production. Think about it, your stomach depends upon tiny insects. We are not independent of the rest of nature, even with our modern harvesters, agribusinesses, and especially our insecticides. Neonicotinoids, which are nerve agents, have been shown to cause a wide range of harm to bees. Predictably, businesses are claiming that there is not enough evidence. Likewise, farmers worry about pests, although without pollinators it will be beside the point. Dave Goulson, Professor at the University of Sussex and author of two charming books on pollinators, believes that the full solution is sustainable farming.[27] This includes less harmful pesticides and more flowery habitats for bees, which means the abandonment of monocultures.

Spare a thought for the useful creepy crawlies. The destruction of wild areas, widespread use of pesticides, and possibly climate change, has resulted in the abundance of flying insects in Germany declining by three-quarters over the past 25 years.[28] While feathers and fur gather some people's attention, insects sit near the bottom of the food chain and pollinate many of our food crops, so they certainly form a boundary.

Introduction of novel entities

One of the things that should be clear from the last boundary is that we are managing to fill the soil and water with chemicals that are harmful. Steffen defines novel entities as

[26] Damian Carrington, "EU agrees total ban on bee-harming pesticides," *The Guardian*, 27 April, 2018, accessed 7 May, 2018, https://www.theguardian.com/environment/2018/apr/27/eu-agrees-total-ban-on-bee-harming-pesticides.

[27] Dave Goulson, *A Sting in the Tale: My Adventures with Bumblebees* (London: Picador, 2015). Dave Goulson, *A Buzz in the Meadow: The Natural History of a French Farm* (London: Picador, 2016).

[28] Damian Carrington, "Warning of 'ecological Armageddon' after dramatic plunge in insect numbers," *The Guardian*, 19 October, 2017, accessed 7 May, 2018, https://www.theguardian.com/environment/2017/oct/18/warning-of-ecological-armageddon-after-dramatic-plunge-in-insect-numbers.

new substances, new forms of existing substances and modified life-forms that have the potential for unwanted geophysical and/or biological effects.

Certainly, the death of bees would be one of these unwanted effects. Steffen and co-authors identify over 100,000 substances in global commerce, excluding plastics. One such chemical is DDT, or Dichlorodiphenyltrichloroethane (you can see why we shorten it). Used to kill pests like mosquitoes to control the spread of malaria, Rachel Carson made it famous with her book *Silent Spring*.[29] The use of DDT was implicated in the death of birds. While never spread in places like Antarctica, it has been found in the shells of Adele Penguins.[30] In Australia, its use was banned in 1987. In 2007, a dramatic increase in the reproductive success of a whole range of birds like Peregrine Falcons was noted.[31] It is still used in parts of the world to control malaria, such as in South Africa in 2013 where mortality rates have been cut dramatically.[32] The Australian story gives us hope that stopping using pollutants like DDT and neonicotinoids can turn things around.

The other chemical making the news of late is plastic. Plastics break down into microplastics, small pieces less than 5 mm long. Microplastics have been discovered in soil across Switzerland. About 70 to 80 per cent of the particles found were smaller than 0.5 mm and are likely windblown.[33] The key concern is whether or not microplastics are getting into our food, and more research is needed. It has been found that plastics in the soil can kill earthworms. These creatures, other than being food for the early bird, are a keystone species in ecosystems. They recycle organic material in the soil, they help aerate and moisten soil

29 Rachel Carson, *Silent Spring* (London: Penguin, 2001).

30 William J. L. Sladen, C. M. Menzie, and W. L. Reichel, "DDT Residues in Adelie Penguins and A Crabeater Seal from Antarctica," *Nature* 210(1966): 670-673.

31 Allison Jess, "DDT Environmental Effects," *ABC Goulburn Murray*, 11 October, 2007, accessed 7 May, 2018, http://www.abc.net.au/local/stories/2007/10/09/2054547.htm.

32 AFP, "Malaria death rate slashed with use of controversial DDT," *The Sydney Morning Herald*, 11 October, 2013, accessed 7 May, 2018, https://www.smh.com.au/world/malaria-death-rate-slashed-with-use-of-controversial-ddt-20131010-2vb7c.html.

33 Damian Carrington, "The hills are alive with the signs of plastic: even Swiss mountains are polluted," *The Guardian*, 27 April, 2018, accessed 7 May, 2018, https://www.theguardian.com/environment/2018/apr/27/the-hills-are-alive-with-the-signs-of-plastic-even-swiss-mountains-are-polluted.

through their tunnelling, and are a measure of soil health.[34] If plastics are affecting them, then we are in big trouble. We also now know that our drinking water contains plastic fibres.[35] We know that the oceans are full of plastic and that thousands of seabirds die consuming it each year.[36] Our addiction to plastic must end!

There are some positive signs as it is slowly becoming the norm in some places for supermarkets to either charge for, or not use, plastic bags.[37] There are also some more imaginative ventures afoot, from 'biodegr(edible)' straws, to clothes made from recycled plastic.[38]

Stratospheric ozone depletion

One of the few good news stories with regards to planetary boundaries is ozone depletion. Over 30 years ago, the Montreal Protocol was signed (as it happens, on my 18th birthday!), signalling the phasing out of industrial gases such as chlorofluorocarbons (CFCs).[39] These chemicals were found to react with ozone in very cold clouds in the

---

34 Sarah Johnson, "Earthworms are more important than pandas (if you want to save the planet)," *The Conversation*, 29 March, 2017, accessed 7 May, 2018, https://theconversation.com/earthworms-are-more-important-than-pandas-if-you-want-to-save-the-planet-74010.

35 Damian Carrington, "Plastic fibres found in tap water around the world, study reveals," *The Guardian*, 6 September, 2017, accessed 7 May, 2018, https://www.theguardian.com/environment/2017/sep/06/plastic-fibres-found-tap-water-around-world-study-reveals.

36 Matthew Savoca, "The oceans are full of plastic, but why do seabirds eat it?," *The Conversation*, 10 November, 2016, accessed 7 May, 2018, https://theconversation.com/the-oceans-are-full-of-plastic-but-why-do-seabirds-eat-it-68110.

37 Aisha Stevens Yaman, "Victoria's plastic bag ban: What does it mean for you?," *Herald Sun*, 13 June, 2018, accessed 15 June, 2018, https://www.heraldsun.com.au/news/victoria/victorias-plastic-bag-ban-what-does-it-mean-for-you/news-story/d4e112215b4aea5d3 3ed95048df70f21. Rebecca Smithers, "England's plastic bag usage drops 85% since 5p charge introduced," *The Guardian*, 30 July, 2016, accessed 15 June, 2018, https://www.theguardian.com/environment/2016/jul/30/england-plastic-bag-usage-drops-85-per-cent-since-5p-charged-introduced.

38 Tim Lewis, "Meet the anti-plastic warriors: the pioneers with bold solutions to waste," *The Guardian*, 22 April, 2018, accessed 17 June, 2018, https://www.theguardian.com/environment/2018/apr/22/meet-the-pioneers-tackling-plastic-waste-loliware-straws-vin-and-omi.

39 Andrew Klekociuk, and Paul Krummel, "After 30 years of the Montreal Protocol, the ozone layer is gradually healing," *The Conversation*, 15 September, 2017, accessed 7 May, 2018, https://theconversation.com/after-30-years-of-the-montreal-protocol-the-ozone-layer-is-gradually-healing-84051.

stratosphere (about 9 km above the earth) over the poles during winter. Then, during spring, this ozone poor air would be circulated away from the poles. The slow decline in the size of the so-called Antarctic Ozone hole is a measure of how successful the protocol was. Luckily too, since CFCs are a greenhouse gas, we've gone a small part of the way to dealing with climate change. The initial reaction from industry was one of denial, something mirrored by the 'controversies' over DDT, tobacco and climate change, as pointed out in the ground breaking book *Merchants of Doubt.*[40]

It turns out that skin cancer rates in Australia, close to the hole, have nothing to do with ozone depletion.[41] However, it has impacted marine animals and plants, and the climate of southern Australia and New Zealand, by shifting further south the track of cold fronts.[42]

Biogeochemical flows

This next boundary includes a variety of chemicals that flow through our environment but mostly focuses on nitrogen and phosphorous from fertilisers. In some parts of the developing world, fertiliser is crap, literally. And this is a problem because it can hold back development.[43] Basically, it comes down to cows not producing enough manure to fertilise crops. As Teo Kataratambi and her husband, Silver, have discovered growing bananas in Uganda, without fertilisers: 'We don't make much money. We can't break even.' Chemical fertilisers can

---

40 Naomi Oreskes, and Erik M. Conway, *Merchants of Doubt: How a Handful of Scientists Obscured the Truth on Issues from Tobacco Smoke to Global Warming* (New York: Bloomsbury Paperbacks, 2012).

41 Terry Slevin, and David Whiteman, "Why does Australia have so much skin cancer? (Hint: it's not because of an ozone hole)," *The Conversation*, 20 March, 2018, accessed 7 May, 2018, https://theconversation.com/why-does-australia-have-so-much-skin-cancer-hint-its-not-because-of-an-ozone-hole-91850.

42 One marine life see The University of Western Australia, "Ozone hole UV impacting marine life: study," *University News*, 25 July, 2012, accessed 7 May, 2018, http://www.news.uwa.edu.au/201207264841/climate-science/ozone-hole-uv-impacting-marine-life-study. On the Southern Annular Mode see Jim Salinger, "New Zealand is drying out, and here's why," *The Conversation*, 7 October, 2014, accessed 7 May, 2018, https://theconversation.com/new-zealand-is-drying-out-and-heres-why-32330.

43 Natasha Gilbert, "Costly fertiliser holds back a green revolution in Africa," *The Guardian*, 5 December, 2014, accessed 7 May, 2018, https://www.theguardian.com/global-development/2014/dec/05/costly-fertiliser-holds-back-a-green-revolution-in-africa.

be too expensive in sub-Saharan Africa. That said, use of chemical fertilisers varies across the region.[44] Not all situations benefit from extra fertilisation, with one World Bank report suggesting that crops like maize in Nigeria deliver minimal extra return, and benefit little from extra nitrogen.[45] Growing legumes helps to introduce more nitrogen to the soil, but the Green Revolution in Africa is still a way off yet.

In the West, we have been using chemical fertilisers for some time and it has had negative impacts. Nitrogen in fertilisers can run-off into waterways, fertilising algal growth, and producing toxic blooms. When algae die, their decay consumes oxygen and results in oxygen poor or dead zones.[46] Nitrogen deposits also cause a variety of ill effects such as soil acidification, some cancers, and 'blue baby disease,' where infants are born with a decreased oxygen carrying capacity in the blood, which can be fatal.[47] Fertiliser overuse in China has increased soil nitrogen between 1980 and 2010 by 60 per cent.[48] Hence, it's a fine balancing act between feeding people and ultimately starving them. Finally, nitrogen based fertilisers also contribute to greenhouse gases by producing nitrous oxide.

Freshwater use

Water is life. Without it, crops die, animals die, trees die, and people die. Quite apart from issues of rainfall decline due to climate change and pollution, the overuse of fresh water is resulting in a decline in the availability of safe water. The causes are many. Around the world, some

---

44 Megan Sheahan, and Christopher B. Barrett, "Ten striking facts about agricultural input use in Sub-Saharan Africa," *Food Policy* 67(1-27): 12-25.

45 Word Bank, "Is Increasing Inorganic Fertilizer Use in Sub-Saharan Africa Profitable? Evidence from Nigeria," accessed 7 May, 2018, http://www.worldbank.org/en/programs/africa-myths-and-facts/publication/is-increasing-inorganic-fertilizer-use-in-sub-saharan-africa-profitable-evidence-from-nigeria.

46 Lee Bryant, "Ocean 'dead zones' are spreading – and that spells disaster for fish," *The Conversation*, 7 April, 2015, accessed 7 May, 2018, https://theconversation.com/ocean-dead-zones-are-spreading-and-that-spells-disaster-for-fish-39668.

47 Vaclav Smil, "Global Population and the Nitrogen Cycle," *Scientific American*, July 1997:76-81.

48 Jane Qiu, "Nitrogen pollution soars in China," *Nature*, 20 February, 2013, accessed 7 May, 2018, https://www.nature.com/news/nitrogen-pollution-soars-in-china-1.12470.

946 million people still go to the toilet outside.[49] Ethiopia achieved a huge decrease in the population practising open defecation, from 92 per cent of the population in 1990, to 29 per cent in 2015. With some 2.4 billion people still lacking improved sanitation, the Millennium Development Goal to extend access to sanitation has not been met. Sustainable Development Goal 6 continues the goal of furthering access to safe water and sanitation, and sound management of freshwater ecosystems.[50]

Aquifers are underground layers of water-bearing permeable rock that can be accessed using wells. In some places, this water was deposited tens of thousands of years ago in wetter times. Those aquifers consist of ancient fossil water and are not readily recharged. Others, like those in sub-Saharan Africa, are slowly recharged by rainfall.[51] Large parts of India, Pakistan, southern Europe, and the western United States, could face depleted aquifers by mid-century due to over extraction for agriculture. Between 2040 and 2060, India's Upper Ganges Basin and southern Spain and Italy could be used up.[52] Rivers are also depleted by overuse, and in Australia, the Murray Darling basin continues to be the subject of political wrangling over environmental limits and water theft.[53]

---

49 Katherine Purvis, "Access to clean water and sanitation around the world – mapped," *The Guardian*, 1 July, 2015, accessed 7 May, 2018, https://www.theguardian.com/global-development-professionals-network/2015/jul/01/global-access-clean-water-sanitation-mapped.

50 United National Department of Economic and Social Affairs, "SUSTAINABLE DEVELOPMENT GOAL 6: Ensure availability and sustainable management of water and sanitation for all," Sustainable Development Knowledge Platform, accessed 7 May, 2018, https://sustainabledevelopment.un.org/sdg6.

51 J. Gonçalvès, J. Petersen, P. Deschamps, B. Hamelin, O. Baba-Sy. "Quantifying the modern recharge of the "fossil" Sahara aquifers," *Geophysical Research Letters*, 40:11(2013): 2673 DOI: 10.1002/grl.50478.

52 Cheryl Katz, " As Groundwater Dwindles, a Global Food Shock Looms," *National Geographic*, 22 December, 2016, accessed 7 May, 2018, https://news.nationalgeographic.com/2016/12/groundwater-depletion-global-food-supply/.

53 Anne Davies, " Murray-Darling basin plan: Labor to decide whether it will back key changes," *The Guardian*, 7 May, 2018, accessed 7 May, 2018, https://www.theguardian.com/australia-news/2018/may/07/murray-darling-basin-plan-labor-to-decide-whether-it-will-back-key-changes. Michael Slezak, and Anne Davies, "Murray-Darling water theft allegations: NSW to prosecute irrigators," *The Guardian*, 8 March, 2018, accessed 7 May, 2018, https://www.theguardian.com/australia-news/2018/mar/08/murray-darling-water-theft-allegations-nsw-to-prosecute-irrigators.

Competition for fresh water is not only between consumers and agriculture, but also due to government mismanagement, and competition with mining and other industries. In Flint, Michigan, a four year ordeal began with a switch from treated water to river water in order to save money. Improperly treated water leached lead from Flint's pipes and, until recently, locals were being supplied with bottled water to avoid lead poisoning.[54] Water supplies can also be polluted with chemicals from fracking, which is the extraction of oil or gas using the injection of chemicals to fracture rocks, itself a questionable practice because it continues our addiction to fossil fuels.[55] Likewise, the plans of Adani in Queensland to use ground water aquifers to wash its coal could amount to up to 4.5 billion litres of water being used per year, permanently draining desert oases.[56] Finally, big businesses like Nestlé extract water to sell cheaply, from drought prone locations like Southern California.[57] Famously, Nestlé Chairman Peter Brabeck has stated publicly that it is extreme to consider access to fresh water as a basic human right: he thinks it is best handled and distributed by a free market![58]

Land-system change

As the human population expands we need more land to feed ourselves. Some of this is driven by basic needs. Some of it is perhaps driven by things we need less of, could substitute, or regulate. Land is perceived of

54 Joe Difazio, " Flint, Michigan, Water Crisis Update: Government Spends Thousand Per Day for Bottled Water," *Newsweek*, 14 March, 2018, accessed 7 May, 2018, http://www.newsweek.com/flint-bottled-water-michigan-lead-flint-water-crisis-844547.

55 Oliver Millman, "Scientists find fracking contaminated Wyoming water after EPA halted study," *The Guardian*, 8 April, 2016, accessed 7 May, 2018, https://www.theguardian.com/us-news/2016/apr/07/wyoming-fracking-water-contamination-dangerous-chemicals.

56 Josh Robertson, "Adani groundwater plan could permanently drain desert oasis, scientists say," *ABC News*, 21 March, 2018, accessed 7 May, 2018, http://www.abc.net.au/news/2018-03-21/adani-groundwater-plan-risks-permanent-damage-to-desert-springs/9569184.

57 CBS News, "Nestlé faces backlash over collecting water from drought-hit California," *CBS News*, 9 Ma7, 2017, accessed 7 May, 2018, https://www.cbsnews.com/news/backlash-bottled-water-nestle/.

58 George McGraw, " Nestlé Chairman Peter Brabeck Says We Don't Have a Right to Water, Believes We Do Have a Right to Water and Everyone's Confused," *Huffington Post*, 25 April, 2015, accessed 7 May, 2018, https://www.huffingtonpost.com/george-mcgraw/nestle-chairman-peter-brabeck-water_b_3150150.html.

as a resource, and so it's clearing for mining, farming, or the expansion for housing, is done often without a thought for what we lose in water filtration, carbon storage, or species loss. So, what do we value?

In 2017, a new species of orang-utan was discovered in upland forests in north Sumatra, in Indonesia: the Tapanuli orang-utan. There are just 800 of the species left and its habitat is rapidly being cleared for palm oil and pulp-wood plantations. There are also plans for a hydropower plant.[59] And what about the rampant clearing of land in the Amazon to make way for soybean and cattle?[60] The Amazon has been called the lungs of the world, although the oceans produce the bulk of our oxygen (about 80 per cent).[61] Loss of the Amazon is not simply the concern of comfortable western environmentalists. Indigenous peoples have been battling against governments, miners, and pastoralists for decades to save their forests and homes. Patricia Gualinga, an indigenous Kichwa from Sarayaku in Ecuador, received death threats in January of 2018 for lobbying for her homeland's protection. Sexual violence and death threats are claimed to accompany oil drilling and mining.[62] Meanwhile in Brazil, three people in four months have been assassinated for their opposition to palm oil plantations.[63]

These sorts of stories are becoming depressingly common. Take, for example, the assassination of Honduran indigenous and environmental

---

59 Andrew Griffin, "Scientists find new orangutan and it is already the most endangered great ape in the world," *The Independent*, 2 November, 2017, accessed 8 May, 2018, https://www.independent.co.uk/news/science/new-orangutan-endangered-tapanuli-great-ape-endangered-extinct-liverpool-a8034036.html.
60 Nikolas Kozloff, *No Rain in the Amazon: How South America's Climate Change Affects the Entire Planet* (London: St. Martin's Press, 2010).
61 Sarah Witman, "World's Biggest Oxygen Producers Living in Swirling Ocean Waters," *EOS Earth & Space Science News*, 13 September, 2017, accessed 8 May, 2018, https://eos.org/research-spotlights/worlds-biggest-oxygen-producers-living-in-swirling-ocean-waters.
62 Dan Collyns, "Keep off our land, indigenous women tell Ecuador's president," *The Guardian*, 24 March, 2018, accessed 8 May, 2018, https://www.theguardian.com/environment/2018/mar/23/keep-off-our-land-indigenous-women-tell-ecuadors-president.
63 Johnathan Watts, "Murdered land activist adds to rising death toll in Brazil's Amazon," *The Guardian*, 18 April, 2018, accessed 8 May, 2018, https://www.theguardian.com/environment/2018/apr/17/murdered-indigenous-land-activist-adds-to-rising-death-toll-in-brazils-amazon.

rights campaigner, Berta Cáceres, in 2016.[64] Her death came only a week after she was threatened for opposing a hydro-electric project, opposition for which she had been awarded the Goldman Environmental Prize. While the police claimed it was a bungled robbery, Cáceres's mother is clear

> I have no doubt that she has been killed because of her struggle and that soldiers and people from the dam are responsible, I am sure of that. I hold the government responsible.

As is often the case, business, government, and law enforcement work together. After a march to protest the dam, Cáceres and others were confronted by the army, police, local mayor and employees of the dam company. Cáceres's death is not unique in Honduras. In 2013, a colleague of hers, Tomás García, was shot and killed at a protest by a military officer.

Closer to (my) home, Australia is among the worst offenders for land clearing in the world.[65] While the western world has largely cleared its forests, we seem unsatisfied with leaving what is left. While activists don't face death in a country like Australia, there have been repeated attempts to curtail the rights of protesters with threats of long jail terms.[66]

Atmospheric aerosol loading

Finally, humans have been polluting the air we breathe with particles for centuries. In describing the air quality of ancient Rome, the philosopher and senator, Seneca, noted that

---

64 Jonathan Watts, "Berta Cáceres, Honduran human rights and environment activist, murdered ," *The* Guardian, 4 March, 2016, accessed 17 June, 2018, https://www.theguardian.com/world/2016/mar/03/honduras-berta-caceres-murder-enivronment-activist-human-rights

65 Joshua Robertson, " Alarming' rise in Queensland tree clearing as 400,000 hectares stripped," *The Guardian*, 5 October, 2017, accessed 8 May, 2018, https://www.theguardian.com/environment/2017/oct/05/alarming-rise-in-queensland-tree-clearing-as-400000-hectares-stripped. Noel D Preece, and Penny van Oosterzee, " Australia is a global top-ten deforester – and Queensland is leading the way," *The Conversation,* 21 November, 2017, accessed 8 May, 2018, https://theconversation.com/australia-is-a-global-top-ten-deforester-and-queensland-is-leading-the-way-87259.

66 Georgie Burgess, "Anti-protest laws found unconstitutional by High Court to be resurrected by Tasmanian Liberals," *ABC News*, 20 February, 2018, accessed 17 June, 2018, http://www.abc.net.au/news/2018-02-19/anti-protest-law-to-be-attempted-again-by-hodgman-liberals/9461252.

No sooner had I left behind the oppressive atmosphere of the city and the reek of smoking cookers, which pour out, along with clouds of ashes, all the poisonous fumes they've accumulated ... I noticed the change in my condition at once.[67]

Aerosols lead to about 7.2 million deaths per year and we have all seen pictures of what major Chinese cities look like.[68] Recently, in Delhi, India, pollution levels were so high they were literally off the charts. And this is months before the peak of their pollution season which begins in October, where cooler temperatures trap pollution closer to the ground. In November 2017, the air was so bad that the quality was the same as smoking 50 cigarettes a day. India is home to 14 of the world's top polluted cities and has the highest rate of respiratory diseases anywhere in India. About half of Delhi's 4.4 million schoolchildren have stunted lung development, according to a 2015 study.[69]

Industry and cars are not the only generators of aerosol pollution. Globally, over 3 billion people presently use solid fuel for meal preparation, just as they did in ancient Rome. This indoor cooking causes an estimated 4.3 million premature deaths annually.[70] Cleaning up of aerosols is a key development goal, which in the case of cooking, requires the provision of electricity, preferably clean and renewable energy. Aerosols have been offsetting some of the greenhouse effect by stopping sunlight from reaching the surface, a phenomenon known as global dimming. An unfortunate side effect therefore of dealing with such pollution is that the amount of sunlight reaching the surface actually increases, raising global temperatures even further. Cleaning up air pollution is easier than dealing with global warming because if we stopped aerosol emissions tomorrow, the air would soon clear up,

---

67 Stephen Mosley, "Environmental History of Air Pollution and Protection," in *The Basic Environmental History* edited by Mauro Agnoletti, and Simone Neri Serneri (Heidelberg: Springer, 2014), 145.

68 Stefen et al., *Planetary boundaries*.

69 Michael Safi, "Delhi's air pollution is now so bad it is literally off the chart," *The Guardian*, 15 June, 2018, accessed 16 June, 2018, https://www.theguardian.com/world/2018/jun/15/delhi-blanketed-by-smog-so-toxic-it-cant-be-measured.

70 Forrest G. Lacey, Daven K. Henze, Colin J. Lee, Aaron van Donkelaar, and Randall V. Martin, " Transient climate and ambient health impacts due to national solid fuel cookstove emissions," *Proc Natl Acad Sci U S A.*, 114:6 (2017): 1269–1274.

whereas carbon dioxide stays in the atmosphere for centuries. We need to deal with both aerosols and carbon dioxide, so a change to renewable energy will cut down on both pollutants and carbon.

We'll Always Have Paris

The planetary boundary framework illustrates just how much damage humanity has done to this world. Climate change is perhaps the best understood of the nine planetary boundaries, and the main focus of this book. Climate change also has the easiest things to measure, like the concentration of carbon dioxide in parts per million, and the global mean average temperature. Our future depends largely on the rate at which we burn through fossil fuels and destroy our forests, and the resulting total amount of greenhouse gases in the atmosphere. This is also affected by various feedback mechanisms in the Earth System and how they in turn release more greenhouse gases.

At the Paris climate meeting in December 2015, ambitious targets were set to keep global mean temperatures below 1.5° C above pre-industrial temperatures. This was at the behest of Pacific Island nations whose futures are threatened by rising sea levels. Given the doubling of the chance of heat waves, observed sea level rise, and the disruption of the Indian monsoon, to name just a few, our nearly 1° C above pre-industrial temperatures is already too much. But sadly, we don't have a time machine, so we deal with what we have. The problem is that no country is on track with its commitments,[71] and consequently the chance of staying below 1.5° C is now very small.[72] Developed nations need to lead the charge in cutting carbon, as they have been polluting for the longest. Justice demands that we pay our way and support developing nations to leapfrog our mistakes. Most economies are cutting emissions, just way too slowly. The US had made small gains but swapping coal for

---

[71] David G. Victor, Keigo Akimoto, Yoichi Kaya, Mitsutsune Yamaguchi, Danny Cullenward, and Cameron Hepburn, "Prove Paris was more than paper promises," *Nature* 548 (2017):25-27.

[72] Oscar Williams, "Paris 1.5°C Warming Limit Could Be Broken In A Decade, Warn Scientists," *Huffington Post*, 5 September, 2017, accessed 16 June, 2018, https://www.huffingtonpost.co.uk/entry/paris-warming-limit-broken-decade_uk_5911a011e4b0104c73523c92?guccounter=1.

natural gas is not a solution. Trump has been an environmental disaster, gutting every agency that cares, from NASA to the EPA.

The transition required is a whole of society one, from large scale changes in diet to lower consumption of animal products, changes in transport, land use, and manufacturing. However, energy generation must lead the way. For example, while announcements by financial institutions that they won't fund new coal fired power plants is heartening, the sheer amount of coal being burnt means that one plant per day must be closed from now until 2040 to meet the Paris agreement.[73]

The Four Horsemen of the 4° C Apocalypse

The cost of inaction is incredibly high. In the absence of any policies, global mean temperatures are expected to rise by 4.1° to 4.8° C by the end of this century. Warming would continue beyond that but most people struggle to think beyond next week, let alone next century. Current policies are in line for about 3.1° C.[74] Even a fairly low threshold of 1.5° C to 2.0° C could be too high, as a recent paper has suggested. Above 2° C could lead to the reaching of a number of tipping points, producing a domino like cascade of feedbacks that raise the temperature even further, and leading to a 'hothouse earth.'[75]

For argument's sake, let's run with a 4° C world. It's not a world we want to contemplate, but this didn't stop oil and gas company, Santos, from basing its business plans on it.[76] Petro-giant, Shell, has been accused of the same thing. So, what might a 4° C world look like? If you like things in dollar terms, there could be losses of up to $72 trillion off the

73 Matt Gray, "Earth to investors: Paris Agreement requires one coal unit to close every day until 2040," *Carbon Tracker*, 3 May 2018, accessed 9 May, 2018, https://www.carbontracker.org/earth-to-investors/.

74 Climate Action Tracker, "Addressing global warming," accessed 9 May, 2018, https://climateactiontracker.org/global/temperatures/.

75 Will Steffen, Johan Rockström, Katherine Richardson, Timothy M. Lenton, Carl Folke, Diana Liverman, Colin P. Summerhayes, Anthony D. Barnosky, Sarah E. Cornell, Michel Crucifix, Jonathan F. Donges, Ingo Fetzer, Steven J. Lade, Marten Scheffer, Ricarda Winkelmann, and Hans Joachim Schellnhuber, "Trajectories of the Earth System in the Anthropocene," *PNAS* http://www.pnas.org/cgi/doi/10.1073/pnas.1810141115.

76 Helen Davidson, "Oil company Santos admits business plan is based on 4C temperature rise," *The Guardian*, 5 May, 2017, accessed 9 May, 2018, https://www.theguardian.com/environment/2017/may/05/santos-admits-business-plan-based-4c-global-temperature-rise.

world's Gross Domestic Product. In 2015, the chairman of AXA, one of the world's largest insurers, vowed 'to divest from the companies most exposed to coal-related activities for the assets managed internally.' The title of the Forbes article in which this was quoted reads 'A 2°C World Might Be Insurable, A 4°C World Certainly Would Not Be.'[77]

A 2009 conference in Copenhagen heard that a 4° C world would mean swaths of southern Europe would be turned to desert.[78] Sea levels will rise up to 2 metres by 2100. This is, no doubt, an underestimate given how rapidly some ice sheets are collapsing. Even modest warming could unleash a carbon 'time bomb' from Arctic soils as defrosting organic material decays, releasing methane and carbon dioxide. We already know that methane is leaking from melting permafrost, although how permafrost thaw will contribute to carbon feedback in recent decades is not well understood.[79] Over 85 per cent of the Amazon rainforest could disappear by 2100, releasing yet more carbon from soils and organic matter.[80]

A 4° C global average rise means temperatures about 5.5° to 6° C warmer over land, especially away from the coast. This would render half the world uninhabitable. Heat waves like the European heat wave of 2003, which resulted in as many as 2000 deaths per day, would occur every summer. Many of our modern cities would be drastically affected: 'heat stress in New York City would exceed that of present-day Bahrain.' In a warming world, outdoor labour becomes more difficult. In the sugarcane region of El Salvador, as many as one-fifth of the population already has chronic kidney disease due to excess sweating in the heat.[81]

---

[77] Dina Medland, "A 2°C World Might Be Insurable, A 4°C World Certainly Would Not Be," *Forbes*, 26 May, 2015, accessed 9 May, 2018, https://www.forbes.com/sites/dinamedland/2015/05/26/a-2c-world-might-be-insurable-a-4c-world-certainly-would-not-be/.

[78] Climate Action Centre, *4 Degrees Hotter* (Melbourne: Climate Action Centre, 2011).

[79] Katey Walter Anthony, Ronald Daanen, Peter Anthony, Thomas Schneider von Deimling, Chien-Lu Ping, Jeffrey P. Chanton, and Guido Grosse, "Methane emissions proportional to permafrost carbon thawed in Arctic lakes since the 1950s," *Nature Geoscience* 9 (2016): 679-682.

[80] Thomas E. Lovejoy, and Carlos Nobre, "Amazon Tipping Point," *Science Advances* 4 (2018). DOI: 10.1126/sciadv.aat2340.

[81] David Wallace-Wells, "Uninhabitable Earth," *New York*, 9 July, 2017, accessed 9 May, 2018, http://nymag.com/daily/intelligencer/2017/07/climate-change-earth-too-hot-for-

Large impacts on global crop yields are expected by the 2080s as we head to a 4° C world: up to 45 per cent global average yield reductions for maize compared to the 1980s, up to 52 per cent reduction for spring wheat, and up to 25 per cent for soybean.[82] Remember that we are expecting 11.2 billion people by 2100, which means increasing, not decreasing, the amount of food we produce. We already produce enough food to feed everyone in the world, yet people still starve due to waste, inequality, war, and corruption.[83] So, how will we manage it with declining yields? The tropics are already at peak yield, which means that a small increase in temperature will have a large impact on crop production. Declining rainfall will be set to produce 'unprecedented droughts nearly everywhere food is today produced.'[84] Megadroughts in the US, like that of the 1930s Dust Bowl, are expected to increase in likelihood and severity. Such droughts could last for three decades and increase to about 60 to 80 per cent likely, depending on whether or not carbon emissions stop mid-century to continue on with business as usual.[85]

Climate change will also increase epidemics. Lyme disease is being billed as the first of many to come.[86] Ticks that can carry the bacteria that causes Lyme can now survive in environments that 30 years ago would have been cold enough to kill them. With rising temperatures, by 2050, 12 per cent of the U.S. population will likely be infected by the Borrelia pathogen. Meanwhile in Europe, as ice and permafrost melts,

---

humans.html.

[82] Delphine Deryng, Declan Conway, Navin Ramankutty, Jeff Price and Rachel Warren, "Global crop yield response to extreme heat stress under multiple climate change futures," *Environmental Research Letters* 9 (2014).

[83] Eric Holt Gimenez, "We Already Grow Enough Food For 10 Billion People — and Still Can't End Hunger," *Huffpost*, 2 May, 2012, accessed 9 May, 2018, https://www.huffingtonpost.com/eric-holt-gimenez/world-hunger_b_1463429.html.

[84] Wallace-Wells, *Uninhabitable Earth*.

[85] Steve Cole, and Leslie McCarthy, "NASA Study Finds Carbon Emissions Could Dramatically Increase Risk of U.S. Megadroughts," *NASA*, 13 February, 2015, accessed 9 May, 2018, https://www.nasa.gov/press/2015/february/nasa-study-finds-carbon-emissions-could-dramatically-increase-risk-of-us.

[86] Gabriela Serrato Marks, "Climate Change is Causing a Dangerous Uptick in Case of Lyme Disease," *Pacific Standard,* 17 April, 2018, accessed 9 May, 2018, https://psmag.com/environment/global-warming-increases-instances-of-lyme.

nasties will be released from cold storage. Researchers have discovered remnants of the 1918 flu that infected up to 500 million and killed as many as 100 million.[87] Meanwhile in a remote part of Siberia, a 12 year old boy died and at least 20 others were hospitalised with anthrax, contracted from a melted 75 year old reindeer carcass.[88] As evolutionary biologist, Jean-Michel Claverie, observes; 'Permafrost is a very good preserver of microbes and viruses, because it is cold, there is no oxygen, and it is dark.' Permafrost has been described as a Pandora's Box. As the region of Siberia opens up to mining for minerals and drilling for oil and gas, the greater the possibility of long dead plagues rising again.

Lastly, climate change drives conflict. In *A Climate of Justice*, I suggested that a six year long drought played a role in exacerbating the Syrian conflict. It is a complex mix of poor management, unstable social, religious, and political factors, and international politics.[89] History shows us that natural climate change can interact with other factors in a complex way. In the case of the Mayan civilisation, drought, access to water and trade routes, interacted with shifting political alliances.[90] There is rarely a simple relationship between changes in climate and human society, but it has been an undeniable factor in the past and will be more so in the future.

Increased conflict, plagues, and declining crop yields, lead to famines and death. Sounds familiar, right? Welcome to the climate apocalypse of our own making, complete with its own four horsemen. Looking forward to God making all things new? It will happen. Read on!

---

[87] Wallace-Wells, *Uninhabitable Earth*.

[88] Jasmin Fox-Skelly, "There are diseases hidden in ice, and they are waking up," *BBC*, 4 May, 2017, accessed 9 May, 2018, http://www.bbc.com/earth/story/20170504-there-are-diseases-hidden-in-ice-and-they-are-waking-up.

[89] Pope, *A Climate of Justice,* Chapter 4.

[90] Peter M. J. Douglasa Mark Pagani, Marcello A. Canuto, Mark Brenner, David A. Hodell, Timothy I. Eglintone, and Jason H. Curtis, "Drought, agricultural adaptation, and socio-political collapse in the Maya Lowlands," *PNAS Early Edition*, April 20, 2015, doi. org/10.1073/pnas.1419133112.

CHAPTER 3 — EAST OF EDEN

Falling from Grace

We have seen already in the first chapter that what we might call the human project is an ambiguous one. The human condition has improved greatly for many but I am yet to be convinced that 'things can only get better.' We then saw in the last chapter that we are now living in the Anthropocene; an age where the present state of the planet bears a strong human footprint, and the fate of the earth is in human hands. That's not to deny eschatology or end times theology, the return of Christ, and so on. But what will Christ find on his return? One of the main aspects of the Anthropocene, and the major focus of what follows, is climate change. How did we get here? What is the problem? And, after all, hasn't the burning of fossil fuels delivered great good to society? Yes, indeed they have, but that doesn't mean that it hasn't come at a cost, as we have seen. So, we need a way of understanding all of this theologically, and this brings us to the doctrine of sin.

In this chapter, I want to look briefly at the ideas of sin and 'the Fall' as they apply to understanding climate change and the Anthropocene as a whole, as well as some of the early voices on what sin actually is, and what it means.

There are four ideas that I think are useful. The first is sin and the Fall as falling short of our human vocation to exercise the image of God, by falling into idolatry. The second is the idea of order and chaos in the Old Testament, and how sin unleashes chaos that can affect the whole of creation. The third idea is Walter Wink's concept of 'the Powers', which represent structural evil and how we relate to it. The last takes up the title of this chapter: our being sent out from Eden because of sin.

Falling short

Pick up any standard textbook on theology and you will find a chapter on sin. Some theological traditions are obsessed with sin, others appear to want to psychologise it away. We've already seen that evil appears to be a part of the world in which we live and that the grammar of evil continues to have currency. What we need is a theological way of understanding it, to enable us to work with God's plan to make all things new. Only by understanding our situation theologically can we speak and act prophetically, and live proleptically, in hope and with expectation of this new world to come. Of course, how you define sin will, in part, determine what you think the solution is, and how you understand the cross. There's no room here to delve into the atonement, or the mechanics of how the cross works, in any depth. Instead, what I'll do in this section is limit the discussion to one understanding of sin and how it sheds light on the problems we face.

One of the most common understandings of sin is the idea of missing the mark. This idea is captured by two words in particular, *chata* in Hebrew, and *hamartanō* in Greek.[1] I can remember going to Kryal Castle, with is a slight kitsch faux medieval castle in country Victoria. My son, who would have been about six or seven at the time, had a little bit of assistance at the archery range and managed to hit the target. I didn't. I missed the mark, by a long way. This idea of literally missing a target is found in Judges 20:16 with regards to a soldier's ability with a slingshot. However, when *chata* and *hamartanō* are used in a moral sense to describe the nature of sin (Lev 4, Rom 3:23), it typically means a deliberate failure. Sin, as Augustine, Thomas Aquinas, and others have observed, is a matter of the will. To 'have sinned and fall short of the glory of God' is more than a lack of ability to hit the target, but also a lack of intent to do the right thing, or as theologian, Sarah Coakley, observes, a misorientation of our desires.[2] This falling short is spelled out as falling short of the glory of God. And what is God's glory? In Greek is the word *doxēs*, from which we get the word doxology (which means the formal or liturgical praise of God). So, in a sense it is hinting at God's praiseworthiness.

---

1 Millard J. Erickson, *Christian Theology, Second Edition* (Grand Rapids, MI: Baker Books, 1998), 586–588.

2 Sarah Coakley, "Sin and Desire in Analytic Theology: A Return to Genesis 3." Filmed AAR & SBL Annual Meetings in San Antonio, Texas 20 November, 2016. YouTube video, 1:30:41. Posted [31 January, 2017]. https://www.youtube.com/watch?v=8oR8C91vqmc.

How does that help us understand sin more? In the Greek translation of the Hebrew Bible, the glory of the Lord (Ex 33) is described a God's *doxēs*. We learn that Moses does not see God's face, but he does see God's *doxēs*, which is closely associated with God's covenant name, YHWH, which in turn reflects God's character as the one who shows mercy. Jump forward to the New Testament, and the glory of God is the Word, the glory of the only son of the Father (Jn 1:14). Indeed, John is echoing Exodus because he mentions Moses by name and points out the superiority of Jesus' revelation of the nature of God as 'grace and truth.' Jesus reveals what God is like. Jesus is the one who, like God in the Tabernacle, pitches a tent among us: the literal meaning of the Greek word skēnoō, usually translated as 'lived' in John 1:14. This is why I think that the Rainbow Spirit Elders capture the idea of the incarnation so wonderfully as God having 'built a humpy among us.'[3]

Paul further picks up on much of the language of John in Colossians 1. While John tells us that no one has ever seen God (Jn 1:18), Paul informs us that is because God is invisible (Col 1:15). Likewise, Jesus is both the only son (Jn 1:18) and the firstborn of creation (Col 1:15). All things came into being through him (Jn 1:3) and all things in heaven and earth were created through him (Col 1:16). And just as Jesus is the glory of God (John) so he is also the image of the invisible God (Paul).

This might seem a slightly long bow to draw (yes, that is the longest pun set-up I have ever used), but it seems to me that the image of God is God's glory, which is the divine character. And so, if sin is falling short of God's glory, it means falling short of God's image. This takes us right back to the beginning, where we read of human beings that they are created in the image of God (Gen 1:26–27)

> Then God said, "Let us make humankind in our image, according to our likeness; and let them have dominion over the fish of the sea, and over the birds of the air, and over the cattle, and over all the wild animals of the earth, and over every creeping thing that creeps upon the earth." So God created humankind in his image, in the image of God he created them; male and female he created them.

---

3 Rainbow Spirit Elders, *Rainbow Spirit Theology: Towards an Australian Theology Second Edition* (Hindmarsh SA: ATF Press, 2007), 59.

So, falling short of the glory of God is to fall short of the image of God, which is to fall short of what it means to be human, made in that image. And that means we are failing in our vocation to bear that image to the rest of creation.

Further to this, theologian, John Walton, describes the creation narrative of Genesis 1 as the setting up of a temple. He connects God's ceasing from his work on the seventh day (Gen 2:2) with the notion of divine rest, as the two are linked together in Exodus 20:11 in the giving of the Ten Commandments. God *rested* on the seventh day and blessed it as a *Sabbath*. Language of rest is associated with temple and divine rule. Psalm 132 is a pilgrim psalm, something that would be sung on the journey up to Jerusalem. Like much Hebrew wisdom literature, ideas are expressed in two ways within the same phrase, known as Hebrew parallelism. Hence, in verses 7–8, God's dwelling place is paralleled with God's resting place, and God's footstool is paralleled with the Ark of the Covenant. Likewise, in verse 14, God's resting place is paralleled with God's throne.[4] The implication we are meant to draw is that creation was intended as a temple, the divine throne room from where God rules the cosmos. This idea is bookended in Revelation 21:22, where the New Heaven and Earth are created from the old, the New Jerusalem descends, and there is no temple, because the Lord and the Lamb are present. So, the Jerusalem temple was designed as creation in miniature, but the end goal was always for God to dwell everywhere. At the end, so as in the beginning.

The last piece of the puzzle is to consider what you find in a temple. An example is the historic Meenakshi Amman Temple in the Indian state of Tamil Nadu. This visually stunning temple complex is adorned with thousands of statues of animals, demons, and gods.[5] Theologian, Rikk Watts, observes that there are close parallels between the formation of human beings out of the clay in Genesis 2:7 and other ancient Near

---

4 John Walton, *The Lost World of Genesis One: Ancient Cosmology and the Origins Debate* (Downers Grove, IL: IVP, 2009), 71–74.

5 Karina Sharma, "This Temple Is Covered in Thousands of Colorful Statues," *National Geographic*, 2 August, 2017, accessed 16 June, 2018, https://www.nationalgeographic.com/travel/destinations/asia/india/meenakshi-amman-hindu-temple/.

Eastern creation stories.[6] Given that there is no mention of a statue or image of God in the garden, the narrative and context points to the idea that humans are installed as the divine image, to be God's presence in the temple–cosmos. But bearing the divine image doesn't mean we sit idly around. Rather, as idols of the living God, we have a job to do. John Walton also notes that the verbs usually translated as 'cultivate' and 'keep' in Genesis 2:15 are best understood as carrying out sacred service.[7] In other words, our tending of creation is holy work. In sinning and falling short of our vocation to bear the image of God in the world, our work of caring properly for creation and for exercising proper dominion is compromised.

How does this come about? For Paul, it is all about idolatry, the giving ourselves over to the worship of things other than God and living in less than a fully human fashion.[8] A full treatment of Paul's argument in Romans will take too long, so I will tease it out in outline. The phrase in Romans 3:23 about falling short, is preceded by what Tom Wright takes as a single section from 1:18–3:20. Human beings are made in the image of God (*imago Dei*) and hence, in worshipping images made with human hands (1:23), humans not only dishonour God, but also degrade themselves. Critiquing pagan idolatry is standard prophetic fare in the Hebrew Bible. In Romans 1:18, wrath is revealed against all ungodliness, just as in verse 16, salvation is available to all who have faith. Wrath, as Tom Wright notes, is not merely against breaking arbitrary laws, but against the rejection of the plain knowledge of God made known in creation and the exchange of the worship of God for created things such as idols. God is the creator and passionate lover of the world, intimately involved with it and known through it.[9]

---

6 Rikk Watts, "The New Exodus/New Creation Restoration of the Image of God: A Biblical–Theological Perspective on Salvation," in *What Does it Mean to be Saved?* edited by John G. Stackhouse, Jnr (Grand Rapids, MI: Baker Academic, 2002), 18–22

7 John Walton, *The Lost World of Adam and Eve: Genesis 2–3 and the Origins Debate* (Downers Grove, Il: IVP, 2015), 104–115.

8 N. Thomas Wright, *Romans*, in Robert W. Wall (ed) "The New Interpreter's Bible: A Commentary in Twelve Volumes, Volume X" (Nashville: Abingdon Press, 2002), 430.

9 Wright, *Romans*, 431.

In verses 19–20, we read that God's 'eternal power and divine nature' have been made known through the created order, so that people are 'without excuse,' for their idolatry. Paul is calling creation as a witness against human idolatry in the same way that Moses did in Deuteronomy 30:19 against Israel. Paul calls on the whole of creation to judge against humanity in its breaking of the creation covenant with God to be divine image bearers (Gen 1:26–28) and to fulfil the creation mandate of ruling as vice regents. Instead, they exchanged God's glory for the worship of a creature. This echoes both the Fall and the wilderness experience with the Golden Calf (Ex 32, Ps 106:20 which also speaks of exchange). Hence, this passage does not merely denounce pagan idolatry, but also that of which God's very own people were guilty.

Romans 2–3 continues the law court setting. The common theme is the impartiality of God in judgement (2:3), and the equality of both Jew and Gentile before God in judgement and salvation (2:10, 3:9). That the Gentiles were guilty of idolatry is beyond question, but in 2:24 Paul writes, 'For, as it is written, "The name of God is blasphemed among the Gentiles because of you."' This is a reference to Isaiah 52:5. The people of Israel were exiled in Assyria and they were mocked all day by their captors. Hence, the result of Israel's idolatry and consequent exile is blasphemy of the divine name. Yet we are not without hope, as Isaiah 52:7 states that the gospel message is that 'Your God reigns' and that all of the earth will see God's salvation (v. 10).

So, by the time we reach Romans 3:23, we understand that falling short of God's glory is giving up our divine vocation as the image of God by worshipping things other than God. While in the ancient world this was things of stone and wood, we have replaced the graven images of animals and phallic symbols with money, sex, progress, knowledge, power and control. The Anthropocene comes out of the naïve understanding that we can control and subdue nature for our own ends. Medieval historian, Lynn White, famously pointed the finger of blame at the text of Genesis 1.[10] However, ethicist, Michael Northcott, makes the case that we have read Genesis 1 through the lens of Francis Bacon for centuries, which allowed humans to manipulate the earth

---

10 Lyn White Jnr, "The Roots of our Historical Crisis," *Science,* 155 (1967): 1203–1207.

as inert, dead matter. Bacon was an English philosopher, statesman, scientist (an anachronistic title but an accurate claim), and author, to name a few roles. He understood scientific knowledge as power over nature. Bacon explains that nature

> exists in three states, and is subject, as it were, to three kinds of regimen. Either she is free and develops herself in her own ordinary course, or she is forced out of her proper state by the perverseness and insubordination of matter and the violence of impediments, or she is constrained and moulded by art and human history. The first state refers to the 'species' of things; the second to 'monsters'; the third to 'things artificial'.[11]

For Bacon, humans can take charge of the 'human–nature relation' and constrain and mould nature, which Northcott ultimately sees as a kind of technology.[12] It is not that technology shouldn't play a role in the way in which we relate to creation. Who wants to be naked when it is cold, rained on without cover, and subject to disease without cures? It is how we perceive of and use technology in our relation to the rest of the creation that requires careful thought. If we have no regard for nature, or see it (and oftentimes as a consequence, other humans) as mere inert matter for our own use alone, we will invariably abuse it. As John Polkinghorne observes, all new technological advances can be understood as a fall upwards, precisely because the new enlarged powers that these technologies give us open up the possibilities of good and evil.[13]

Chaos Unleashed

When I was a kid, I used to watch a lot of TV. It doesn't appear to have done much damage. One of my favourite series was the American spy comedy, *Get Smart*. A Mel Brookes classic, it poked fun at Cold War anxieties, with Don Adams playing the bumbling, yet ultimately effective spy, Maxwell Smart, agent 86. He worked for the government agency, *Control*, fighting against the agents of the spy agency, *Chaos*. Chaos describes the state of a house with young children, the political

---

11 Michael S. Northcott, *A Political Theology of Climate Change* (Grand Rapids, MI: Wm. B. Eerdmans Publishing Co, 2013): 102.

12 Northcott, *A Political Theology of Climate Change*, 117.

13 John Polkinghorne, *Belief in God in an Age of Science* (New York: Vail-Balou Press, 1998), 92.

situation in countries like Syria, and was used in the ancient world to describe the world without the ordering of the gods.

The first thing to acknowledge is that in wanting to communicate theological truths, the biblical writers (and ultimately the Holy Spirit who inspires) used ideas that were commonly understood and drew from the cultural air that their readers breathed. In other words, the bible is not merely another piece of ancient Near Eastern literature, simply stolen and adapted from Israel's neighbours. And yet, scripture was not written in an historical vacuum.[14] This means we don't have to panic and go into a defensive huddle when we see similarities between the Babylonian *Enuma Elish* and Genesis 1, or between the Noahic Flood and the Akkadian *Atrahasis* and Babylonian *Gilgamesh* sagas.[15] The similarities will help us better appreciate the differences.

The second thing to realise is that Genesis 1 shares an understanding of the world with its contemporaries, in particular that, as John Walton has found

> people in the ancient world believed that something existed not by virtue of its material properties, but by virtue of its having a function in an ordered system.[16]

Order is the key: order brought out of chaos. It is lack of order that is described in Genesis 1:2, where the word typically translated as formless (*tōhû*) means waste or wilderness, a place of no agricultural value (Deut 32:10). In six days, God brings order to this chaos in a series of separations: light from dark to create time, waters from waters to create space, and dry land from waters to create food.[17]

Now let's consider the text's cultural background. The breath of God broods over the deep (Hebrew *tehom*) like a mother bird over her chicks. The Akkadian equivalent of *tehom* is *ti'amat* (Tiamat). In the Babylonian story *Enuma Elish*, Tiamat is the personification of saltwater. She is killed by the storm god, Marduk, who makes the earth

14 Peter Enns, *Inspiration and incarnation* (Grand Rapids: Baker Academic: 2005), 15.

15 Enns, *Inspiration and incarnation*, 27.

16 Walton, *The Lost World*, 24.

17 John Walton, *The Lost World of Adam and Eve: Genesis 2–3 and the Origins Debate* (Downers Grove, IL: IVP, 2009), 35–45.

out of her body. So, in Genesis, Tiamat is demythologised to become *tehom*, not a god, but still representative of chaos in creation. Yet, on day five, sea monsters (*tanninim*) make an appearance, as creatures of God (v. 21). Chaos is still present in creation, but firmly under divine control. Some notion of a battle against chaos is retained in Psalm 74: 14, 16–17. Here, we read that day and night belong to God (a reference to the first day of creation), and that he smashed the heads of Leviathan. God is master of the chaos monsters.[18]

If we then think about the biblical flood, chaos is released. The earth was corrupt and filled with violence (Gen 6:11) and so the great deep burst open, the windows of heaven opened, and the ordering of day two was undone (Gen 7:11). The waters don't subside until the divine breath blows over it (Gen 8:1–3), echoing the original ordering act of Genesis 1:2 (see also a likely allusion in Psalm 104:30). Even after the flood, the chaos monsters lurk in the background. A frustrated Job calls out for those who can rouse Leviathan to unleash the forces of chaos once more and make the world as if he'd never been born (Jb 3:8).

Furthermore, the language of the uncreation of the Flood appears in judgement on the people of Israel. For example, in Isaiah 24, the earth dries and withers so that it is useless for agriculture (v. 4), because like Genesis 6:11, the earth is polluted by covenant violation (v. 5). The curse of verse 6 is that the inhabitants of the earth dwindle; the reverse of the blessing of multiplication and fruitfulness in Genesis 1:28. Finally, in verse 18, we read that windows of the firmament are opened, just as in the Flood. Hence, acts of divine judgement throughout the Old Testament are envisioned using a similar vocabulary as the Noahic Flood; that of uncreation reducing order to disorder and chaos.

It takes little imagination then to think of climate change in general, and sea level rise in particular, as an undoing of God's created order as a consequence of human sin. Rather than exempting us from divine judgement, the flood narrative gives us a framework for understanding our present situation. Michael Northcott suggests that we needn't

---

18 For a fuller discussion on the chaos monsters and the contemporary backstory to Genesis 1, see Gregory Mobley, *The Return of the Chaos Monsters – And Other Backstories of the Bible* (Grand Rapids, MI: Wm Eerdmans Publishing Co., 2012), chapter 1.

understand the link between our sin and climate chaos as one where God has the divine finger on the smite button ready to punish. Instead, there is an order of creation that bears the divine will for how things are to operate, which is 'set into the character and structure of creation.'[19] This means that the accumulation of wealth in the West brings about judgement by disrupting the natural order God has placed in the creation. Sadly, judgement on the sins of the rich is indiscriminate and falls disproportionately on the poor (Jer 2:34).[20] In particular, and profoundly unjustly, the chaos of sea level rise has been unleashed on the inhabitants of Oceania. Not because of their sin, but because of ours.[21]

The Powers that Be

The Fall and the effects of human sin are often thought of in purely individual terms. This leaves much to be desired and falls short (pardon the pun) of the biblical witness on the topic. Climate change is not simply the result of a collective of individuals gone wrong, but the whole structure of society and its power structures. The Fall narrative doesn't end with Adam and Eve ejected from the Garden, but with the scattering of the people of Babel. Theologian and activist, Walter Wink, has written extensively about the fallen nature of the power structures of society, including its spiritual elements, and so his approach is worth examining.[22] Wink identifies the Powers that we read of in the bible as

the systems themselves, the institutions and structures that weave society into an intricate fabric of power and relationships.[23]

The Powers themselves are necessary for an ordered society but they can also be a source of great evil. Wink dismisses as 'gross literalism'

---

19 Michael Northcott, *A Moral Climate: The Ethics of Global Warming* (Maryknoll, NY: Orbis Books, 2007), 12–13.
20 Northcott, *A Moral Climate,* 41.
21 Mick Pope, "The Sea is Eating the Ground: A Theology of Sea Level Rise," *Anglican Theological Review*, 100:1 (Winter 2018): 79–92.
22 Walter Wink, *Naming the Powers: The Language of Power in the New Testament* (Philadelphia: Fortress Press, 1984). Walter Wink, *Unmasking the Powers: The Invisible Forces That Determine Human Existence* (Philadelphia: Fortress Press, 1986). Walter Wink, *Engaging the Powers: Discernment and Resistance in a World of Domination* (Minneapolis: Fortress Press, 1992). Walter Wink, *The Powers that Be* (New York: Doubleday, 1998).
23 Wink, *The Powers that Be*, 1.

the idea that the Powers are angelic or demonic beings and yet, at the same time, wants to dismiss materialism, the idea that the Powers are nothing but an aspect of material reality that a sociologist could study. Instead, he sees, for example, the angels of the seven churches in Revelation 2–3 not as supernatural beings, but as 'the corporate personality of the church, its ethos or spirit or essence.'[24] On the one hand, Wink helps orient us correctly to examine the spirituality of systems and organisations, to understand that they can take on a life of their own that transcends the total of the individuals within it. He also points to why it is not enough to convert individuals in order to end oppression, but rather, to change systems. He points out that good and necessary systems can go bad and become oppressive. Their angel becomes a demon. I don't buy entirely into his understanding, but find the approach useful. I'm a little more with C.S. Lewis, who wrote in *The Screwtape Letters*

> There are two equal and opposite errors into which our race can fall about the devils. One is to disbelieve in their existence. The other is to believe, and to feel an excessive and unhealthy interest in them.[25]

One of Wink's key texts is Colossians 1:16,

> for in him all things in heaven and on earth were created, things visible and invisible, whether thrones or dominions or rulers or powers—all things have been created through him and for him.

All things, including the Powers, were created through and for Christ.[26] The words translated as thrones, dominions, rulers, and powers are used in many places to describe human institutions. For example, ruler and rule (Greek *archē*) can refer to that of a human governor (Lk 20:20). Eighty-seven of the one hundred and two New Testament uses of power (Greek *exousia*) are impersonal and refer to the actions carried out in an office, that is, it is structural, the authorities (plural) of a synagogue (Lk 12:11).[27] Yet, some words are ambiguous. The Greek word *thronos* can be used of earthly thrones, or of the throne of God and surrounding thrones of a heavenly council (e.g. Dan 7:9, Rev 4:4).

---

24 Wink, *The Powers that Be*, 3.

25 C. S. Lewis, *The Screwtape Letters* (Glasgow: Harper Collins, 2001), ix.

26 Wink, *Naming the Powers*, 64–67.

27 Wink, *Naming the Powers*, 15.

What Wink concludes then is that these terms are mostly human ones. When we add 'all things in heaven and on earth' and 'things visible and invisible', he believes we are to understand that the Powers include human institutions and the spiritual realm.

Wink goes on to claim then that the spiritual powers are

the inner aspect of material or tangible manifestations of power, precisely because we 'encounter them primarily in reference to the material or "earthly" reality of which they are the inner most essence.'[28]

This means that human institutions have both a material reality that needs to be changed, and an inner spirituality than needs to be challenged. Together, these form the Powers.

Perhaps Wink's most useful insight is that in Ephesians 3:10 the church makes known God's wisdom to these Powers.[29] He reads the Powers in this context as the angels of the Gentile nations but the overall point is that to be the church, living by Christ's self–sacrificing and serving nature, is a testimony to these Powers that their sovereignty is not absolute. Hence, our mandate in Ephesians 3:10 can't be merely materialistic but must be spiritual as well. Evangelism is always social action and social action is always evangelism. Proclaiming the sovereignty of Christ over the Powers is an act of critique of idolatry and empire.[30] While the Powers can be considered in isolation, together as an overarching network, they form the domination system.[31] Wink identifies this domination system as *kosmos*, 'the human sociological realm that exists in estrangement from God.'[32] The *kosmos* is created by God (John 1:1–5), fallen (John 1:11c), but it is redeemable (John 12:47).

Applying this then to the problem of climate change, for example, we need to address the fact that the Powers in this case are big energy companies who either deny, or deliberately obscure, the truth about what they are doing. Rather than serving the good of the cultural mandate of Genesis 1:26–28, they continue to commit the evil of damaging God's good creation because their spiritual aspect has become corrupt, driven

---

28 Wink, *Naming the Powers*, 105.

29 Wink, *Naming the Powers*, 89f.

30 Wink, *Naming the Powers*, 117.

31 Wink, *The Powers that Be*, 39.

32 Wink, *Engaging the Powers*, 51.

by the desire to maximise profit. Exxon apparently knew about climate change 40 years ago but at best sat on the knowledge, now claiming that their conclusions were not as stark as made out. And yet, they have been implicated in funding think tanks that promote climate change denial.[33] The American Enterprise Institute, which is funded by fossil fuel companies, actively obscures and denies the science.[34]

What this shows is that the spirituality of a system can be so wrong that individual conversion to faith is not enough: the very spirituality of a system needs to be changed. Exxon Mobil could invest in renewable energy. As a company, it must either change or go out of business. Justice must be done and corruption must be rooted out. Exxon's spiritual intransigence is seen in its counter-suing lawyers who are suing it because Exxon 'denied findings of climate change scientists despite knowing that the use of fossil fuels posed "grave risk" to the planet.'[35] We cannot totally demonise the company or its employees, but a spade is a spade, sin is sin, and change, non–violently achieved, is essential. Prayer will be a big part of this and so will all sorts of sacrifices. This is, after all, how the Powers have always been challenged.

But there is a little more to say on the topic. We can identify the evil that has produced climate change and the other aspects of the Anthropocene with our political institutions, big business and so on. Indeed, there is a strong element of truth to this insofar as that when we are told that we should all switch our light bulbs to more efficient ones – while the government can't move from coal to wind and solar – we are being conned by the system. But individuals can't be let off the hook either. When Walter Wink visited Apartheid South Africa in 1986, four

---

33 Shannon Hall, "Exxon Knew about Climate Change almost 40 years ago," *Scientific American*, 26 October, accessed 16 April, 2018, https://www.scientificamerican.com/article/exxon–knew–about–climate–change–almost–40–years–ago/.

34 On denial see Jeffrey Sachs, "How the AEI Distorts the Climate Debate," *Huffpost*, 2 August, 2014, updated 6 December, 2017, accessed 16 April, 2018, https://www.huffingtonpost.com/jeffrey–sachs/how–the–aei–distorts–the_b_4751680.html. On funding of AEI by big oil see, Ian Sample, "Scientists offered cash to dispute climate study," *The Guardian*, 3 February, 2007, accessed 16 April, 2018, https://www.theguardian.com/environment/2007/feb/02/frontpagenews.climatechange.

35 Bon Van Boris, "Exxon Sues the Suers in Fierce Climate–Change Case," *Bloomburg Business Week*, 13 February, 2018, accessed 16 April, 2018, https://ww\w.bloomberg.com/news/articles/2018–02–13/exxon–sues–the–suers–in–fierce–bid–to–defeat–climate–lawsuits.

years before Nelson Mandela was released, black people knew they were fighting not just white people but an oppressive system. They also knew that they had to tell some people that they were 'supporting the system.'[36] Wink recognised that support of the system can be active or passive, done by the perpetrators or those being oppressed. And much of our passive support of the systems that are wreaking havoc on the planet are fairly banal.

The idea that evil acts can be utterly banal goes back to Hannah Arendt and her examination of the trial of Nazi, Adolf Eichmann.[37] Eichmann pleaded that he was but a small cog in a big machine. Indeed, the horror that was the Holocaust, with its ruthless efficiency and the enormity of the horrendous task it performed, could only be carried out by a big machine. In Arendt's words, the court thought they had found the actual motor.[38] Whatever the best metaphor, he was guilty. And as Arendt observes, all cogs in an evil machine are guilty, even if their contribution is passive support. And here is the kicker of the Anthropocene: so long as we actively support the consumerism and individualism of our society, and buy into the myth of endless growth, we too are cogs in what Brian McLaren calls the suicide machine.[39] While we are not examining closely our diets, our travel, or contacting our politicians to urge them to action, we are allowing ourselves to be swept along in the stream, following the current that leads to the falls. It's time to resist the system, to come out of Babylon (Rev 18:4).

Moving out of Eden

The title of this chapter is East of Eden. This is a phrase that appears twice in Genesis 3–4. There are many parallels between these two 'Fall' accounts as bible historian, Cynthia Edenburg, observes.[40] Both Adam

---

36 Wink, *The Powers that Be*, 39.

37 Hannah Arendt, *Eichmann and the Holocaust* (London: Penguin Books, 2005).

38 Arendt, *Eichmann and the Holocaust*, 116.

39 Brian D. McLaren, *Everything Must Change: Jesus, Global Crises, and a Revolution of Hope* (Nashville: Thomas Nelson, 2007), 55.

40 Cynthia Edenburg, "From Eden to Babylon: Reading Genesis 2-4 as a paradigmatic narrative," in Thomas B. Dozeman, Thomas Römer, and Konrad Schmid (eds), *Pentateuch, Hexateuch, or Enneateuch : Identifying literary works in Genesis through Kings* (Atlanta: Society of Biblical Literature, 2011): 155-167.

and Eve (Gen 3:23–24) and Cain (Gen 4:14) are sent east of Eden for their sin. Humanity are made homeless wanderers in the ark (Gen 7). The inhabitants of Babel are scattered over the earth (Gen 11:9). Indeed, in his book *The Land,* Walter Brueggemann suggests that Genesis 1–11 follows a landed people on their way to landlessness, and Genesis 12–50 describes a landless people on the way to landedness.[41] The whole drama of the Hebrew Bible is a people in search of a home under God's rule, and this extends into the New Testament, reaching its crescendo in the descent of the New Jerusalem and the New Heavens and Earth.

However, the point is that there is a link between idolatry, sin, and expulsion in the Hebrew Bible that forewarns us about our modern idolatry and sins, and their impact on the planet. The Anthropocene is a sign that we are being made homeless in judgement over our failures to bear the divine image and tend the garden. It's time to repent as we hope and wait for our own return from exile.

---

41 Walter Brueggemann, *The Land* (Philadelphia: Fortress Press, 1977).

Chapter 4 — Beam Me Up, Goddy

It's just a game?

When I was 16, handheld computer games first became a thing. Nintendo had released its Game and Watch series that featured handheld games with an LCD screen. It ranged from Donkey Kong, the angry barrel tossing ape, and an as yet not famous Mario, to a variety of titles done in bad taste. I still own (albeit, a not fully operable) copy of Fire Attack, which isn't really acceptable by today's standards. I owned an Atari 2600 and still have it tucked away along with half-a-dozen old consoles. I played text adventures and the early 3D shooters like Doom. My teenager continues in the tradition with his Xbox, Nintendo 3DS, and Steam downloads onto his laptop. So, I don't have an issue with games per se. However, one significant issue with computer games is the way that violence is portrayed, in particular what Walter Wink calls the 'myth of redemptive violence.' This myth suggests that violent acts can solve problems, save people, and bring lasting peace.[1] Violent computer games have been implicated in mass shootings, but I don't think we can scapegoat them directly. Rather, these games represent or embody the broader Powers as Wink would describe them. There is, however, perhaps something even larger that the prevalence of computer games can tell us about our culture.

In 2015, in Taiwan, two men died within days of each other after playing computer games nonstop for three and five days respectively. A 32-year old, identified by his family name Hsieh, appears to have gone into cardiac arrest.[2] On January 6, he entered an internet café in Kaohsiung, Taiwan's second largest city, and was found motionless and sprawled on a table at 10 a.m. on January 8. The man had been

1 Walter Wink, *The Powers that Be: Theology for a New Millennium* (New York: Galilee Doubleday, 1999), 49.

2 AFP, "Man dies after three-day internet gaming binge," *Sydney Morning Herald,* 17 January, 2015, accessed 8 April, 2018, https://www.smh.com.au/technology/man-dies-after-threeday-internet-gaming-binge-20150117-12sg0a.html.

unemployed for a long time and was a regular customer at the café, often playing for days. His family noted that he would often disappear for two to three days at a time.[3] Gaming has come a long way from the days of watching pixelated dots move across the screen. Online games are immersive and highly interactive: they can also be highly addictive. Why do people want to spend so much time in games and not in the real world?

The title of this chapter is borrowed from comments made when Gene Roddenberry, the creator of the classic 60s TV science fiction series, *Star Trek*, died. *Star Trek*, in its various franchises, depicts a future where human beings have made contact with aliens and taken their place in the galactic community of beings. It is an age where the consumption of animal protein has disappeared, replaced by computer created versions. Alcohol is likewise a thing of the past in its original form. Humans have transcended money and pursue art, science, and other forms of culture. It is a secular paradise. Roddenberry was an atheist and this came through very obviously in a number of the stories. Religion is either ignored or dismissed as irrelevant in the series. In the episode, *Who Mourns for Adonis?* a being claiming to be the Greek god, Apollo, demands that the crew of the Enterprise worship him.[4] The star of the show, Captain James T. Kirk, responds to Adonis' desire for worship with 'We've out grown you. You asked for something we could no longer give.' After Roddenberry's death, this hard-nosed atheism becomes less obvious and spirituality makes a reappearance in various guises. The joke is that, upon Roddenberry's death, a widely circulated internet meme was 'Beam me up, Goddy', after the phrase 'Beam me up, Scotty.' The latter phrase was never actually used in the TV series, but the meme has stuck.

So, what is the point of this short anecdote other than to show that I am a geek (some of you already knew that)? Well, in *Star Trek*, a device known as a transporter is able to disassemble people atom by

---

[3] Katie Hunt, and Naomi Ng, "Man dies in Taiwan after 3-day online gaming binge," *CNN*, 19 January, 2015, accessed 8 April, 2018, https://edition.cnn.com/2015/01/19/world/taiwan-gamer-death/index.html.

[4] Gene Roddenberry (creator), and Gilbert Ralston, "Who Mourns for Adonis?" *Star Trek*, NBC, New York, 22 September, 1967.

atom and transport them almost instantaneously over a large distance. It is a standard plot device that characters in *Star Trek*, and other science fiction series like the BBC's late 70s dystopian *Blake's 7*, are rescued at the last minute by being 'beamed up.'[5] Such a device is illustrative of the modernist idea that technology and secularism can rescue us from all of our human limitations and dangers, both external and internal. And this is the role computer games often play in modern culture.

Reality can be kind of dull. American game designer, Jane McGonigal, claims that 'reality is broken' and that games can change the world![6] Reality is broken compared with games because they provide us with meaningful challenges. McGonigal thinks we should 'create more happiness by structuring real work like game work', an exercise known as gamification. Likewise, why 'should we needlessly spend the majority of our lives in boredom and anxiety?'[7] Games can save the world, making it a more interesting place. But is boredom and anxiety the main thing we need saving from? To be sure, McGonigal recognises that the world faces real problems, like peak oil. No problem. We already have experience of managing complex problems from playing 'God games', games which allow the player to shape civilisations, the development of life, and the future of planets. We're smart enough with our gaming experience to finds solutions to all of life's problems. After all, McGonigal claims

> Humanity is now stuck with a planet stewardship role ... We are gods and *have* to get used to it.

Cyberheaven

Games and the internet are, for some, a replacement for heaven. This is the thesis of Margaret Wertheim's *The Pearly Gates of Cyberspace*.[8] This comparison unfortunately trades on a misunderstanding that

---

5 Personally, I like the humorous twists on this in the Star Wars spoof *Space Balls* direct by Mel Brooks, and the Star Trek spoof *Galaxy Quest* starring Tim Allen, Sigourney Weaver, Alan Rickman, and Tony Shalhoub.

6 Jane McGonigal, *Reality is Broken: Why Games Make Us Better and How They Can Change the World* (London: Vintage Books, 2012).

7 McGonigal, *Reality it Broken*, 36.

8 Margaret Wertheim, *The Pearly Gates of Cyberspace: A History of Space from Dante to the Internet* (Sydney: Doubleday, 2000).

Wertheim has about heaven. But then it's the same misunderstanding that many Christians have as well. She understands the vision of Revelation 21 as describing the heavenly city as

> the final reward: an eternal resting place of peace and harmony, above and beyond the troubled material world.[9]

While her understanding is biblically inaccurate, the comparison of this idea of heaven with people's approach to technology seems spot on. Wertheims' description of cyberspace as techno-heaven relies on a number of parallels.[10] Following Umberto Eco, she sees America as a kind of Rome (not an original comparison as you will see) in its state of decline, and hence, I might add, a target for the criticisms levelled at Babylon in Revelation. Just as mystery religions and Christianity were able to take hold in a spiritually bereft society, so too cyberspace has gained traction in a boring and anxious one, just as McGonigal suggests. Social inequality is growing, and cyberspace offers the kind of democratic spirituality that the vision of heaven gives us (Rev 5:9). The ability to connect with many people online mimics medieval iconography of a heaven full of angels. However, the dream of cyberspace as a place where we can finally rid ourselves of 'the ballast of materiality' owes more to Gnostic and Platonic thought than it does that of first century Judaism or the early church. It is a mistake to take the vision of Revelation 21:4 of no crying, mourning, or death as a denigration of the flesh as mere 'meat' or a prison. This is not a Christian vision, but a Platonic one.[11]

Wertheim sees cyberspace as a real space, going through an inflationary period just as the real universe has done.[12] Cyberspace emerges from physical reality, in that it is dependent on the physics of electronics, electromagnetism, and the properties of silicon. However, according to Wertheim, 'cyberspace is not ontologically rooted in these physical phenomena, it is *not subject to the laws of physics*.'[13] In other words, in essence, cyberspace is not tied to the physical world that

---

9 Wertheim, *The Pearly Gates of Cyberspace*, 18.

10 Wertheim, *The Pearly Gates of Cyberspace*, 22f.

11 Wertheim, *The Pearly Gates of Cyberspace*, 259.

12 Wertheim, *The Pearly Gates of Cyberspace*, 224.

13 Wertheim, *The Pearly Gates of Cyberspace*, 228.

gave it birth, but transcends it. This sounds a lot like Walter Wink's understanding of the Powers, and is for Wertheim, a shift back to medieval dualism, a relationship between heaven and earth that the Enlightenment rejected. Bereft of a spiritual reality, we are left with scientist Carl Sagan's 'The Cosmos is all that is or was or ever will be.'[14] However, in cyberspace, our location is no longer fixed, and neither is our sexual identity, as we can be anywhere, and become anybody. This is truly a liquid modernity, a liquid self, a techno-Gnosticism.

If Eden is presented to us (via Augustine) as a state of innocence, the New Jerusalem is a state of wisdom and knowledge. Likewise, cyberspace is rooted in information, according to Professor of architecture, Michael Benedikt.[15] Maybe someone should explain to Benedikt that information alone is neither knowledge nor wisdom. However, such insight appears lacking in discussion about a cyber future. Knowledge is replaced by big data, and faith in God is replaced by faith in technology and our endless ability to improve ourselves. Such is the vision of *Singularity*. According to Ray Kurzweil, singularity is the 'merger between human intelligence and machine intelligence' that will result in 'something bigger than itself. It's the cutting edge of evolution on our planet.'[16]

The idea of singularity goes back to mathematician, physicist, and computer scientist, John von Neumann, who wrote of the

> accelerating progress of technology and changes in the mode of human life, which gives the appearance of approaching some essential singularity in the history of the race.[17]

The positive vision, advanced by futurist, Ray Kurzweil, is that Artificial Intelligence (AI) will augment our humanity for the better. Technology is already being used to replace degraded sections of our brain, with neural implants for Parkinson's Disease, and cochlear implants for profound to severe hearing loss. Soon, Kurzweil expects

---

14 The words of Carl Sagan in Carl Sagan, Ann Druyan, and Steven Soter, "The Shores of the Cosmic Ocean," *Cosmos*, Public Broadcasting Service, Arlington, September 28, 1980.

15 Quoted in Wertheim, *The Pearly Gates of Cyberspace*, 258.

16 Ray Kurzweil, "Singularity," *Edge*, 24 March, 2001, accessed 8 April, 2018, https://www.edge.org/conversation/ray_kurzweil-the-singularity.

17 Stanislaw Ulam, "Tribute to John von Neumann," *Bulletin of the American Mathematical Society* 64 (1958):1-49.

a complete map of the human brain, allowing us to enhance our own intelligence using nanobots; tiny robots at or close to the scale of a nanometre (10^{-9} metres). Human and technology will no longer be separate, but one. If you've ever seen the anime series *Ghost in the Shell*, you'll get the picture of enhanced humanity, together with the stigma attached to the unenhanced. It's really an updated version of Aldous Huxley's *Brave New World*, where 'John the Savage' simply seeks to live like we do now. His simplicity is met with incredulity. Why would you remain unmodified when 'machine intelligence will appear to biological humanity to be their transcendent servants'?[18]

What is the foundation of this thinking? Firstly, Kurzweil thinks that from an economic point of view, only information has value, insofar as it reflects knowledge and not just data. He believes that 'the knowledge component of products and services is asymptoting towards 100 percent.' This means that the exponential growth in technology is a good thing: it's an increase in economic value. We will, he believes, be able to 'create virtually any physical product and meet all of our material needs' out of sand and some metals. I wonder if this works for food for over 10 billion? Additionally, I think his idea of reducing everything to information falls short of wisdom, or relationship, to say nothing of the fact that the economic point of view is not the only consideration in human life. Or indeed, that this stunning technology has, to date, had a large impact on the environment in which we live and rely upon for life!

The other important ethical issue to rise is whether or not AI will be conscious. How will we relate to AI and indeed will it be our saviour or will Skynet activate and bring a Terminator future? What does it really mean to be human if we can manipulate our genes or merge with AI? Kurzweil sees humans as special as we are the only species to survive in the technological evolutionary niche; technology that evolves over time. And yet, he also states that 'Patterns are the fundamental ontological reality, because they are what persists, not anything physical.' You can hear echoes of Wertheim's analysis in this. Cyberspace over physical space; AI mergers over the mere biological. Indeed, 'Even our basic existence as people is nothing but a pattern.' Rather reductionist, don't

---

[18] Kurzweil, *Singularity*.

you think? It also begs the question of why my pattern should seek to persist? Apparently, Kurzweil is waiting for his own personal techno-heaven; he reportedly takes one hundred and fifty pills a day and is intravenously injected weekly so that he can live the fifteen years or so until singularity, and be assured of external life.[19]

This entire vision seems to rest on the assumption that we have been better, and will continue to get better, as a species. It is a secular premillennialism, where society increasingly gets better until the dawning of a new age. This idea of the progress of humanity finds its champion in cognitive psychologist, Steven Pinker, as discussed in chapter 1.

The Geoengineered Heavenly City

It seems to me that a good deal of the secular gospel is blind to the impacts that we have had on the planet. And even when it isn't, it seems to think that technology will provide the magic beans to fix all our ills. Now, don't get me wrong: when it comes to climate change, technology will play its role, but exactly what role is the key question. Geoengineering is 'the intentional manipulation of planetary systems at a global scale.'[20] What this means in practice is that it is a 'possible means of preventing the potentially catastrophic consequences of climate change.'[21] There are two main techniques. One designed to cool the planet by reflecting sunlight back into space, otherwise known as solar radiation management (or SRM for short). The other is the direct removal of planet warming carbon dioxide from the atmosphere, known as carbon direct removal (or CDR for short).

---

19 Carole Cadwalladr, "Are the robots about to rise? Google's new director of engineering thinks so…," *The Guardian,* 23 February, 2014, accessed 8 April, 2018, https://www.theguardian.com/technology/2014/feb/22/robots-google-ray-kurzweil-terminator-singularity-artificial-intelligence.

20 Stephen M. Gardiner, "Why geoengineering is not a 'global public good', and why it is ethically misleading to frame it as one," *Climatic Change,* 121 (2013):513–525

21 David P. Keller, Ellias Y. Feng, and Andreas Oschlies, "Potential climate engineering effectiveness and side effects during a high carbon dioxide-emission scenario," *Nature Communications,* 5 (2014) Article number: 3304 (2014) doi:10.1038/ncomms4304.

The problems with SRM are numerous.[22] Because it blocks sunlight to cool the planet, it doesn't deal with the build-up of carbon dioxide in the oceans, which is making them more acidic, and hence, making life difficult for animals that make shells.[23] Do you like pretty reefs and oysters? Then be concerned about ocean acidification. Some of the SRM techniques are also impossibly expensive, like launching a flotilla of mirrors into space. Others, like injecting sulphur into the upper atmosphere, can cause ozone loss and negatively impact the Indian monsoon. It's also worth noting that if we were to stop SRM suddenly, the warming would be very rapid and highly disruptive to natural systems. It also goes without saying that blocking sunlight will be bad for agriculture, and for solar power, one of the technologies that will power our future.

The kinds of carbon removal technologies that are usually discussed typically have a small impact on climate, except schemes to green the centre of Australia and the Sahara via irrigation. These techniques actually warm the planet by making the earth's surface darker and hence absorb more heat. Other techniques involve fertilising the oceans to encourage the growth of plankton. The idea is that they will absorb more carbon out of the atmosphere and take it with them to the bottom of the ocean when they die. The impacts of these techniques appear minor, with the side effects of making regions of the ocean oxygen poor, since decay of organic matter consumes oxygen. It can also increase the acidity of the ocean floor by adding extra carbon dioxide. While we will need to remove carbon dioxide directly from the atmosphere to return the atmospheric concentration to close to pre-industrial levels, geoengineering is no replacement for the rapid decarbonising of our economies. There are better ways to remove carbon, such as better agriculture practices, and artificial photosynthesis that does not rely upon messing with natural cycles.[24]

22 Ken Caldeira, Govindasamy Bala, and Long Cao, "The Science of Geoengineering," *The Annual Review of Earth and Planetary Sciences*, 41 (2013): 231-256.
23 UNEP, *UNEP Emerging Issues: Environmental Consequences of Ocean Acidification: A Threat to Food Security* (Nairobi: United Nations Environment Programme, 2010).
24 Paul Hawken, *Drawdown: The Most Comprehensive Plan Ever Proposed to Roll Back Global Warming* (New York: Penguin Putnam, 2017).

Ultimately, apart from the risks and ineffectiveness of such technology, one of the key problems is spiritual. Recall the story of the prophet, Elijah, against the prophets of Baal. The Israelites had turned to Baal worship under King Ahab and his foreign wife Jezebel (1 Ki 16:29–34). Baal (master or lord) was a prominent deity in Canaanite religion. As the storm God, he was tied to the winter rains by a repetition of his death at the hands of Mot, the god of death, following by an annual rising again. For the Israelites, to worship Baal as well as YHWH (the Lord) was to have an each way bet on obtaining good harvests. So, Elijah brings judgement on this apostasy by declaring a drought where there would be neither rain, indicating a failure of the rainy season (October to April), nor dew, which brought water to crops in the summer.[25] When Elijah challenged the prophets of Baal on Mount Carmel, they turned to Baal for help (1 Ki 16:26–29), the very cause of their woes in the first place. The competition ends as a victory of YHWH and his faithful, with rains then returning (1 Ki 18:33–45).

In a sense, manipulation of Baal to bring the rains was an ancient form of technology, because technology is the production of tools to manipulate our environment to suit our needs. This makes geoengineering a form of Baalism because it looks solely to technology for our salvation; the very technological thinking that has caused all of our problems and which can't deliver on its promises.

Now that we have looked at secular heaven, what about secular apocalypse?

It's the end of the world as we know it (and I feel fine)

America is an amazing country. It produces extremes of everything. This is made clear in the TV series, *Doomsday Preppers,* which was an American reality television series that profiled various survivalists or 'preppers': people preparing to survive the end of civilisation. I watched an episode to get a feel for the sort of people who become preppers and their issues of concern.[26] Steve H is expecting the collapse

---

25 Denis Baly, *The Geography of the Bible* (New York: Harper and Row, 1974): 43, 52.
26 Alan Madison, Kathleen Cromley, and Matt Sharp (executive producers), "Top Survivors," *Doomsday Preppers*, National Geographic Channel, Washington DC, 3 November, 2013.

of the American economy and believes that 'the entitlists' will come for his stuff. The entitlists remain unidentified but I assume that Steve is no believer in taxation or the welfare state. He has a cabin hidden away, stockpiled with an AK-47, a Glock pistol, and hunting guns. He provides target practice for his 8 year old son to teach him how to kill people. Steve has armour piercing rounds and uses readily available explosives to practice blowing up approaching vehicles. His paranoia is such that when he visits his cabin on weekends to stock it with supplies, he and his family walk in armed and not via the main road, to catch any squatters by surprise.

David Appleton is a stand-up comedian, with a distrust in human nature. He is expecting an earthquake, even though he lives in an area where there is no immediate risk. David builds survival tools out of scrap and is often found roaming the streets looking for bits and pieces to prep on the cheap. His prepping forms part of his comedic act. It isn't that funny. Meanwhile, Suzanne describes herself as a lifestyle prepper. Like others, she thinks that the US economy is in trouble (and with its debt to China, who's to argue). She is preparing for a bartering economy by accumulating goods she thinks would be good to barter, growing her own food, and so on. Unlike many others who seem to think that violent protection is part of the economic apocalypse, she turns to non-violent means, using paintballs as opposed to real firearms. Firearms do appear to be a common theme in the show, indeed in American society in general! Where does this obsession come from, along with the expectation of imminent societal collapse?

The end of the world is a theme that pervades popular culture. Take a TV series like *The Walking Dead,* for example (indeed you can take it – it's certainly not my cup of tea). Author Michael Totten believes the show is typical of our obsession with zombies, which are in turn a reflection of our age of anxiety.[27] The period 2003 to 2013 he believes was the golden decade for zombies, with movies like *World War Z* and video games like *Dead Rising 3.* The Walking Dead is now in its eighth

27 Michael J. Totten, "The Walking Dead in an Age of Anxiety: Why we're obsessed with zombies," *City Journal*, Autumn 2014, accessed 8 April, 2018, https://www.city-journal. org/html/walking-dead-age-anxiety-13688.html.

season. The series is based on a long running comic book that looks at life in the zombie apocalypse. One of the central characters is sheriff's deputy, Rick Grimes, who wakes up from a coma to find that a virus has animated the dead with the urge to consume human flesh. Civilisation has collapsed as a result. It's nothing new. I once sat rather unwillingly through *The Return of the Living Dead,* which was a poor taste horror comedy.

Zombie movies symbolise our anxiety about our own destruction. In the season one finale, a doctor from the Center for Disease Control exclaims, 'This is what takes us down. This is our extinction event.' The series is not really about zombies per se, but rather about how humans respond to crisis. The depressing thing about the series for me, as opposed to the tongue in cheek *Army of Darkness* where everyone bands together to defeat the evil, is that so much of the action centres around distrust and competition among the survivors. The forms of government that appear range from relatively benign to cannibalistic. Indeed, civilised people find it hard to survive in a world where civilisation itself has collapsed.

So, where does the anxiety come from? Totten grew up with Cold War anxiety and believes that it is over. However, with Trump in the White House, Putin as ruthless as ever, China ever willing to rattle the sabre, and North Korea willing to make nuclear threats to get attention, we perhaps shouldn't feel so secure. Nuclear disarmament has not been achieved. Thankfully, it is still on the agenda for some. The International Campaign to Abolish Nuclear Weapons (ICAN) won the 2017 Nobel Peace Prize

> for its work to draw attention to the catastrophic humanitarian consequences of any use of nuclear weapons.[28]

Sadly, none of the nuclear powers paid much attention to the award and the Australian government largely ignored this Australian born movement.[29] Indeed, US President Donald Trump has called for

---

28 "The Nobel Peace Prize 2017," *Nobel Media AB 2014*, 8 April 2018, accessed 8 April, 2018, http://www.nobelprize.org/nobel_prizes/peace/laureates/2017/.

29 James Glenday, "Nobel Peace Prize: Does an Australian-born anti-nuke group's award achieve anything?," *ABC News*, 11 December, 2017, accessed 8 April, 2018, http://www.abc.net.au/news/2017-12-09/does-the-nobel-peace-prize-achieve-anything/9242626

greater flexibility in its nuclear deterrent options, including 'low-yield' options.[30] But low-yield does not mean usable: a study found that a limited war involving one hundred Hiroshima sized bombs would devastate the world's food supplies. As journalist, Matt Taibbi, points out, Trump's demonisation of North Korea with human rights abuses (no doubt they do occur) mirror George H.W. Bush's comments about Iraq before the first Gulf War, or indeed any comment by an American president before some form of action. Yet, in the next breath, Trump is praising Kim Jong-un and saying, 'He's the head of a country, he's the strong head, don't let anyone think anything different.'[31] Perhaps we should still be anxious about 'the bomb'!

However, Totten identifies the beginning of the zombie craze with the movie *28 Days Later*, which was released about a year after 9/11. We fear social collapse and a terrorist attack seems to figure fairly highly in this concern. After all, how else do governments motivate us to engage in an endless 'war on terror' unless we are constantly, if subconsciously, feeling terrorised? Ostensibly, the 'Be alert, not alarmed' advertising campaign in Australia was not designed to frighten the ordinary Australian, and yet raising the issue of suspicion over your neighbour does put a sense of unease in your mind.[32] The media constantly brings before us the crimes of 'them' (typically Islamic terrorists) but there are also natural disasters like Hurricane Katrina, the Fukushima tsunami and nuclear disaster, and various pandemics such as bird flu. These all serve to remind us that we are not really in control.

We are ever more afraid of our neighbours, as *Doomsday Preppers* makes clear. Urbanisation is a mark of the Anthropocene. Zombie contagion captures this well and our neighbour soon becomes a gibbering monster wanting our brains. Or a Jihadist wanting an infidel dead. Be

30 Matt Taibbi, "Donald Trump's Thinking on Nukes Is Insane and Ignorant," *Rolling Stone,* 9 February, 2018, accessed 8 April, 2018, https://www.rollingstone.com/politics/news/taibbi-donald-trump-on-nukes-is-insane-ignorant-w516568.

31 Martin Pengelly, "Trump praises Kim on Fox & Friends: 'I want my people to do the same'," *The Guardian*, 16 June, 2018, accessed 16 June, 2018, https://www.theguardian.com/us-news/2018/jun/15/antsy-and-bored-trump-nearly-left-kim-summit-in-peril-report-says.

32 Linda Morris, "Be alert, not alarmed - grins replace guns on anti-terrorism ad," *The Sydney Morning Herald*, 28 December, 2002, accessed 8 April, 2018, https://www.smh.com.au/articles/2002/12/27/1040511177155.html.

alert, not alarmed. The unprecedented comfort, ease, and freedom from violence that Steven Pinker boasts of, is perhaps not as stable as we might think. Whether or not you believe climate change played a role in Hurricane Sandy, the fact that some residents in New York City armed themselves with booby traps, baseball bats, and bows and arrows in *The Walking Dead* style to protect themselves from potential looters, shows that our civility is paper thin. As climate change and the Anthropocene threaten us, what might the church look like, should society start to crumble around us?

CHAPTER 5 — IT'S NOT THE END OF THE WORLD

It's all about me (not)

When my son was younger, I wrote him a few pieces about various things he might ask about his faith, like is Genesis true, and if so, how? He read them but I'm not sure how useful he found them. Now that he is a teenager, I'm tempted to write him something about the temptations and struggles of the teen years, how I found them, and what got me through. It has been a few years since I was a teen but I do remember how painful those times were. Imagine if I did write such a letter, then some other teen boy read it. Might he find it useful as well? Perhaps. Some of the comments would reflect the distinct relationship between my son and I, other observations would be more general. What about a teen boy from another generation, say in thirty years? As time separates myself and my son from new readers, more work needs to be done to extract the meaning. The letter will contain truths about the teen years for a young man, but will always be a letter from me to my son. It was written to him, but it could be for other boys as well.

Turning to the book of Revelation, a problem arises with our reading of the text when we make the mistake of not understanding that the bible was written for us, but not to us. What I mean is that there were original human authors who wrote to original audiences. They shared experiences, a world view, and spoke the same language. The bible was written to other people. Paul wrote letters to individuals and churches. Luke and Acts were written to Theophilus. The Hebrew Bible was compiled for the Jews and edited for them during the exile. And the book of Revelation was written to seven churches in Asia (Rev 1:4) by John. I can hear the 'but, buts' happening. We believe in divine inspiration, and indeed the book of Revelation was a vision (Rev 1:1–2). Surely this means Revelation is relevant for us? Absolutely it does! But this doesn't mean we can read it simply as if the original recipient doesn't matter. We are not free to randomly twist the text to our situation in a way that is not faithful to the original meaning. So, we need to understand this book is for us, for our instruction, our encouragement, and our warning. But to properly understand it, we also need to remember that it was written to someone else.

John and his readers

Revelation is a letter from John (Rev 1:4, 9), in exile on the island of Patmos due to his persecution 'because of the word of God and the testimony of Jesus.' This persecution was under Rome, who expected that all people would join in the Caesar cult. It was unpatriotic to not do so, and hence more than just frowned upon. John of Patmos appears to be very familiar with the churches of Asia Minor. Michael Gorman claims that, due to stylistic differences, he is unlikely to be John the apostle, or the author of the gospel that bears his name, but certainly has a prophetic office, and is one who is 'theologian, poet, and pastor.'[1] Joseph Mangina attests to the long-standing Christian tradition, particularly among Eastern Christianity, that indeed it was John, the beloved disciple, as does Leon Morris.[2] Regardless of which John it is, he claims authority on the basis of his vision (Rev 22:8, 18). Most scholars date the book during the reign of the Roman Emperor Domitian (AD 81–96), a tradition dating back to Irenaeus.[3] After the fall of Jerusalem in AD 70, Jews and Christians began calling Rome Babylon (Rev 18:2). It is the context of Roman rule that we need to take seriously, as I discuss further below.

What the heck am I reading?

Revelation is a weird book. I mean, who hasn't had nightmares like this from overheating, or a meal that disagreed with us? Playwright, George Bernard Shaw, said that it was the 'curious record of the visions of a drug addict.'[4] Martin Luther worried that the symbolism veiled Christ and could confuse the average Christian. He wasn't wrong!

---

1 Michael J. Gorman, *Reading Revelation Responsibly: Uncivil Worship and Witness. Following the Lamb Into the New Creation* (Eugene, Or: Cascade, 2011), 28.

2 Joseph L. Mangina, *Revelation* (Grand Rapids, MI: Brazos Press, 2010), 33. Leon Morris, *Revelation: An Introduction and Commentary* (London: The Tyndale Press, 1969), 26.

3 Gorman, *Reading Revelation*, 26; Mangina, *Revelation*, 33.

4 Gorman, *Reading Revelation*, 2.

Revelation might be a book you've not spent much time in, or else (and much worse) you've read through the lens of *The Left Behind* series! It is important to know what we are reading before we think about how to read it. Michael Gorman identifies five kinds of genre in Revelation.[5] No wonder it is confusing.

The first word in the Greek text of Revelation is *apokalypsis*, from which we get the English word apocalypse, which means revelation or unveiling. The Cambridge Dictionary defines apocalypse as 'a very serious event resulting in great destruction and change' and that 'in the bible, the total destruction and end of the world.'[6] This is a great misunderstanding, one that far too many Christians share. Jesus 'making all things new' implies much more than this. A more thorough definition of apocalypse comes from John Collins

> a genre of revelatory literature with a narrative framework, in which a revelation is mediated by an otherworldly being to a human recipient, disclosing a transcendent reality which is both temporal, insofar as it envisages eschatological salvation, and spatial insofar as it as it involves another, supernatural world.[7]

There's quite a bit in this definition, so let's briefly unpack it. Firstly, apocalyptic literature like Revelation, Daniel, and Mark 13, reveals something. It isn't about hiding things. This means that, while the language may be coded, the original readers would have had an 'aha' moment, or a series of such moments. There is a narrative framework, or a story or big picture. In the bible, this big story is God's plan to make 'all things new', to 'renew our world.' This was through the line of Adam to Noah and his ark, then the line of Abraham and the people of Israel, and then finally through Jesus, and in him, the people of God; both Jew and Gentile. It is not a narrative of destruction, but rather of renewal of that which 'in the beginning' was considered 'very good' (Gen 1:1–31).

---

5 Gorman, *Reading Revelation*, chapters 2 and 3.

6 Cambridge Dictionary, *Apocalypse*, accessed 31 March, 2018, https://dictionary.cambridge.org/dictionary/english/apocalypse.

7 John Collins, "Introduction: Towards the Morphology of a Genre." *Semeia* 14 (1979): 1–20, 9.

The next element is the otherworldly being. In Daniel 8, we see the angel Gabriel act as Daniel's interpreter (Dan 8:16). In Revelation, it is 'one like a son of Man' (Rev 1:13), which in turn is a reference to Daniel 7:13 and the key behind understanding Jesus' own use of the term (eighty-seven times in the gospels). Note that while some English translations (e.g. the NRSV) use 'one like a human being' to be inclusive, it obscures the connection. So, the role of the son of Man is to reveal things to John.

What does transcendence mean? People are always looking for ways to go beyond themselves, whether it is extreme sports, sex, meditation, or a great cause. Gurus or cult leaders claim insight into hidden secrets. Augustine identified this longing for transcendence with our need for God: 'You made us for yourself, and our heart is restless until it finds its place of rest in you.'[8] As Collins states, this transcendence is about both time and space. In time, Revelation talks about eschatological salvation. Salvation is a familiar word: it means being saved from something. We normally think about being saved from sins, from judgement, and so on. Eschatology simply means the study of the last things, although we need to be careful what we mean by last things, since Revelation tells us that Christ is making 'all things new.' But eschatology implies that 'history is a linear movement towards a goal' and that this goal is the fulfilment of God's 'purposes for his creation.'[9] So, the last things to which the apocalypse points is that all things are made new. We are saved with, and not from, creation. Indeed, we are being saved with creation right now. But more of that soon.

The other aspect involves space: a supernatural world. In the Hebrew Bible, the cosmos is portrayed with a three-tiered structure. The solid earth is set on foundations (Ps 104:5). In its depths is Sheol, the realm of the dead (Jb 17:16). The waters above are separated from the waters below by a dome or firmament (Gen 1:6–8; Ps 19:1). In the heavens is the sun, which rises and sets from end to end of the heavens (Ps 19:6), and the moon and stars, which have the function of marking seasons

---

[8] St Augustine, *The Confessions of St Augustine: Modern English Version* (Grand Rapids, MI: Baker Book House, 2005), 15–16.

[9] Richard J. Bauckham, "Eschatology," in *The New Bible Dictionary: Second Edition*, ed. J. D. Douglas (Leicester: Inter-Varsity Press, 1992), 342.

(Gen 1:14–18). Finally, the heavens are set on beams in the waters, and are God's chamber or temple (Ps 104:3). In this cosmology, heaven is up and hell is down. And yet, this word picture points to transcendence; a way that must transcend its very own limitations. Soviet cosmonaut, Yuri Gagarin, was the first person in space. He is alleged to have said that 'I looked and looked and looked, but I didn't see God.'[10] However, it is more likely that this is another example of 'fake news' and a reflection of Soviet anti-religious propaganda. It has even been suggested that Gagarin was a Christian. The point is, however, that heaven simply isn't 'up there' in modern cosmology. But this doesn't mean that heaven isn't real. Christians do get very confused about heaven but, consistent with Collin's definition of apocalyptic literature, we see that heaven is where the action is; where we learn what is really going on down here on earth.

What else do we learn from apocalyptic literature? According to Gorman, it is full of dualisms. For me, dualism is usually a dirty word. Dualism is the tacit belief that many Christians hold that heaven is more important than earth, the spirit more important than the body, and life after death is more important than life on earth. All of these things seem right because they contain half-truths, but they also contain some dangerous half untruths! I'll get back to these ideas later. For Gorman, apocalyptic literature contains cosmic dualism, the idea that there are good forces (God and his angels) and evil forces (Satan and his demons); historical dualism, which reflects the cosmological dualism in history as battles between the children of God (in Revelation, the early church, identified as Jerusalem) and the children of Satan (the Roman empire, also referred to as Babylon); and ethical dualism, the arguments put forth by each side to inform our choices.[11] These are ideas we will come back to again and again in subsequent chapters. We will explore how they might be appropriated for considering the damage we have done to God's world, how people and creation suffer unjustly, and our mission to live out God's plan to make all things new and to renew our world.

---

10 Marc Bennetts, "Soviet Space Propaganda Was Atheistic — But Putin's Cosmonauts Fear God," *Business Insider*, 24 July, 2014, accessed 13 March, 2018, http://www.businessinsider.com/strange-connection-between-russian-astronauts-and-god-2014-7?IR=T.

11 Gorman, *Reading Revelation Responsibly*, 15–16.

Part of the problem of reading Revelation is that all of these dualisms are embedded in language that can be hard to read from a perspective so far removed from the original historical events. Remember, Revelation is written for us but was originally written to the seven churches as a pastoral letter. This is another of Gorman's genres in Revelation. The symbols of Revelation are not the message of the book but 'carry and embody the message.'[12] The symbolism is like a political cartoon that exaggerates features in a way that would be familiar to its first readers but could be lost on us without extra help.[13] Imagine someone one hundred years from now reading about Tony's 'budgie smugglers' or 'the human cheeto'?[14] You may not even know what I mean without the explanation in the footnote! How could people in the future know what was meant without the proper sources? We need to take care not to always want to project our situation onto the text in a rather wooden manner, or to bring our question to the text before we have understood the original context.

The third of Michael Gorman's genres in Revelation is prophecy. Revelation is a prophecy to hear and keep (Rev 1:3; 22:7), to be made open to read (Rev 22:10), and not to be added to (Rev 22:18–19). But what is prophecy? Is it about telling the future? Prophecy may be described as both forth-telling and foretelling.[15] That prophets speak about things in the future is undisputed: there was, after all, a condition that what a prophet predicted had to come true for them to be a true prophet (Deut 18:22)![16] However, the main function of a prophet is not foretelling the future but forth-telling the character of God and calling his people back to faithfulness. Or as Leon Wood writes about the prophets

---

12 Paul J. Achtemeier, Joel B. Green, and Marianne Meye Thompson, *Introducing the New Testament: Its Literature and Theology* (Grand Rapids, MI: Wm. B Eerdmans Publishing Company, 2001), 562.

13 Achtemeier, Green, and Thompson, *Introducing the New Testament*, 565.

14 Former Australian Prime Minister Tony Abbott is a surf lifesaver and wears a particular style of swimwear referred to vulgarly as the "budgie smuggler" which is a comparison of male genitalia to a small Australian parrot. Likewise, the "human cheeto" refers to American President Donald Trump's fondness for spray on tans.

15 Thomas Hale, and Stephen Thorson, *The Applied Old Testament Commentary: Applying God's Word to Your Life* (Colorado Springs, CO: David Cook, 2007), 80.

16 Leon J. Wood, *The Prophets of Israel* (Grand Rapids, MI: Baker Book House, 2001), 112.

They were really like the preachers of today, urging people to live in a manner pleasing to God.[17]

As John himself writes, 'blessed are those who hear and who keep what is written in it; for the time is near' (Rev 1:3). This means that reading Revelation is less about guessing the details of the future as communicated using obscure first century symbolism, and more about seeing the character of God as faithful, and a call to live in hope and obedience to God's will. But this becomes clearer when we look at two of Gorman's other genres in Revelation.

What's the big idea?

The first genre recognises that there is a lot of music in Revelation; songs of worship. This is a point I'll return to in the final chapter because the songs we sing in church do affect our theology. Gorman points out that worship means acknowledging the worthiness of God and the Lamb, explicitly stated in Revelation 4:11, 5:9 and 5:12.[18] Indeed, the acclamation of the worthiness of the Lamb who was slain in Revelation 5 demonstrates that the gospel is central to the logic of this book. Graeme Goldsworthy affirms this point in his appropriately named *The Gospel in Revelation*.[19] It is for this reason that Gorman considers Revelation to be a liturgical text.

The centrality of worship in Revelation, with its focus on the exclusivity of allegiance to God and the Lamb, is politically subversive. It was written of Augustus that he was

> a **savior** for us and those who come after us, to make **war to cease**, to create order everywhere ...; the birthday of the **god** [Augustus] was the beginning for the world of the **glad tidings** that have come to men through him ...(emphasis added).[20]

Note all of the pretensions: good news, peace, saviour, divinity (cf. Rom 1:1–4, 5:1)? To confess God and the Lamb alone as divine was to

---

17 Wood, *The Prophets of Israel*, 68.

18 Gorman, *Reading Revelation Responsibly*, 34.

19 Graeme Goldsworthy, *The Gospel in Revelation* (Flemington Markets: Lancer Books, 1984), 34.

20 Quoted in Tom Wright, *What Saint Paul Really Said: Was Paul of Tarsus the Real Founder of Christianity?* (Oxford: Lion Publishing, 1997), 43.

be unpatriotic or unRoman and made you an atheist in the first century world. In practice, it meant separation from 'normal Greco-Roman religious, social, and political activity' where the acknowledgement of pagan divinities and Caesar as divine was a part of normal life.[21] For example, the earliest state sponsored temple for the worship of the emperor was in Pergamum.[22] Jesus acknowledges that 'Satan's throne' is in Pergamum and some scholars suggest that this is a reference to this temple.

Gorman, however, finds no evidence in Revelation of systematic persecution: such a thing was past – during the reign of Nero – and also in the future. John himself was exiled for preaching 'atheism' in this pagan context and so it appears as if the target of his critique is imperial idolatry and injustice, or simply everyday empire. In other words, Revelation is not just a liturgical text that reminds us of who God and the Lamb are, but it is a *theopolitical* text. To declare the Lamb is worthy of the same worship as God is to declare that Caesar is not to be worshipped.

Gorman then brings together several ideas to call Revelation a Theopoetic, Theopolitical, Pastoral-Prophetic text.[23] It reminds us that the Lamb is God in liturgy (theopoetic), and therefore that Caesar is not God (theopolitical). If offers comfort when we suffer or are excluded from society for the faith (pastoral) and it encourages us to be faithful to the New Covenant (prophetic).

Most outlines of Revelation look roughly similar, so I have followed Gorman's division, though I have changed his summaries a little to suit the current context

1. Chapters 1–3 Opening vision and the seven pastoral-prophetic letters
2. Chapters 4–5 God and the Lamb are in charge now
3. Chapters 6–20 Visions of judgement of empire with interludes
4. Chapters 21–22 The Lamb makes all things new

21 Gorman, *Reading Revelation Responsibly*, 32.

22 Michael Wilcock, *The Message of* Revelation (Leicester: Inter-Varsity Press, 1975), 47.

23 Gorman, *Reading Revelation Responsibly*, 59.

The main focus of this book is on the Lamb making all things new, hence, we will examine chapters 21 and 22. However, there are a few other places in Revelation that will be important to examine to build the case that Revelation is a text that can be applied to the problem of climate change, along with closely related social, economic, and political issues.

Reading Revelation today

When we come to the text today, the key question is how to properly read it. I have already alluded to the fact that in taking the text to be historically grounded, we need to avoid trying to match individual details of the text to events today. This is what Gorman calls 'text as code.' Instead, reading the text as lens, our strategy of reading the text (exegetical principles) should be analogical. In particular, Gorman notes that Rome is identified as Babylon and that this suggests that applying Revelation to Rome is not exhaustive, that is to say, we can think of all empires in a similar fashion. This means that while we can't willy-nilly apply the text, neither is it consigned purely to the first century world of John and his audience. Remember, since the gospel is central to Revelation, it is written for us, even as it was written to the seven churches.

Uncomfortably for some, the blow torch of application blows close to home. Gorman applies the anti-empire critique to American civil religion; the awkward combination of Christianity with nationalism.[24] A generation earlier, William Stringfellow attacked the Vietnam War and the treatment of African-Americans, Latinos, and other non-whites with whom he worked as a lawyer, identifying the US with Babylon.[25] In this book, we will apply this anti-empire critique more broadly to include those aspects of modern culture that have led to the Anthropocene: those things that keep us from identifying climate change as a threat to human existence, and that need a gospel-centred critique.

---

24 Gorman, *Reading Revelation Responsibly*, 48.
25 William Stringfellow, *An Ethic for Christians & Other Aliens in a Strange Land* (Waco, TX: Word, Incorporated, 1973).

CHAPTER 6 — WHO'S THE BOSS?

Looking at the world today, you could be forgiven for thinking that God is largely absent and that maybe things are not going according to plan. I don't mean the loosening grip of Christianity on the reins of power in the West, I mean Egyptian Christians who have suffered persecution by ISIS. Take, for example, the story of Michael Nabil Ragheb. One Sunday, Michael, who was a church deacon, went to the front of the church at the start of the service to perform his duties. A few minutes later, the church was rocked by a large explosion. It filled with smoke and the sound of screams as everything went dark. Michael left behind his widow Sara and a three-year-old daughter. He had recently told his wife he thought he would soon be 'among the martyrs in heaven.'[1] Or think about the African-American Christians living in Charlottesville, Virginia, who have had to deal with angry white supremacists marching through their town.[2] These racist protests resulted in three deaths and yet received only a vague statement from the US President denouncing bigotry and violence 'on many sides' rather than roundly condemning fascism and white supremacy.[3] How comforting for black Americans when their president fails to call out evil for what it is.

And then there are those facing an escalating climate apocalypse, like Tuvaluan Christians, who think that when climate change affects their fishing for their 'daily bread', 'God's providence has failed them.'[4]

---

[1] Brian, "Widow of Palm Sunday Martyr: 'He asked me to wait for him … But he never came back," *Open Doors*, 12 April, 2017, accessed 9 May, 2018, https://www.opendoorsusa.org/christian–persecution/stories/egyptian–widow–of–palm–sunday–martyr–speaks–out/.

[2] Jonathan Blitzer, "How Church Leaders in Charlottesville Prepared for White Supremacists," *The New Yorker*, 15 August, 2017, accessed 9 May, 2018, https://www.newyorker.com/news/news–desk/how–church–leaders–in–charlottesville–prepared–for–white–supremacists.

[3] Jelani Cobb, "The Battle of Charlottesville," *The New Yorker*, 13 August, 2017, accessed 9 May, 2018, https://www.newyorker.com/news/daily–comment/the–battle–of–charlottesville.

[4] Ruth Moon, "Teaching Natural Theology as Climate Changes Drown A Way of Life." Posted 14/2/2012, accessed 11 November, 2013, http://www.christianitytoday.com/ct/2012/february/natural–theology–climate–change.html.

I suspect in a way it is hard for many white western Christians (like me) to read Revelation because we simply don't fit the bill of those suffering under empire: we are too deeply embedded in it. That said, we are oppressed by empire. We have so absorbed the message of empire that we have become rich and prospered, yet have also become lukewarm and internally impoverished (Rev 3:15–17). So, while western Christians learn to identify our spiritual poverty as we examine our complicity with the status quo, we also need to hear the message for those who are poor, and yet are rich. And that message is that God is in charge in the midst of the mess of the world, while the Powers claim to be in control. Knowledge of that helps us to realise that the Lamb is making all things new, that we are called to join in renewing our world, to speak and act prophetically to our world, and to live proleptically and hopefully.

Turning back to the book of Revelation, we learn that God is firmly in charge. After the letters to the seven churches, we are translated into a vision, a 'peek into heaven', as Michael Gorman says.[5] What we see is a picture of worship. I will talk more about this vision of heaven in the last chapter, but for now it is worth stressing that worship is central to the life of the church, and a not simply to entertain us. I recognise the tension between worship in church as professional, good quality music, and the unhelpful tendency for it to fall into performance. We must keep worship central to our life as a church: to balance both the intellectual and the 'emotional', to remind us that God and the Lamb reign now, and that we are called to faithful witness. So, let's look at these passages.

Gorman points out that the language of ruling is important. The word throne appears forty-three times in Revelation, and nineteen times in chapters 4 and 5. The Lamb, also mentioned twenty-eight times, is one who sits on the throne. The New Jerusalem of Revelation is the bride of the Lamb. But the marriage is not all in the future, as we will see.

---

5 Michael J. Gorman, *Reading Revelation Responsibly: Uncivil Worship and Witness. Following the Lamb Into the New Creation* (Eugene, Or: Cascade, 2011), 103.

God reigns now

Chapter 4 begins with 'after these things' that Grant Osborne sees as a rhetorical rather than temporal device. In other words, every time the phrase is used (also 7:1, 9; 15:5; 18:1) it means a progression in the vision rather than a timetable of events.[6] The scene in verse 1 reminds me of the climax of the 80s movie *Ghostbusters*. For those unfamiliar with the original, three former university academics go into business catching ghosts in New York. Their business is a huge success as paranormal activity increases dramatically. Central to the plot of the movie is the impending return of the fictional Mesopotamian god Gozer, who is returning to bring the end of the world. Atop a large gothic apartment block stood a huge door into a spiritual realm. As Egon, one of the Ghostbusters explains

> After the First World War, Shandor decided that society was too sick to survive. And he wasn't alone. He had close to a thousand followers when he died. They conducted rituals up on the roof, bizarre rituals intended to bring about the end of the world.

At one point in the movie, another of the Ghostbusters quotes Revelation 6:12, though mistakenly referring to it as 7:12, to describe the spectral events from which they were profiting. The point is that in Revelation 4:1, a door stands open and, like the movie, has been opened from the inside, that is, we assume, by God. The use of 'must' in verse 1 points to the divine will in what follows. There is a plan and it will unfold.[7] Not for a giant marshmallow man to destroy the earth, but for the Lamb to make it new.

At the time I am writing this, there has recently been the royal wedding between Prince Harry and Meghan Markle. The idea of royalty seems to still attract attention in a world that has largely moved past such ideas, probably because there is a lingering 'princess myth' in popular culture (much thanks to Disney). With royalty comes the idea of a throne and the authority that it represents. The Greek in verse 2 literally says 'sitting on the throne.' We are left to fill in the details. Clearly, the unnamed someone on the throne is God. John is deferential

---

6 Grant R. Osborne, *Revelation* (Grand Rapids, MI: Baker Academic, 2002), 223.

7 Osborne, *Revelation*, 225.

to the Divine person, recalling the command of Exodus 20:4 to not make an image of God. This throne room scene contains a good deal of symbolism worth teasing out.

The throne of God sits at the centre of concentric circles of a rainbow, twenty-four elders, and four living creatures. God is the centre of the action, the focus of this scene.[8] The outer rainbow takes us back to Genesis 9:13–16, where we are given the promise of no further earth-flooding judgement and a divine covenant with the whole of creation. In a book dealing with the end times and care of creation, especially the problem of climate change, you can see why this is noteworthy. The throne itself is made of jasper. When the Lamb finishes making all things new, and the New Jerusalem descends, it too is made of jasper (Rev 21: 11, 18, 19). In other words, there is a link to this scene of God's rule now and the future that God intends to bring about!

There is some debate as to whether the twenty-four elders are human, in which case they could represent the twelve tribes of Israel and the twelve apostles, linking the promises to Israel with its fulfilment through the Lamb and through his apostles to the New Testament church. They could also be angels. The important thing here, however, is their role, which is to worship God. Finally, the four living creatures are clearly drawn from Ezekiel chapter 1. Again, there is much scholarly debate as to what precisely they represent but it is clear that, like the twenty-four elders, their function is to worship God.

While drawing on Hebrew Bible imagery, there is the context of the readers to consider. Michael Gorman points out that there are numerous similarities between this scene and those of the Roman imperial court. The emperor was attended by lesser kings giving him golden crowns, hymns and songs of praise. He even had a travelling throne on which he was carried.[9] The twenty-four elders fall down before God and cast their crowns of gold before the throne. J Nelson Kraybill points out a similar scene in the history of Rome.[10] Tiridates, the king of Armenia,

---

8 David Aune, *Word Biblical Commentary Volume 52: Revelation 1–5* (Dallas, TX: Word Incorporated, 1997), 286.

9 Gorman, *Reading Revelation Responsibly*, 106.

10 J Nelson. Kraybill, *Apocalypse and Allegiance: Worship, Politics, and Devotion in the Book of Revelation* (Grand Rapids, MI: Brazos Press, 2010), 16f.

made a long trip to see Nero in Rome. In wanting to become a vassal of Rome, he intended to place his crown before Nero so he could take it back up again. Nero threw a party in expectation, spending 300,000 sesterces out of the annual imperial budget of 800,000. As Tiridates approached the throne, he knelt with both his hands on his breast. He announces himself as Nero's slave and says, 'I have come to you, my god, worshipping you as I do [the sun god] Mithra.' To which Nero responds that Tiridates has done well to come to 'enjoy my grace', that he declares him king of Armenia, and that he has 'power to take away kingdoms and to bestow them.'

So, the scene we get in Revelation 4 is politically charged. The gospel is political because it resists all other attempts at worship. John is telling us from this vision of heaven that God is in charge: not just sometime in the future, but right now! Jesus said that the ruler of this world has been cast out (Jn 12:31) and all authority sits with the Lamb (Matt 28:18–20). God rules, not Caesar. And Rome is under divine judgement.

Consider a modern example. The United States is a militaristic culture. And I don't mean the simple, quiet gratitude for defence of lands, but a country much like Rome that often turns to military force as foreign policy and to advance their material wealth. Empires do this sort of thing by definition. While I could attack the former Soviet Union for this, at length, at least they never claimed to represent the free world. One of the ways in which this militarism is celebrated is the practice of standing to the American national anthem at football games. The first occurrence of standing for the Star–Spangled Banner at a sporting event was at a baseball game in 1862, although it wasn't the official national anthem until 1931. It was played at football games during WWII and the tradition continued after the war as an ongoing mark of respect.[11]

However, it wasn't until 2009 that players were mandated to be on the field for the playing of the anthem, and the 2017 rulebook didn't

---

11 Olivia B. Waxman, "Here's How Standing for the National Anthem Became Part of U.S. Sports Tradition," *Time*, 25 September, 2017, accessed 10 June, 2018, http://time.com/4955623/history–national–anthem–sports–nfl/.

state that players had to do anything while the anthem was being played. Now we find that players have to stand because the

Department of Defense had spent $6.8 million on what they called "paid patriotism" between 2012 and 2015. This money was spread out among 50 pro teams from the NFL, NBA, MLB, NASCAR, MLS and others.[12]

So, when quarterback Colin Kaepernick kneeled during the national anthem at protest of social injustice, particularly the deaths of African-Americans at the hands of police, the firestorm that followed should never have occurred.[13] Yet, when you challenge the idols and mythology of a nation, expect a backlash. Accusations of disrespect towards soldiers who fight for freedom are ill–founded. In western culture in general, and in America in particular, black men are only permitted to be visible for their sporting performances and not their political views. Australian readers will remember similar reactions to Aboriginal Australian Rules footballer, Adam Goodes, for representing his culture and attacking racism among fans.[14] It is no coincidence that at least seven of the thirty-two NFL franchise owners have donated funds to Donald Trump and he has been very vocal about the protests. These protests are now banned.[15] This represents a suppression of 'free speech' that is only free for the powerful. Such a ban illustrates what happens when people refuse to join in the worship of civil religion.

Now we turn our attention to the content of the worship in Revelation 4. What are the four living creatures and twenty-four elders saying about God? In verse 8 we see that God is holy, drawing on imagery from Isaiah 6:3. This too is a throne room scene, including a message

---

12 A.J. Willingham, "The national anthem in sports (spoiler: it wasn't always this way)," *CNN*, 25 September, 2017, accessed 10 June, 2018, https://edition.cnn.com/2017/09/25/us/nfl–national–anthem–trump–kaepernick–history–trnd/index.html.

13 John Branch, "The Awakening of Colin Kaepernick," *The New York Times*, 7 September, 2017, accessed 10 June, 2018, https://www.nytimes.com/2017/09/07/sports/colin–kaepernick–nfl–protests.html.

14 See Mick Pope, *A Climate of Justice: Loving Your Neighbour in a Warming World* (Reservoir: Morning Star Publishing, 2017), chapter 5.

15 Ed Maylon, "NFL to fine players for kneeling in protest during the national anthem," *Independent*, 23 May, 2018, accessed 10 June, 2018, https://www.independent.co.uk/sport/us–sport/national–football–league/nfl–anthem–protest–kneeling–donald–trump–colin–kaepernick–a8365336.html.

of judgement upon Israel and a prophetic calling for Isaiah. It seems to me then the message of verse 4 is fourfold. Firstly, God is utterly other, thrice ascribed holy. God is the eternal one, who was, who is, and who is to come. Osborne stresses that God is sovereign over history.[16] Secondly, this means that the church should therefore purify itself. You will recall that chapter 4 immediately follows the letters to the seven churches in chapters 2 and 3. While this purification will necessarily involve the usual sorts of moral issues that plague individuals, the call to worship God is a call to stop worshipping Caesar and the trappings of Rome. This is a message to the compromised church, the colonised church. So long as we buy into the myths of the empires of the world and the worship of its gods, we have need to come out of Babylon. More on this later.

Thirdly, the church should not fear. As I said earlier, most of us do not face genuine persecution. In China, Christianity is seen as a Western philosophy that is a threat to the Communist party's authority.'[17] This has resulted in the arrest of Christians, the confiscation of bibles, and the dynamiting of churches. In Australia, we get the occasional rather pathetic attempt to be provocative, like an upside down neon cross as part of a trendy arts festival.[18] Most of us are not excluded from employment for our faith. Personally, I don't count being called out for refusing to ice a cake for a same-sex wedding on the same level as having your church bombed by Islamic terrorists. This is not to say that there isn't a creeping exclusion from public life happening in the West. But that said, when the church was at the centre of power, the results were very mixed! So, we should neither embrace persecution as a good in and of itself, nor embrace being at the centre of power. Instead, be a faithful witness wherever you are. And here's the fourth point: the church is called to be a prophetic witness to the present reign

---

16 Osborne, *Revelation*, 237.

17 Russell Goldman, "Chinese police dynamite Christian megachurch," *The Sydney Morning Herald*, 13 January, 2018, accessed 10 June, 2018, https://www.smh.com.au/world/chinese–police–dynamite–christian–megachurch–20180113–h0hujr.html.

18 Stephanie Convery, "Dark Mofo: Mona founder unperturbed by controversy over inverted crosses," *The Guardian*, 9 June, 2018, accessed 10 June, 2018, https://www.theguardian.com/culture/2018/jun/09/dark–mofo–mona–founder–unperturbed–by–controversy–over–inverted–crosses.

of God. This is not a call to theocracy or an imposition of values, nor a triumphant boasting. Instead, it is a call to faithful witness to the fact that God is in charge and history is headed somewhere. We achieve that by continuing to meet together to worship God. Chinese Christians do this often at great risk and cost to themselves, as does the persecuted church everywhere.

Prophetic Calling

I think that a prophetic lifestyle – or better still, a prophetic calling (as 'lifestyle' is the pretentious rubbish of so much TV and glossy magazines these days) – is in both word and action: we speak and act prophetically. One example of prophetic action is petitions. I realise that this can seem somewhat pedestrian but many countries have regulations about the reading of petitions in assemblies when they reach a number of signatories. We have to put our money where our mouth is, but if allegiance is all important to politicians, then signing something that says your allegiance is conditional can speak powerfully.

In 2017, TEAR Australia, through its *Renew Our World* campaign, joined with a group of faith-based organisations in a Community Climate Petition focused on letting politicians know how passionate Christians are about government action on behalf of the global poor and a changing climate. In only a few months, the collaborative, multi-electorate, 'pen and paper' petition was raised simultaneously in one hundred federal electorates and signed, by hand, by 28,000 people. I had the pleasure of visiting Peter Khalil, Labor member for Wills, in Melbourne. Petitions like this draw attention to our politicians that Christians are interested in key issues. The church actually still has some influence in the West and so we should be like Esther and make the most of our position.[19] As I write, there is also a petition that *Renew Our World* is running globally at http://renewourworld.net/actions/petition/ to encourage world leaders to follow up on the promises of the Bonn Conference of the Parties (COP 23) at the upcoming COP 24, to be held in Poland in November 2018.

---

[19] Renew Our World, "Democracy in action! Climate petitions handed over to MPs," *TEAR Australia*, accessed 17 June, 2018, https://www.fortomorrow.org.au/renewourworld/action/democracy-in-action-climate-petitions-handed-over-to-mps2.

To world leaders:

As Christians across the globe we are calling for action on climate change. The changing climate is causing great damage to people and planet right now, and we are particularly concerned about hunger and poverty hitting the most vulnerable communities, who did least to cause it.

We urge each nation's leaders to keep the promises they made in the Paris Agreement, to restore the natural balance.

Please use the COP23 global climate talks in Bonn, Germany this November, for each country to make significant progress to:

Set targets for the world to reduce our greenhouse gas emissions fast enough to limit global warming to the safe level of 1.5 degrees.

Invest in 100% clean energy, particularly using local grids so it reaches those in poverty beyond the reach of national electricity grids.

Support more sustainable, low emission agriculture, to stop communities going hungry, and help them cope better with more floods and droughts caused by climate change.

Publish national country plans in 2020 showing how each nation will move to zero emissions.

Please follow up at the COP24 climate talks in November 2018, in Poland.

This is our generation's challenge, a significant part of how we love our neighbours.

We're committing to respond as Christians by living more sustainably, praying, and raising our voices; we're asking every member of the church – the world's largest network – to join in, alongside many others, and every national leader to lead the way.

Join us.

The *Renew Our World* global campaign engaged Christian influencers to add their voice to a similar letter to the one above and used the influence of the signatories to influence officials in the lead up to the UN talks. The signatories to the letter petition came from thirteen countries included an award-winning human rights activist, five Anglican Primates (Australia, Brazil, Central Africa, Polynesia and Southern Africa) representing the whole Anglican Communion, US worship artists, the director of the World Evangelical Alliance, authors, climate scientists, theologians and church leaders. The UNFCCC blogged about the letter petition and outlined the demands, and there were many influential opportunities to speak about climate change, sustainability, and the role of Christians in particular, in tackling it with country officials during the UN talks.[20]

Being prophetic sometimes requires action: symbolic action that speaks to a particular situation. Prophets, being people of the Spirit, have often been given over to 'dramatic behaviour' and, by the power of the Spirit, to physically bring about their message.[21] The dramatisation of the spoken word, or 'prophetic symbolism', is a natural extension of the prophetic message. It is as the old adage says: 'actions speak louder than words'. Elijah's attire, taken up later by John the Baptist, was a symbolic protest against royal opulence (2 Ki 1:8). The dying Elisha tells King Joash to fire a symbolic arrow of victory over the invading Syrian army (2 Ki 13:14–19). Isaiah wandered naked and barefoot for three years before Assyria took Ashdod (Is 20:2). Ezekiel lay on his side for 390 days (Ez 4) to symbolise God's punishment and exile. Hosea's action was a little more than just symbolic, since he was told to take 'a wife of harlotry', he embodied God's relationship with an idolatrous nation (Hos 1:2).

One recent prophetic symbolic action happened in 2017. Christian peace activist, Jarrod McKenna, had been smuggled onto Manus Island, located off mainland Papua New Guinea, to see first-hand the conditions under which people were living in the detention centre. There, the Australian government has been holding asylum seekers under long-term mandatory detention.[22] The treatment of asylum seekers on Manus

---

20 United Nations Climate Change, "Archbishops Call for Climate Action Ahead of COP23," 18 October, 2017, accessed 22 July, 2018, https://unfccc.int/news/archbishops-call-for-climate-action-ahead-of-cop23.

21 Jack R. Lundbom, *The Hebrew Prophets: An Introduction* (Minneapolis: Fortress Press, 2010), 208.

22 Luke Cooper, and Alana Calvert, "Christian Leaders Arrested For Kirribilli House Protest Over Manus," *Huffington Post*, 27 November, 2017, accessed 10 June, 2018, https://www.

is at odds with Article 31 of the UN 1951 Convention relating to the Status of Refugees.[23] What Jarrod saw shook him to the core, and so he, with four other Christians, chained themselves by the neck to the front gate of Kirribilli House (the Sydney residence of the Prime Minister of Australia). The message behind chaining oneself to a symbol of a government (a Prime Ministerial residence) that keeps the desperate in chains could not be clearer. There are many injustices that require similarly imaginative, non-violent, prophetic acts.

A last thing to note from this chapter of Revelation is the content of the praise of the twenty-four elders. Worship is ascribing worth to God. We all go around with an unexamined view of the world, failing to appreciate the lens through which we view things. This lens helps us ascribe value to things and to people. It tells us what is important. Do we put career first, or family? What do we see as a good person, or a successful life? Where should we spend our money? When we acknowledge the worth of God, we are making a powerful statement about the ultimate nature of reality and our place in it. Like the twenty-four elders, all of our pretensions to power need to be cast aside before God. What we take up again is authority: authority to live lives freed from fear, 'free from the need to follow the kings of this world', free to bear prophetic witness to God.

All glory goes to God, all honour, and all power. And what is the reason? It is because

> You are worthy, our Lord and God, to receive glory and honour and power, for you created all things, and by your will they existed and were created (Rev 4:11).

This is why a solid creation theology is so important, because it is tied up in the person and glory of God. Note what the elders affirm. Firstly, that God created all things. The title of this book is *All Things New*. God creates all things, and in Genesis 1 we see that all things

---

huffingtonpost.com.au/2017/11/27/christians-chain-themselves-to-kirribilli-house-to-protest-manus_a_23288811/.

23 Stephanie Anderson, "How is the Government changing Australia's immigration policy?" *ABC News*, 7 November, 2016, accessed 26 February, 2017, http://www.abc. net.au/news/2016-11-07/how-is-the-government-changing-australias-immigration-policy/7996964. See *A Climate of Justice*, chapter 4.

are very good. This is not a moral statement but a functional one. All things fit together according to divine will and purpose. It is human sin that releases chaos into the order of creation. A challenge to this order of creation is a challenge to divine will, which is a strong theological reason to take climate change so seriously. Creation theology is at the heart of the Hebrew Bible; think of Psalm 19 or Psalm 104, for example.

Secondly, the creation and existence of all things is an exercise of divine will. Contingency is involved in the way in which the world operates, but there is a divine intent behind the created order. Sometimes it is hard to get at. This is the story of Job; that a righteous man can suffer misfortune and yet it falls under divine sovereignty. Thirdly, if all things were created by God, then God will make all things new. This means *all* things. What was initially fit for purpose, has been marred by human sin, and was created out of chaos to reach divine order, will find its Amen in the resurrection. This is the message of Romans 8 and we will examine that passage in more detail in later chapters.

The Lamb Reigns Now

In Revelation, after chapter 4 comes chapter 5 . Funny that. While chapter 4 establishes that God reigns now from the throne room, and that we are not to fear but to speak and act, chapter 5 speaks of the Lamb. One of the ideas that is central to both the Hebrew Bible and the New Testament is that the creator is also redeemer. For example, in Psalm 96:5 we read, 'For all the gods of the peoples are idols, but the Lord made the heavens'. And then in verse 10, the Psalmist proclaims

> Say among the nations, "The Lord is king! The world is firmly established; it shall never be moved. He will judge the peoples with equity."

There is only one creator: the Lord. Tom Wright calls this creational monotheism. This God is judge of the earth. He is coming to save his people. Wright calls this covenantal monotheism.[24] There are other places where this is clear. Take for example the pairing of Psalm 103 and 104. Psalm 104 speaks of creation and how it points to divine

---

24 N. T. Wright, *The New Testament and the People of God* (Minneapolis: Fortress Press, 1992), 248–252.

wisdom and majesty. Yet there's an ambiguity in Psalm 104 when it speaks of the waters in verses 5–9. Is this a reference to the creation of dry land, or the receding waters after the Flood, or both? Is creation or the renewal of creation as salvation in view? And then there's the odd ending, mentioning sinners being 'consumed from the earth' (v. 35). Psalm 103 speaks of covenant faithfulness and God's *hesed* or covenant love. The theological link between Psalms 103 and 104 is that God's dwelling is in the heavens (Ps 103:19; Ps 104:1–3). The point is that these two Psalms are thematically linked: we can't worship God as saviour without considering God as creator as well.

That's a slightly longish preamble to considering Revelation 5 and the genius of New Testament monotheism. Here we see the Lamb brought into the centre of Jewish monotheism as the one who saves and is worthy of the same praise as God. Let's unpack that briefly. Firstly, we see the drama of the scroll in verses 1–4. Again, there are echoes of Ezekiel (chapter 2) where God hands over a message of judgement to the prophet.[25] Here in Revelation 5, the scroll contains 'the eschatological plan of God to judge and save the world.'[26] Who would be able to open this and, hence, begin God's saving plan? The answer is the heart of the gospel, which is that Israel's long promised Messiah has come to usher in the Messianic age. The Hebrew Bible points to and is summed up in Jesus as Christ. The dying Jacob blessed his sons and he described Judah as a 'lion's whelp.' Jesus carries with him the Abrahamic blessing down through Isaac, Jacob, and his line to be a blessing to the whole world (Gen 12:1–3). One people were chosen but all people were to be blessed. Now that blessing is fulfilled in the Messiah, where all people can be included in the people of God, not just Israel. As the root of David (Is 11:10), Jesus is the true king. This was an affront to the Chief Priests, to Herod, to Pilate, to Caesar, and to all who claim ultimate authority.

What follows next requires a double take. We expect a Lion but get a Lamb. We expect a victor and we see a victim. Yet, given the contrasts we have already seen between imperial pretensions and divine reality, such an inversion should not be a surprise. So, what do we learn?

---

25 Osborne, *Revelation*, 247.

26 Gorman, *Reading Revelation Responsibly*, 108.

Firstly, let's focus on the divine status of the Lamb. The Lamb takes the scroll from the right hand of God. The right hand was a position of authority. We might say that the Lamb is God's 'right hand man.' As such we see a transfer of authority from God to the Lamb.[27] With this authority is the right to be worshipped, or the ascription of divine worth or value to the Lamb. The Lamb is worthy to take the scroll and break the seals because he was slain (v. 9). The Lamb receives the prayers of the saints (v. 8). The Lamb is not just worthy of glory and honour and power, but also honour and riches and blessing (v. 12). Finally, the Lamb is worshipped with God (v. 13). So, true worship is not given to an imperial, militaristic potentate any more than it should be given to communist demagogues or self–obsessed narcissists. More than that, as Michael Gorman notes, the 'nature of power is being redefined.'[28] This should be our guide to the way in which we relate to others.

Note also that in Revelation 5:13 there is a link back to God as creator (4:11). The praise for God and the Lamb comes not from the angels, twenty-four elders, or four living creatures alone, but from every creature

> in heaven and on the earth and under the earth and in the sea, and all that is in them

Every created thing praises God and the Lamb. The creation recognises its creator and redeemer: yes, all of creation! When we are to behold God making 'all things new' we recognise, with the rest of creation, that this is so. Therefore, we cannot ignore the plight of all of creation, of every created thing. We must care about climate change, about air pollution, about plastics and pesticides, because all things praise their creator and all things will be made new. Here is an ecotheology, a view of God shaped by God's creation of, care for, and redeeming of, creation. It is an ecotheology shaped by a love of those made in God's image who suffer, not at the hand of divine judgement on their sins, but via the effects of our sins. There's a vision for your Sunday morning worship music!

---

27 Osborne, *Revelation*, 257.
28 Gorman, *Reading Revelation Responsibly*, 109.

Note again how highly missional this all is. Why is the Lamb able to open the scroll and unleash God's plan to make all things new? The Lamb's authority comes from his being slain, purchasing with his blood people from every tribe, tongue, people, and nation for God. And what were these people purchased for? We have been purchased to be 'a kingdom and priests to our God; and they will reign upon the earth' (v.10). We are part of a kingdom. And not the kingdom of this earth or its rulers. Given what we have seen about sacrifice and the reversal of power, we should understand that kingdom values are non-violent ones. Recall when Jesus said that his kingdom was 'not of this world' (Jn 18:36)? The word in the Greek is *ek* or 'out of'. Jesus' kingdom is concerned with the world (think the Lord's Prayer) but it does not derive its values or purpose from the *kosmos*; human society set in opposition to God. Such an understanding will shape our prophetic witness as non-violent, and creative: like being sued for your outer clothes and walking out of court naked (Lk 6:29) or chaining yourself to the gates of government!

Our priestly role is one of mediation between God and the world. And what a bad job we have done of this. When church leaders abuse women and children and try to cover it up, we do not mediate between the world and God. When we join with empire to oppress indigenous peoples and take it upon ourselves to try to extinguish their culture and languages in the name of the gospel, we do not mediate between the world and God. When we refuse to acknowledge that we worship on stolen land, we do not mediate between the world and God. When we sell a message of consumerism that looks little different to that which the world offers, we do not mediate between the world and God. When we treat the environment as disposable and ignore the fact that we are undermining the beauty and variety of the natural world, and ability to support human flourishing, we do not mediate between the world and God. I can remember going to my priest (minister, if you will) to discuss going to bible college as an ordination candidate. He advised against it. Becoming a capital P Priest is a high calling. Well, guess what? So is being a small p priest, and we need to get a lot better at it.

Note also the promise of reigning on the earth. Does that excite you? Many Christians in the West want to do that now. We elect the candidate we think is best going to support Christian values and often that's a fairly narrow (which is not to say important) set of values. Regardless of which end of the political spectrum you sit, it must be said that it is a tragedy that a man who has no conception of or use for truth, who happily maligns Afro–Americans who protest their mistreatment in a simple non-violent act of kneeling, casts Mexicans as rapists, describes African countries as s**tholes, repeals environmental protections, and covers up acts of adultery, still has the support of Evangelicals? No person is perfect apart from Christ, but do you see a problem here?

Let's face it: the sorts of Christians who most want the power to reign on earth are the ones who should be casting their crowns before the throne. Here in Revelation 5:10 is a message of encouragement for those who suffer under the impacts of war, famine, climate change, human misrule and cruelty. It is a message for Palestinian Christians who suffer under Israeli rule while American Christians fund the resettlement of the Holy Land in an attempt to bring about the Apocalypse. It is hope for Kiribati Christians whose homes are disappearing beneath the waves. It is hope for Chinese Christians persecuted by their government, and Sara Ragheb, who lost her husband. It's time we started to feel uncomfortable in Babylon if we want to feel comforted about ruling on Earth.

So, when does the ruling begin? In Revelation 20:4, we read that the martyrs come to life and reign for a thousand years. Likewise, in Revelation 22, we return to the throne room scene of Revelation 5 where God and the Lamb are present. The name of God and the Lamb will be on the people's foreheads (Rev 22:4) as opposed to the mark of the beast (Rev 20:4). The people of the Lamb will be illuminated by the presence of God and the Lamb and will reign forever. So, what about now?

No Millennium But Now

Revelation 20:4 is one of those problematic verses that divides denominations within the body of Christ. What does the thousand years, or millennium, refer to? Much ink has been spilled on this topic. A useful book is Stanley Grenz's *The Millennial Maze*.[29] Following him, I will briefly outline three major views.

The first view is Premillennialism, which teaches that the one thousand years comes *before* Christ returns.[30] This period of peace is not achieved by humans but by the working of the Holy Spirit and the preaching of the gospel. We saw earlier that secular versions abound, but a genuinely orthodox view places the emphasis on divine action. Augustus Hopkins Strong articulates it as the idea that the preaching of the gospel enlarges the boundaries of the kingdom until Christianity largely prevails throughout the Earth, including Jew and Gentile.[31] This represents a smooth transition from the present into the millennium. You can see the appeal in this view. The gospel spreads and human evil retreats. And, as Grenz notes, there are implications for the environment

as humans engage in the task of proper management of the earth assigned to them before the fall, a marvellous transformation will occur in nature.

We could certainly use such a transformation right now.

The second view is postmillennialism, where the one thousand years reign follows Christ's return. Postmillennialism is typically presented in its Dispensationalist form. Dispensationalism is the view that history is split into distinct epochs, where God's will is progressively revealed. Some schemes have seven such epochs, others as few as two. A basic tenet is a fundamental split between Israel and the church. Another fundamental idea is the expectation of a political and earthly restoration of Israel.[32] This is the centre of so much controversy, as many see a final conflict in Israel as being the biblical Armageddon described in Revelation 16:16. Ronald Reagan said in 1983 that

I find myself wondering if we're the generation that is going to see that come about. I don't know if you've noted any of those prophecies lately, but, believe me, they certainly describe the times we're going through.[33]

29 Stanley J. Grenz, *The Millennial Maze: Sorting out Evangelical Options* (Downers Grove, Il: InterVarsity Press, 1992).

30 Grenz, *The Millennial Maze*, 68.

31 Grenz, *The Millennial Maze*, 70.

32 Grenz, *The Millennial Maze*, 97.

33 Quoted in Grenz, *The Millennial Maze*, 19–20.

So, the seven years of tribulation and the millennium that follows are tied up with Israel. There will be a pretribulation rapture of the church, which will be a spur for the mass conversion of Israel.

I'll deal with the rapture in more detail in the next chapter, but ask yourself for a moment why you would deal with justice issues in general, and climate and other environmental issues in particular, if this view were true? I'm certainly not arguing backwards here by saying we must do justice, therefore this view is wrong. What I am saying is that I find it difficult to square being beamed up to heaven while the earth goes to hell, while working to embody kingdom values of justice here and now. Dispensationalist premillennialism treats Revelation as a strict chronology and we've dealt with the difficulty of doing that in chapter 5. The major problem with this system is that it requires a literalistic reading of texts rich in symbolic meaning and dealing in the first instance with the first century world.

The last view of the millennium is pan-millennialism. Everything will pan out in the end. No wait: that's a joke from my friend and mentor, Rev Dr Gordon Preece! The last view is actually amillennialism, which dates back as far as premillennialism, and started with Augustine. The Reformers backed this view against the millennial hopes of the 'enthusiasts' for something safer.[34] However, properly understood, amillennialism is anything but safe, given that it is meant to propel us into the world, while premillennialism draws us away from the world. Simply put, amillennialism says there is no literal one thousand year earthly rule of Christ prior to judgement. Instead, the millennium is symbolic of the church age, the age in which we now live. We live with the tension of both good and evil existing side by side. We live with the church being a mixed community of those who genuinely follow Christ, and more cultural Christians.

The chief advantage of the amillennial view is that it follows the simple chronology of the whole New Testament, rather than turning to speculative readings of Revelation.[35] It usually follows a less literalistic reading of Revelation that doesn't press the details of the symbolism.

---

34 Grenz, *The Millennial Maze*, 150.
35 Grenz, *The Millennial Maze*, 173.

It also has neither the pessimism of premillennialism, nor the optimism of postmillennialism. A bone of contention is the role of the state of Israel. Premillennialist evangelicals look for war in the Middle East and support Israel, quite unthinkingly, in their oppression of Palestinians (which includes Christians!)[36] Amillennialists recognise that Paul's hope for all Israel doesn't mean separating them off from the rest of the church, as he discusses at length in Romans 9–11. Indeed, there is no Jew or Gentile now (Gal 3:28).

Why is this important? For me, postmillennialism can be a kind of Pelagianism that says the world will get better by our efforts. You can argue that the Spirit does all of the work, but the reality is at best that postmillennialism is a pipedream that doesn't take evil seriously enough. Evil requires an eschatological interruption of the present order. We should live with a postmillennialism zeal and fight hard to 'make the world a better place', but should expect that our victories won't always be long lasting. Premillennialism can easily be used as an excuse for not caring, for simply ignoring the problems of climate change and the suffering of the poor, and as incidental to getting 'people on the bus', as in preaching the gospel – code for some particular form of individualism, or Jesus as my afterlife insurance policy. Others will even go so far as to say that environmental destruction is a sign of the end, all the while ignoring their (and my) role in that very sign. If it is a sign of the end, we, like the Assyrians, whom God used to judge Israel, will be judged for our overzealous carrying out of the task (Is 10). Remember: when God returns in wrath, it will be time 'for destroying those who destroy the earth' (Rev 11:18)!

The amillennial view recognises that God is in charge now and the message of Revelation is one of hope. We live proleptically in the light of the coming consummation of the kingdom and do not fear in the present. Not occupied by trying to read the signs of Christ's return but understanding he will come back like a sneaky thief (Matt 24:42–44; 1 Thess 5:2). So, let's get on with living as if the future were in the

---

36 Bethany Allen–Ebrahimian, "Evangelicals side with Israel. That's hurting Palestinian Christians," *The Washington Post*, 23 December, 2016, accessed 10 June, 2018, https://www.washingtonpost.com/posteverything/wp/2016/12/23/evangelicals–side–with–israel–thats–hurting–palestinian–christians/?noredirect=on&utm_term=.9d35e788a7ac.

present. I have more to say about this in coming chapters but it seems to me that William Stringfellow had it right. For him, Revelation is not a timetable. The focus of his work is ethics, which he defines as '*how to live humanly during the Fall'*, or under its conditions.[37] God is in charge, so let's get on board with his plan to make all things new.

37 William Stringfellow, *An Ethic for Christians & Other Aliens in a Strange Land* (Waco, TX: Word, Incorporated, 1973), 55.

CHAPTER 7 — BEAM ME UP, GODDY — PART 2

Did you hear the one about?

You might be familiar with this old joke, or a similar version of it. A man is walking out at low tide from the beach to an island just off the coast. The fellow just happens to be a Christian. As he is walking back, he finds himself caught by the tide coming in. His feet begin to get stuck in the sand, which because it is wet is like quicksand. A burly fellow with big biceps walks past and offers to help pull the man free. Instead, the Christian responds, 'No that's fine. My God will save me.' The tide continues to come in and the water rises to our man's waist. Someone paddles past in a row boat, offering to pull the man free and save him from drowning. But again, he responds, 'No that's fine. My God will save me.' Finally, the man is up to his neck in water, and a rescue helicopter lowers someone on a rope in order to save him. But his final words, as the water rises over his head, are, 'No that's fine. My God will save me.'

Our next scene has the faithful, trusting Christian in heaven. He arrives at the pearly gates to be greeted by St Peter himself but he is looking somewhat downcast. 'Why so glum, my friend?' asks Peter. 'Well,' responds the man, 'I thought that I would be rescued earlier than I was.' Peter looked at him sagely and said, 'Well. Our Lord sent you a strong man, a row boat, and a helicopter to rescue you. What more did you want?'

You might ask why I am opening this chapter with such a bad joke. Apart from liking bad jokes – just ask my students, past congregations, Facebook friends, and others – it does illustrate a point made by the title of this chapter. You'll recall than in chapter four, we saw that some people are looking to be rescued from real or perceived threats without the actual bother of having to go through difficult times. 'Beam me up, Goddy' is our escape clause. The problem is that some Christians do this too. It's called the rapture.

Beam me up

For some Christians, I've no doubt that the idea of the rapture seems obvious from texts like 1 Thessalonians 4. For others, perhaps their church tradition has consistently taught and emphasised it. There is certainly a strong tendency in many streams of Christianity to make our ultimate salvation about reaching heaven when we die. It seems to be what the bible teaches and it is comforting because it means we avoid all of the suffering that Revelation suggests will happen during the tribulation. It supports the idea that all earthly solutions to the world's problems are futile. Indeed, it isn't much of a step from the rapture to a theology that says, *why bother dealing with 'social issues' because it is all destined for destruction anyway?* (except for the elect who will be raptured). You might believe in doing good to all; that loving our neighbour doesn't discriminate between Christian and non–Christian. And yet, if the world is destined for destruction and Christians will escape before the scatological hits the eschatological fan, isn't there a risk of being demotivated to care? This is not an inevitable consequence but, at the very least, leaves it open to the charge of significant inconsistency.

So, let's deal with the rapture first as an idea, and briefly with the idea of heaven. While it is often assumed that the book of Revelation is the key source of our idea of the rapture, the text where the idea is picked up is 1 Thessalonians. The church in Thessalonica had been subject to persecution (1 Thess 1:6). Paul writes of a coming wrath from which the Thessalonians would be saved (v. 10). The Greek Thessalonians had turned from idols and now waited for the Son of God out of heaven, who God had raised from the dead. The resurrection of Jesus is the fundamental linchpin of Christian hope. In 1 Corinthians 15, for example, we learn that the death, burial, and resurrection is of first importance (v. 3). Note that the cross does not stand alone for Paul but must be followed with the resurrection. Without the resurrection there is no forgiveness of sins (v. 17). In Romans 1:4, Jesus is declared to be the Messiah, the Son of God, by his resurrection. A crucified and dead Messiah is no Messiah at all!

Notice too that the Thessalonians were waiting for Jesus from heaven, or literally 'out of heaven.' This is a reference to the ascension in Acts 1:9–11

When he had said this, as they were watching, he was lifted up, and a cloud took him out of their sight. While he was going and they were gazing up towards heaven, suddenly two men in white robes stood by them. They said, "Men of Galilee, why do you stand looking up towards heaven? This Jesus, who has been taken up from you into heaven, will come in the same way as you saw him go into heaven."

This idea that heaven is up in the sky is part of the ancient three-tiered model of the universe, where God 'walks on the dome of heaven' (Jb 22:14). This dome separated the waters above from the waters below (Gen 1:6–8). This was a common ancient view and yet we now know this is not the case. There is ample scientific evidence from both ground-based and space-based observations that the Earth is not flat. Neither is the Earth the centre of the physical universe. The theology behind this three-tiered model is what we want to preserve, while the physical picture is best understood as a cartoon representation, a word picture, of the spiritual nature of reality. Another way of saying it is that we need to demythologise this picture, which is simply to say that we need to appreciate and understand the theological point that is behind the mythic language. Note that this does not mean reducing anything in the bible to mere story without any basis in 'fact.'

The consistent message of the New Testament is that Jesus was raised bodily from the dead to a new physical existence. Indeed, after over seven hundred pages of examination in his book *The Resurrection of the Son of God*, Tom Wright concludes two things. Firstly, the only thing that first century Jews could understand about the resurrection was the bodily rising from the dead. The second is that the thing that makes the most sense of the rise of the early church is that it *actually happened*.[1] The resurrection is something that happened in human history.

Jesus' ascension is also something that is said to have happened in history but precisely what we are to think about what happened to Jesus once he was hidden by the cloud is another thing. The ascension makes perfect physical sense in a physical three-tiered universe, but we know now that we don't actually live in this kind of world. Instead, the

---

1 N. T. Wright, *The Resurrection of the Son of God (Christian Origins and the Question of God, Vol. 3)* (Minneapolis, MN: Fortress Press 2003).

biblical picture presented points to the transcendent nature of heaven. Jesus went somewhere else that is at once close but also 'far away' from where we are. He is now immanent to us, or near, particularly through the Spirit, but he also transcends where we are now. We can't just jump into a rocket and fly to heaven. That reality transcends our own.[2] We are to expect Jesus to return in the same way he went away, again not because he comes down to earth like a meteorite from the heavens, but that in 'descending from above' he will return as he left. And when he does return, Jesus is bringing heaven with him!

When we read 1 Thessalonians 4:13–18, we understand the return of Christ from heaven (v. 16) to be on the 'last day,' because from then on, a new era in history will inevitably begin. The last day is a first day! The pastoral context for the letter to the Thessalonians is the grief some of them were feeling over those who had died in Christ. Did they expect that Jesus should already have returned? Did they wonder where the dead in Christ were? Paul doesn't answer this question directly. We might expect from Revelation 7 that the dead in Christ 'descend from heaven' (noting this is a metaphor for a richer reality) with him. Indeed, we read in 1 Thess 4:14 that 'through Jesus, God will bring with him those who have died.' And yet, this bringing is not from heaven, but from the earth by resurrection, as 'the dead in Christ will rise first' (v. 16), not descend first. This might pose a question about whether the 'soul descends' and the 'body ascends', but Jews tended not to think in such dualistic categories. Perhaps it is best not to speculate or theorise too much?

The dead rise first, and those who are alive at the time

will be caught up in the clouds together with them to meet the Lord in the air; and so we will be with the Lord for ever' (v. 17).

That sounds a lot like a rapture of sorts, doesn't it? But the text doesn't say that we meet the Lord to ascend into heaven with him. There is no sense that being rescued from the coming wrath means being beamed up to avoid the events of the end times. We need to be careful about what we read into the text. Yes, we are raptured, but not as some Christians have understood.

2 Tom Wright, *Paul for Everyone: Galatians and Thessalonians* (London: SPCK, 2002), 125.

It is also helpful to understand one of the words that Paul uses to better understand what he is saying. The phrase 'the coming of the Lord' in verse 15 uses the Greek word *parousia*. As Tom Wright notes, the secular use of the Greek word *parousia* is important. When Caesar appeared or arrived at a Roman colony, the dignitaries would go out to greet him, not to go off with him back to Rome, but to welcome him into the city![3] This is further confirmed by another word, *apantēsin*, translated as meet.[4] The same word is used in a couple of places in the New Testament. In the parable of the ten bridesmaids (Matt 25:1–12), which is about people responding to Jesus, the five wise bridesmaids were able to respond to the call to go and meet (*apantēsin*) Jesus because they had oil for their lamps (vv. 6–7). The bridegroom was coming, and they were there to meet him and escort him in. Likewise, in Acts 28:15, Roman believers come to meet with Paul, not to take him anywhere, but to welcome him into Rome. Hence, Paul is saying in 1 Thessalonians 4 that yes, those alive in Christ are meant to be raptured into the air, but not to be taken away from earth and into heaven, because when Christ returns, heaven is coming to earth! Accordingly, these believers function as the welcoming committee.

Where does the word rapture even come from? The Greek of 1 Thessalonians 4:17 is the word *harpadzō*, which means snatch, catch up, or seize. In the Latin translation of the New Testament, this was rendered as *raptio*, from which we get the word rapture.[5] Given what we have already seen, there is no way this rapture can mean anything like it has been understood to mean. The idea that the rapture is into heaven is not very old, having come from the vision of a fifteen year old girl in Scotland in 1830, and taken up by the British preacher John Nelson Darby. The idea was popularised by Cyrus Scofield in his *Scofield Reference Bible*, an annotated King James Version. In it, history is broken into seven 'dispensations', or intervals in time, for God's dealing with the world. These dispensations are based on a less than literal reading of a passage in Daniel 9. This is then applied to

---

3 Wright, *Galatians and Thessalonians*, 125.
4 Barbara R. Rossing, *The Rapture Exposed: The Message of Hope in the Book of Revelation* (New York: Basic Books, 2004), 176.
5 Rossing, *The Rapture Exposed*, 22.

Revelation in a way that dismays some writers. Barbara Rossing describes it as 'bits and pieces to be cut up and pasted into an end–times formula.'[6] While we all tend to string passages together to make some kind of sense out of a lot of information, seeing that the traditional idea of rapture literally has us going in the wrong direction allows us to redeem the idea and gain a lot more in the process.

Rapture in reverse

One of the many problems with the idea of the rapture is that it gets heaven wrong. But isn't heaven where God dwells and rules? The Lord's Prayer asks that God's kingdom come and that his will be done 'on earth as it is in heaven' so that heaven becomes manifest on earth, that is to say the rule of God is extended to earth (Matt 6:9–13). We see that Jesus declares that this has been fulfilled in the Great Commission (Matt 28:18–20), and likewise in Revelation 5. And yet, there is a future time written of in Revelation 21, when the city of God descends to earth. There is no temple because the city itself is a temple, and God and the Lamb are everywhere. Heaven and earth meet where God's kingdom has come and where his will is done. In this passage, the new heavens and new earth replace the old (Rev 21:1), but this replacement is one of character or nature instead of physically, as such; in this new order there is no more death or mourning or pain, for God dwells with people.

So, not only is there no rapture in 1 Thessalonians, as it is traditionally understood, it's not in Revelation either! We have already begun to touch on the motif of all things new, the new heavens and the new earth. Barbara Rossing refers to the vision of Revelation 21–22 as a 'rapture in reverse,' and God's vision for renewing the world.[7] What precedes these chapters is also important. Judgement is important. Evil cannot be allowed to continue unabated. But judgement is not the end of the story. What is the world for? What is its future? And what are we meant to be doing now? If the Lamb is in charge now, and there is no rapture set to pluck us out of the path of danger, be it climate related disasters,

---

6 Rossing, *The Rapture Exposed,* 42.
7 Rossing, *The Rapture Exposed,* chapter 10.

persecution for being Christians, or whatever you can think of, then what is our mission?

Rossing sees the vision of Revelation 21–22 as a mystical journey inward and a homecoming outward journey to the world. The mystical journey inward is indeed what the whole book of Revelation is: a vision in heaven to understand what is really going on and where history is really headed. This was as true for those who were victims of empire in the first century as in the 21st century. So, what does the rapture in reverse look like?

The first thing to note is that God and the Lamb are raptured downward to 'dwell' with humans. This is neither 'heavenism' — the idea that salvation is all about going to heaven when we die — or a form of escapism. The word 'dwell' is also used in John 1:14, where the Word comes and dwells with humans. It literally means to pitch one's tent, and refers back to the Tabernacle, which was a portable temple. This is a vision of the future and yet we already know that the kingdom of our world has become the kingdom of our Lord and of his Christ (Rev 11:15). As I'll touch on in the last chapter, I challenge all modern artists to aim as high as the majesty of George Frideric Handel's Messiah in proclaiming this truth. Revelation 21–22 is a taste of, a glimpse of, what is true now, 'even while we wait to fully unfold in the future.'[8] This means we live in the now and not yet tension between the ages. Rossing observes that God's time is not linear, for the Lamb is the Alpha and the Omega, the beginning and the end (Rev 21:6). What we see in Revelation is a vision that takes in that sweep of history.

This sense of living in the present in anticipation of the future is known as prolepsis. To live proleptically is to understand that the future is one of God and the Lamb pitching their tent among us, not us being raptured to heaven, but that heaven has come (the incarnation and coming of the Spirit) and is coming to earth (the eschaton or last day). Think about walking through a long, dark tunnel. At one end is the dim light of the entrance. That's the resurrection of Jesus. At the other end is the light of our destination. That's the resurrection of the dead and the New Heavens and Earth.

---

8 Rossing, *The Rapture Exposed,* 149.

So, what is this like? Well, as we know, Jesus tabernacled among his people in John 1 just as God tabernacled among the Israelites in the wilderness. In the New Jerusalem we see there is no temple, for the city itself is a temple. As John Walton has discussed at length, and as I wrote about in chapter 3, Genesis 1 describes the formation of a temple. So that we don't miss it, the New Jerusalem contains Eden, with the river flowing out from the throne of God. This is an expanded picture of Ezekiel 47; expanded because, while in Ezekiel 47:12 the fruit of the trees is for healing, in Revelation 22:2 it is for the healing of *the nations*. No longer is this a national message only: it is international, the whole world is now included in God's plan! The honour of the nations will be brought into the city (Rev 21:25–26), which echoes the reality that every tribe, people, and tongue make up the people of God (Rev 7). How can all things be made new, if not all nations?

And what is our future in all of this? In Revelation 22:3–5, we read that our future is one of worship in the throne room of God and the Lamb, and we will reign forever. Not Caesar, not the Powers, not empires, but us. This is an appealing message but remember it was written to the powerless, not the privileged. Some of us need to think about this more, but that's for another chapter.

Remember when Rossing said that accompanying the journey inward into the vision of the present and future rule of God and the Lamb is a journey outward and back to earth? Thinking about my analogy, how do we walk through the tunnel with the light we have seen guiding us on? One might say that accompanying our expanded imagination of what the future looks like, we need an expanded ethical imagination to picture what this looks like in the present. To once more quote Rossing

> God's beloved city in Revelation 21–22 is not primarily a vision for after we die, or for after Jesus returns. It is rather a vision that can transform the way we live out God's reign in the world today.[9]

This is not to say that the final return of Christ is unimportant, unnecessary, or a myth. It is precisely to say that knowing that Christ rules now, and will bring that rule to fruition in the future, can and must shape how we live in the here and now.

---

9 Rossing, *The Rapture Exposed,* 164.

Climate change is no joke

I began this chapter with a bad joke, which highlighted the idea that the rapture is a form of escapism, an easy way out. Certainly, there are trials along the way, although not as part of some kind of tribulation as popularly understood. However, we do see in climate change a judgment upon humanity being revealed, and often an undiscriminating one. Take, for example, Anote Tong, who was the President of the Pacific Island nation of Kiribati from 2003 to 2016. For some time, he has been travelling the world, pleading on behalf of his nation, and that of other Pacific Island nations, for the developed world to take action on climate change. Kiribati is made up of three island groups that straddle the equator and the International Date Line. They are all coral atolls, no more than two kilometres wide and two metres above sea level. They are incredibly vulnerable to sea level rise. Rising seas mean a loss of land and the enhanced impacts of ocean swells. Erosion, land loss, and loss of fresh water are all hazards of sea level rise. In 2016, the people of Kiribati experienced their very first cyclone. Life is changing for them and not for the better.

Kiribati is predominantly Christian and yet we don't hear from them cries for the rapture. It would be scarce comfort to them to be told that their homes were going to be destroyed anyway, or even to suggest the rising seas were part of the end times and they should just wait to be raptured. And while their ultimate salvation lies in the return of Christ, their attachment to place is strong, and rightly so. They are considering the possibility of floating islands, as a preference to being relocated. Technology may be a poor saviour but it can be a useful tool. As soon as we think more about being beamed up rather than being saved with the places we love (instead of from them), we begin to abandon our connection to place and from those who want to maintain it. Compassion for the people of Kiribati would be to help them stay where they are until Christ returns to make all things new. Even more than that, combating climate change by making the necessary changes as a society would mean that the changes that Anote Tong and his people have to make would be less dramatic and costly. We owe them that.

Chapter 8 — All Things New

A few years ago, controversial American pastor, Mark Driscoll, said during a conference presentation that, 'I know who made the environment and he's coming back to burn it all up. So yes, I drive an SUV."[1] I'm not targeting Driscoll as an individual, but his comments are representative of what many Christians believe. Many will cite 2 Peter 3:10 in support of this view

> the heavens will pass away with a loud noise, and the elements will be dissolved with fire, and the earth and everything that is done on it will be disclosed.

But does this passage really mean that God will scrap the whole creation and start from scratch? How do we balance this with texts like Romans 8, where there appears to be a much stronger sense of continuity between this world and the next? And how difficult is it to take matters of injustice seriously, while believing that it's all destined for the furnace? Gale Heide nails it when he writes

> If this earth on which we live is going to be completely destroyed, as many evangelicals believe it is, then we have little more responsibility to it than to act as good stewards of the resources God has given us. But if this world has a future in God's plan, being renewed rather than re-created ex nihilo, then perhaps we have a much greater responsibility than to merely act as good managers.[2]

What if there was another way to understand Peter that is faithful to the text and consistent with other parts of the bible? What I want to do in this chapter is establish from a few places in the New Testament that when John writes that Jesus is 'making all things new,' this means two things. Firstly, all things really does mean all things. Not just the soul but the entirety of your humanity. And not just human beings as

---

[1] Russ Pierson, and John Roe, "Mark Driscoll: Gas–Guzzlers a Mark of Masculinity," *Sojourner*, 5 September, 2013, accessed 26 April, 2018, https://sojo.net/articles/mark–driscoll–gas–guzzlers–mark–masculinity.

[2] Gale Z. Heide, "What is New about the New Heaven and the New Earth? A Theology of Creation from Revelation 21 and 2 Peter 3," *JETS* 40/1 (March 1997): 37–56.

individuals, as much as this is also true. But all things. Human society. The non-human world. This is important when we think about the work that we do in the justice space and, in particular, climate justice. The second idea is all things new means all things renewed, hence, the subtitle of the book and the global campaign, renew our world. For example, if we think 2 Peter 3 speaks of the literal burning up of the world, then the new heavens and earth are literally *brand* new. But if all things are renewed, then there is a sense of continuity as well as discontinuity between what we do now and what is to be when Christ returns. It adds a theological richness and depth to our work now.

Burn baby burn[3]

We have already been introduced to the idea of apocalyptic literature in chapter 5. It is important that we understand what we are reading and what a text is saying in its context and through its genre. Otherwise, we will thoroughly misunderstand it. For many Christians, 2 Peter is the tricky text for our project to renew our world because it appears to suggest that God is going to scrap it and start again. But what about Genesis 1, for example? Didn't God make a good creation? To be sure humans have made a mess but is the solution to the marring of the new creation to scrap it, or renew it?

We firstly need to remember that apocalyptic language is highly symbolic, and describes these worldly events, or as Tom Wright puts it

> to evoke the cosmic or theological *meaning* of events in the space–time world by means of a sometimes complex system of metaphors.[4]

In other words, as Walter Wink often observes, what happens on earth is mirrored by what happens in heaven, so the language is cosmic and mythic. What happens here on the earth is reflected in heavenly ways. So, when we read about the destruction of Babylon in Isaiah 13:10, we see that 'the sun will be dark at its rising, and the moon will not shed its light.' The destruction of the Jerusalem temple was to be accompanied

---

3 The title of this section is taken from a 70s discos song by *The Trammps*. The section is an extension of part one of Claire Dawson, and Mick Pope, *A Climate of Hope: Church and Mission in a Warming World* (Dandenong: Urban Neighbours of Hope, 2014).
4 Tom Wright, *The Millennium Myth* (London: SPCK UK: 1999), 27.

by earthquakes (Mk 13). And when, in Revelation 6, we see the wrath of God being revealed with the opening of the sixth seal (vv. 12–14)

> there came a great earthquake; the sun became black as sackcloth, the full moon became like blood, and the stars of the sky fell to the earth as the fig tree drops its winter fruit when shaken by a gale. The sky vanished like a scroll rolling itself up, and every mountain and island was removed from its place.

None of these texts is to be understood to explain literal astronomical or geological events, but how the heavens reflect earthly events. This should shape our expectation of how 2 Peter 3 should be read.

So, how *do* we read it? Note that we are in the last days, where the word for last is *eschatōn*, from where we get the word eschatology, which is the branch of theology that deals with the last things. Peter is telling his readers that the end is close. Indeed, he is encouraging them that those who scoff at the thought (vv. 3–4) do so because they are more interested in their own indulgent lifestyle than Christ coming in judgement. Likewise, they are running off the wrong timetable, we simply don't know when Christ will return (vv. 8–9). The imagery of a sneaky thief appearing unexpectedly is a saying of Jesus (e.g. Matt 24:43) and found in Revelation as well (Rev 3:3; 16:15). But, when Jesus does return, everyone will know about it. It will be earth shattering (2 Pet 3:10).

Why is the return of Christ delayed? Because God doesn't want anyone to perish but instead for people to repent. Look at verse 10 and the phrase 'the elements will be dissolved with fire, and the earth and everything that is done on it will be disclosed.' There are versions that contain the phrase 'burned up' instead of disclosed, but these are suspect and don't reflect the earliest manuscripts.[5] The Greek word translated as disclosed gives us our English word heuristic, which refers to a method of finding things out.[6] The point of the fire then is not the literal destruction of all things but the revealing of sinful behaviour. Earlier in verse 7, Peter says that the fire is kept for the destruction of the godless,

---

5 Heide, *What is New about the New Heaven and the New Earth?* 53.
6 Steven Bouma–Prediger, *For the Beauty of the Earth: A Christian Vision for Creation Care 2nd edition* (Grand Rapids: Baker Academic: 2010), 68–69.

not the creation. Now the language is all-inclusive, but the significance narrows down to human evil, precisely because of our impact on the earth, not a doing away with creation.[7]

In this sense, fire is not about literal destruction of all that we see, though it is cast in that dramatic, mythic language. Fire is for purification of the earth from sin. Going back to 1 Peter 1:7, we read that fire is for refining,

> so that the genuineness of your faith—being more precious than gold that, though perishable, is tested by fire—may be found to result in praise and glory and honour when Jesus Christ is revealed.

The expression 'may be found' is the same word from 2 Peter 3:10. So the language of destruction in verses 11–12 should be understood in the context of refining and judgement. The new heavens and earth are where righteousness is at home. Hence, the message of fire is a warning to the church to purify itself: to live now in a manner consistent with the future renewed world. Church fathers such as Irenaeus and Origen held this view because they recognised that the idea of a cosmic destruction was pagan and not at all biblical![8]

Barbara Rossing reads Revelation 21:7–8 in the same way. Here we read about two groups of people: those who conquer the temptations of the world and those who live according to them. The vision is twofold: a new heavens and earth where there is no more mourning, crying, or death, and where the one on the throne is 'making all things new' (vv. 1–6). And then there is the lake of fire, which is the second death for those who continue in sin. Notice again the use of fire in the burning up of unrighteousness.

We also need to observe Peter's use of the story of the flood. He draws parallels between the fire that burns up the elements and the waters in which the world perished. The order of creation was overwhelmed by the release of chaos in the flood. The waters above the earth and the oceans, which were separated at creation, come together in an act of 'uncreation.' The world returns to the formlessness of Genesis 1:2,

---

7 Jonathan Moo, and Robert White, *Hope in an Age of Despair: The Gospel and the Future of Life on Earth* (Nottingham: Inter-Varsity Press, 2013), 136.

8 Heide, *What is New about the New Heaven and the New Earth?* 49.

before it functioned in an ordered fashion. If we think about this as material destruction we are missing the point. The Earth was washed clean of sin in the same way the Earth will be purified by fire. In Genesis 6:11–12 we read

Now the earth was corrupt in God's sight, and the earth was filled with violence. And God saw that the earth was corrupt; for all flesh had corrupted its ways upon the earth.

The corruption was washed away and the world was both recreated in a functional sense — made new — but also renewed because there was continuity: order was bought out of the disorder of the initial creation. Notice too that *all things new* here not only means all things *renewed* but that *all* things are made new. Peter knew full well his readers understood that renewal meant choosing a remnant of humanity as well as saving living creatures. The animals went in two by two. Hurrah! God cared about human and non-human alike because he was making all things new. The earth was made new because the waters and land were separated again, re–enacting the creation event from day three. And the heavens were made new because the waters from the sky were taken back above the firmament as in day two of creation. You see, God is in the business of making all things new!

All really does mean all

We can all be rather selective about the way in which we read the bible. We can get fixated on single words. For example, Martin Luther couldn't get around the 'is' in the sentence 'this is my body,' and hence developed a view that was similar to, but not entirely the same as, what the Catholic church taught about the Lord's Supper. Paul does this too. When he wrote to the Galatians (3:16), he makes a big thing that the promise to Abraham was made to his offspring (literally seed) rather than his offsprings (literally seeds), hence reading it as being about Christ. So, when in Revelation 21:5 we read that Jesus is 'making all things new', it really does mean *all things*.

Further evidence for the all-inclusiveness is found in Colossians 1. This passage contains a great hymn to the 'Cosmic Christ.' Jesus is the first born or better the pre-eminent one in *all creation* (v. 15), the same creation that groans in birth pains in Romans 8. *All things*, whether in heaven or on earth have been created in, through, and for, Christ (Col 1:16). As noted earlier, the phrase 'in heaven and on earth, visible and invisible' ensures that the thrones, dominions, rulers, and powers include human institutions and the spiritual realm. One lies behind the other. This also means that the spiritual realm was created for Christ, even if it contains fallen angels. It means that now-corrupt institutions were originally created for Christ to maintain an ordered society but then became corrupt. It means that the idea of government per se is not bad, it was created by and for Christ, and yet often goes wrong when it is apart from Christ. Indeed, history is littered with 'Christian governments' that were Christless. Colossians 1:16–17 points out the powers were made through and for Christ, and therefore must have initially been good and created for our good.

Christ is also before *all things*, which might be temporal, but is certainly again a statement of pre–eminence. We also learn than in Christ *all things* hold together or 'receive their systemic place' from the Greek *synistēmi*. Human life needs social structures to bring order to life, and these things also come from Christ, even though they can and often are twisted by human desire for power and control.[9] Finally, *all things*, whether those things in heaven or on earth, are to be reconciled to Christ by the cross (v. 20). Richard Bauckham observes then that 'Jesus' full significance is found in relationship to all creation.'[10] Richard Middleton goes further and claims that this passage 'does not myopically limit the efficacy of Christ's atonement to the individual or even to humanity.'[11] Such an understanding goes against much of what we have been told. It is right to stress individual response to the gospel and that the cross (and resurrection) suffices for *my* sins. But if our understanding of the cross ends there and doesn't include the

---

9 Walter Wink, *Engaging the Powers: Discernment and Resistance in a World of Domination* (Minneapolis: Fortress Press, 1992), 67.

10 Richard Bauckham, *Bible and Ecology: Rediscovering the Community of Creation* (London: Darton, Longman and Todd Ltd, 2010), 156.

11 J. Richard Middleton, *A New Heaven and a New Earth: Reclaiming Biblical Eschatology* (Grand Rapids, MI: Baker Books, 2014), 158.

reconciliation of all things, both human and other than human, then we sell the gospel short.

The inclusive nature of heaven and earth in Colossians 1 recalls the promise of Revelation 21:5 that Jesus is 'making all things new.' This includes the powers behind the powers, the spirituality of nations, corporations, government. In Revelation 21, the nations are mentioned twice. The New Jerusalem is the light by which the nations will walk (v. 24), and they will bring their glory and honour to the city (v. 26). In chapter 22, the tree of life is for the healing of the nations (v. 2).

Our social structures, nations, and corporations can all be made new and can be reconciled to Christ. This has implications for the way in which we approach dealing with issues like climate change as the church. There are limits to the sorts of actions we can take, and yet non-violence has proven very effective in resisting things like oppressive governments or changing segregation laws. Indeed, the nonviolence of the cross saved humanity from sin and death. We will discuss this more in chapter 10. For now, it is enough to realise that the making of all things new is not simply about individuals, although it is obvious enough that you can't save a nation if you don't save the people in it. Unless you challenge the culture and the spirituality of a group, it is never enough to simply convert the individuals and hope for the best. The goal of converting a culture is so that people will live in harmony with each other and with the other than human creation, which Christ will also reconcile to himself.

The Great Deliverance

Romans 8 is a Christian environmentalist's favourite text. I will have more to say on it in chapter 10 but, for now, I want to discuss the idea that the creation itself looks to be delivered. The title of this section is taken from a sermon preached by the English priest and theologian, John Wesley.[12] His basic idea was that creation fell with humans, claiming

---

12 John Wesley, *The Great Deliverance*. Accessed 30 May 2015. http://wesley.nnu.edu/john–wesley/the–sermons–of–john–wesley–1872–edition/sermon–60–the–general–deliverance/. I discuss his sermon in more detail in Mick Pope, "With Heads Craning Forward: The Eschaton and the Nonhuman Creation in Romans 8," in *Ecotheology in the Humanities: An Interdisciplinary Approach to Understanding the Divine and Nature*, ed.

What did the meaner creature suffer, when man rebelled against God? It is probable that they sustained much loss, even in the lower faculties; their vigour, strength and swiftness.

This even included insects and worms. While this might seem a little naïve from our perspective, Wesley was trying to deal with the problem of natural evil. After all, even if predation seems to be very useful for ecosystem functioning, it is also altogether brutal at times.[13] Take, for example, the scene from the 2001 BBC documentary series *The Blue Planet,* narrated by David Attenborough, involving a grey whale calf. A pod of about fifteen killer whales chased a grey whale and her calf for several hours before the calf finally died. The assistant producer on the site described the scene

> It was quite distressing to watch this poor creature being hunted for so long. Towards the end we were just thinking, 'Just kill it and put it out of its misery'. But at the same time, it was exhilarating to watch this great drama being played out at sea.[14]

Many viewers found the scene quite disturbing. Wesley describes some predators as 'unrelenting monsters' and, no doubt, many Christians would agree. Alan Jacobs, in his essay *In on the kill,* counsels against watching such scenes for entertainment.[15] I have argued elsewhere that his case is overstated.[16] Regardless of the future state of creation, predation is part of the order as it exists now (Ps 104:21). But what Romans does tell us is that things are not the way that they should be.

So, what is wrong? The creation waits with eager longing for the revealing of the sons of God (v. 19). Note that while some translations read children instead of sons, I have kept sons because of the understanding of adoption and sonship in the ancient world. The

---

Melissa J. Brotton (Lanham: Lexington Books, 2016).

13 On the value of predators in Yellowstone National Park, see George Monbiot, *Feral: Searching for Enchantment on the Frontiers of Nature* (London: Allen Lane, 2013), 84. Note that some of what has been claimed about the re–introduction of wolves has been much overstated.

14 David Harrison, "Pack hunt by killers of the sea filmed for first time," *The Telegraph*, 9 September, 2011, accessed 2 May, 2018. https://www.telegraph.co.uk/news/worldnews/northamerica/usa/1340036/Pack–hunt–by–killers–of–the–sea–filmed–for–first–time.html.

15 Alan Jacobs, *A Visit to Vanity Fair* (Grand Rapids, MI: Brazos Press, 2001),

16 Mick Pope, "Christ and the Camera Lens," *Zadok Papers* S141 (Spring, 2005).

sons of God are identical in this sense to the children of God (v. 21). This revelation or apocalypse of the children of God will happen at the resurrection (v. 23). This occurs at Christ's coming (1 Thess 4:15). For now, the creation has been subjected to futility, and it is clearly God who has subjected it. This might not seem like much of an environmental text but the subjection has a purpose. Interestingly though, the word for futility is also found in Romans 1:21, where it refers to the futility of the thinking of idolaters.[17] The likelihood is that creation suffers because we make idols out of it (Rom 1:23). This is as much a warning to those of us who engage in the theology of creation care, known as ecotheology, as anything else. But the subjects of our idol making includes both humans and non-humans, as well as power, money, sex, progress, and so on. All of these things damn the creation to futility under our fallen dominion. There is no moral failure on the part of creation, even while it is less than it should be.

The subjection of creation is in hope that it will be set free from bondage. Both the bondage of creation and the redemption of our bodies (Rom 8:23) speak of slavery. Neither humanity nor humans are fully free. Creation is enslaved to our idolatry and its consequences. Likewise, our idolatry leads to sin and enslaves us to itself and ultimately to death (Rom 7). When we are redeemed at the resurrection, something about our renewed natures will mean that creation itself is renewed. The future of creation is tied up with ours because the word for groaning, *sunōdinō*, is typically associated with childbirth.[18] When the earth, which is our tomb, becomes our womb, our rebirth will be its salvation.

In between times, there is an interesting play on groaning. The whole creation groans in birth pains, awaiting our rebirth and suffering under us. Then, while we await this rebirth, we too groan inwardly. Finally,

---

17 Cheryl Hunt, David G. Horrell and Christopher Southgate, "An Environmental Mantra? Ecological Interest in Romans 8:19–23 and a Modest Proposal for its Interpretation," *Journal of Theological Studies* (2008) NS.

18 N. Thomas Wright, "Romans," in *The New Interpreter's Bible: A Commentary in Twelve Volumes, Volume X*, edited by Robert W. Wall (Nashville: Abingdon Press, 2002), 597. Walter Bauer and Frederick William Danker, *A Greek–English Lexicon of the New Testament and Other Early Christian Literature* (University of Chicago: University Of Chicago Press, 2001), 977.

and sometimes hidden by some translations, when we can't articulate our prayers, the Spirit groans in intercession for us (v. 26). The word in verse 26 is *sustenadzō* which means to groan together with.[19] While some scholars disagree, Robert Jewett believes that we groan together with creation and he draws a link in Job 31:38–40 where the land groaned against Job.[20] So, creation and Christians groan together, and the Spirit and Christians groan together. Can it be said also that the Spirit groans with the creation? I would suggest so, particularly when the church both repents of its idolatry, laments the damage it has done to creation, and empathises with it imaginatively. This should lead us to both prayer and activism.

This all begs the question of what the future will be like and what that looks like proleptically. The vision of a new heavens and earth and New Jerusalem in Revelation 21 has its origins in Isaiah 65:17–25. There, a vision of peace includes (v. 25)

> The wolf and the lamb shall feed together, the lion shall eat straw like the ox; but the serpent—its food shall be dust!

I have always read this as metaphor for peace, particularly given the allusion to the serpent of Genesis 3. Such texts lead some Christians to vegetarianism or veganism. That may yet prove to be one of the best ways to deal with climate change and to co–groan with the rest of creation, even if it is just your stomach that is groaning, and even if eating no meat is a reality at the return of Christ. Prolepsis means working for the redemption of the non-human now, relieving its groaning under the various aspects of the Anthropocene, working for conservation, and limiting our diet so that other creatures can live.

At the very least, Romans 8 tells us that all things new means all things non-human, and that 'God saves us *with,* and not *from,* creation.'[21] We share a future hope and that hope should inform our

---

19 Bauer and Danker, *A Greek–English* Lexicon, 978.

20 In disagreement with the idea of co–groaning see Douglas Moo, *The Epistle to the Romans: New International Commentary on the New Testament* (Grand Rapids: Wm. B Eeerdmans Publishing Company, 1996), 518; Thomas R. Schreiner, *Romans: Baker Exegetical Commentary on the New Testament* (Grand Rapids: Baker Books, 1998): 437. In support see Robert Jewett, *Romans: A Commentary* (Minneapolis: Fortress Press, 2007), 516.

21 Mick Pope, *Preaching to the Birds? The Mission of the Church to the Creation* (Eastwood:

ethics. Jürgen Moltmann, in *Ethics of Hope,* urges us to become more earth-centred, and not only human-centred or God-centred in our ethical considerations.[22] We should let live and let grow, rather than rule and subdue.[23] This is to follow Christ's example of what authority and rule looks like and to place love at the centre of our ethic. This is an eco-centred view. A God-centred view recognises the divine possession of creation, which means that we are not permitted to damage or destroy the Earth.[24]

All things new

This brings us back to our key text from Revelation 21. Now that we see that all things really must mean all things by looking at other bible passages, we can unpack the vision that John gives us. By now, we've seen some pretty intense stuff in Revelation, with the defeat of the beast and the dragon (Rev 19:17–21; 20:7–10) and the judgement of the dead (Rev 20:11–15). Revelation 21:1–8 is a summary of the new heavens and earth, with the details filled in (21:9–22:5).[25] Straight away we need to be wary of literalistic readings. Verse 1 could be the ultimate bummer for surfers: no more sea? More than that, what does it mean for the first heavens and earth to have passed away? Is the new creation really out of nothing, *creatio ex nihilo,* as they say in Latin? As Gale Heide notes, the idea of 'passed away' is not a literal destruction, and we've already dismissed this idea based on a more nuanced and careful reading of 2 Peter 3. In Revelation 20:11, we read that before the throne of God 'the earth and the heaven fled from his presence, and no place was found for them.' What follows is the judgement of the dead. So, concludes Heide, when we read of the passing away of heaven and earth, they have departed from John's sight.[26] We might say that this scene has

---

Morling Press, 2013), accessed May 12, 2015, http://www.morlingcollege.com/sites/default/files/files/2013%20Annual%20Lecture%20Booklet.pdf. Also published as Mick Pope, "Preaching to the Birds? The Mission of the Church to the Creation," in *Speaking of Mission: Volume 2,* edited by Michael Frost, 107–120. (Eastwood: Morling Press, 2013).

22 Jürgen Moltmann, *Ethics of Hope* (London: SCM Press, 2012), chapter 10.

23 Moltmann, *Ethics of Hope,* 150.

24 Moltmann, *Ethics of Hope,* 149.

25 Mark B. Stephens, *Annihilation or Renewal* (Tübingen: Mohr Siebeck, 2011), 228.

26 Heide, *What's New about the New Heaven and the New Earth,* 43.

been done with, the action has moved on. What is not being described is any physical destruction of the world. As Heide says, 'God is not making all things anew. He is making all things as new.'[27] Heavens and Earth 2.0. Upgraded with all new features.

Back to the imagery of no sea. As Heide notes, in Revelation, one of the beasts emerges from the sea (Rev 13). He sees that this emergence from the sea implies an ungodly origin and opposition to God. Certainly, the idea of a creature from the sea carries echoes of the sea monsters from the Hebrew Bible as agents of chaos (see chapter 3). So, the removal of the sea simply means that 'old order/system and the power of evil have been removed from John's sight.'[28] What follows then should be an account of a world of order and peace. We've already seen in chapter 7 that the descent of the New Jerusalem is a rapture in reverse. Mark Stephens describes it as having a threefold significance.[29]

Firstly, the New Jerusalem is a 'reverse Babel.' Remember that Babel represents an attempt for humanity to make a name for itself (Gen 11:4), resulting in confusion and a scattering of the nations (Gen 11:7–9). For Walter Wink, the story of the Fall doesn't finish with Adam and Eve being ejected from the garden but with the story of Babel.[30] This reverse Babel means that peace and unity are not achieved by unaided human efforts, nor according to human agendas. As Terry Eagleton notes, 'Messianic time is thus at odds with the doctrine of progress.'[31] Remember, Houston, we have a problem, and it's not going away. The return of Christ is an event that 'breaks violently, unpredictably, into the human narrative, upending its logic, defying its priorities, and unmasking its wisdom as foolishness.'[32] So, there is going to be genuine change that is surprising to those both inside and outside of the church. However, this is not to say that people have lost the image of God, or don't follow God's plan at times (Rom 2:15). What it does mean is that

---

27 Heide, *What's New about the New Heaven and the New Earth*, 44.
28 Heide, *What's New about the New Heaven and the New Earth*, 45.
29 Stephens, *Annihilation or Renewal*, 233–4.
30 Walter Wink, *Unmasking the Powers: The Invisible Forces That Determine Human Existence* (Philadelphia: Fortress Press, 1986), 97.
31 Terry Eagleton, *Hope Without Optimism* (New Haven: Yale University Press, 2015), 33.
32 Eagleton, *Hope Without Optimism*, 27.

the people of God are supposed to live as if Babel has fallen, yet the scattering is being reversed. The New Jerusalem as the Bride of the Lamb is made up of many nations, tribes, peoples, and tongues (Rev 5:9). While Babel was a unity, New Jerusalem is a unity in diversity, something we will come back to shortly.

The second significance of the reverse Babel is the collapse of dualism. Apocalyptic literature is a peek behind the curtain, as it were; a look at the spiritual significance of worldly events. We need the angelic witness to help us understand this as things are not always clear. We see in part, dimly as in a mirror (1 Cor 13:12). Heaven and earth finally merge, as anticipated in the Lord's Prayer with its 'Your will be done, on earth as it is in heaven (Matt 6:9–13). looks forward to. There is a cosmic wholeness. I'm reminded a little of the movie *The Dark Crystal*, where the evil Skeksis and benevolent Mystics are re-joined to find wholeness and immortality once more. Peace and order then return to the planet Thra. Thirdly, and relatedly, there is a transfer of sovereignty, as Stephens calls it. We know that since the resurrection, 'All authority in heaven and on earth has been given to me [Jesus]' (Matt 28:18). Now it is plain for all to see.

To tease this out some more, let's think of two related themes: temple and garden. In Revelation 21:22 we read that 'I saw no temple in the city, for its temple is the Lord God the Almighty and the Lamb.' The issue of temple is one that we see throughout scripture, as we discussed briefly in chapter 3. Creation is a temple in Genesis 1. The wandering Israelites carried a portable temple with them (Ex 25). Solomon built a temple at God's command but recognised that neither heaven nor earth, let alone a building, could contain God (1 Ki 8:27). This temple is sacked and the people taken off into exile, but Ezekiel promised that God's presence would return to the temple (Ez 43:6). In the New Testament, God's people are God's temple on Earth (1 Cor 6:19–20). Finally, when all things are made new, the whole world becomes God's temple once more.

In the New Jerusalem we see Eden incorporated; the original temple of God. The river of life flows from the throne of God and the Lamb, just as the four waters found their origin in Eden (Gen 2:10). The tree of life, once forbidden to sinful humanity (Gen 3:22–24), is now freely available for the nations, producing fruit year round. Even the leaves bring healing to the nations now they are no longer enslaved to Babylon and the ways of godless empire. Such a right is given to the one who conquers empire through the Lamb (Rev 2:7). Rossing makes the point that this bounty of the tree represents a new economy which is

> In contrast to the economy of Babylon/Rome, which was characterized by famine and hunger and an exploitative system of taxation that squeezed peasants and the poor. God's holy city has enough food for all.[33]

I'll have more to say about economics in chapter 9 and food in chapter 10. For now, we need to understand that this garden metaphor was a powerful message to those subjugated by empire in John's day, as it is in ours. I, and most of those who will read this, are not victims of empire in the way the original readers were. We are colonised, to be sure, but not literally colonised as if by an invading military force. Instead, we are colonised in our hearts and minds, and mostly in a way with which we are quite comfortable.

This brings us to the work of Kenyan Anglican Priest and lecturer, Humphry Waweru.[34] Waweru recognises that the 'bible legitimated the imperial assumption of control of African culture.'[35] This could easily be said about any majority world country or the indigenous people of the western world. In response to this history of control, post-colonial readings have developed because 'we have all been thoroughly constructed by imperialism to perceive each other from a particular stance.'[36] This should mean that post-colonialism can be deeply liberating for both the colonised and the coloniser. For the colonised, post-colonialism means 'a resurrection of the indigenous people who were once marginalised and oppressed.' For the coloniser,

---

33 Barbara R. Rossing, *The Raptured Exposed: The Message of Hope in the Book of Revelation* (New York: Basic Books, 2004), 155.

34 Humphry Waweru, "Postcolonial and Contrapuntal reading of Revelation 22:1–5," *Churchman* 121/1 (2007):23–38. Humphry Waweru, "Postcolonial and Contrapuntal reading of Revelation 22:1–5: Part 2," *Churchman* 121/2 (2007):139–162.

35 Waweru, *Postcolonial and Contrapuntal reading*, 24.

36 Waweru, *Postcolonial and Contrapuntal reading*, 28.

we are relieved of the need to act as if we were superior, freed from our collaboration with the powers and principalities. It means we answer the call to come out of Babylon. Waweru puts it this way

> What we need to do is to explore how to allow the culture of the coloniser and our own culture to interact and to move beyond the limitations of both cultures.[37]

This means finding genuinely African Christianities (and Aboriginal Christianities, and North American indigenous Christianities) that are not simply a clone of western culture. This is echoed in the Moltmann call that

> An ethics of hope for the fullness of life resists the unified global culture and preserves cultural multiplicity because it is in that the potentiality for the future lies.[38]

In order to do this, Waweru advocates a contrapuntal reading of Revelation 22:1–5. Contrapuntal is a musical term that refers to two melodies played at the same time. He sees Revelation as a myth, in the sense not of something untrue, but of a powerful metaphor explaining reality, one which 'offers hope and utopia in a colonised world.' This hope is 'a total social and political discontinuity and a reversal of roles rather than piecemeal changes.'[39] That last phrase should give us pause for thought. If African Christians have suffered at the hands of western empires, and Revelation offers that the first shall be last, then that's a clear warning for us. Waweru's contrapuntal reading is between Revelation 22:1–5 and the Kikuyu story of a garden given to the people by God. The goal is to synthesise and develop a contextual reading for Kenyans. Waweru finds many parallels between the two stories; they play a similar melody. There are trees and rivers from God, a habitable land that is a gift to God's people, and an imperialism to be resisted. Waweru finds discordance between the Kikuyu myth, which holds that the future is not radically different from the present, from Revelation, which he believes foretells immediate destruction.[40] We have seen that

---

37 Waweru, *Postcolonial and Contrapuntal reading*, 29.
38 Moltmann, *Ethics of Hope*, 162.
39 Waweru, *Postcolonial and Contrapuntal reading: Part 2*, 140.
40 Waweru, *Postcolonial and Contrapuntal reading: Part 2*, 155.

this latter claim is untrue, but it does point to the suggestion that a contrapuntal reading helps us challenge false readings of Revelation.

For Waweru, the God of Israel is also found in Kikuyu mythology and hence God 'is the ultimate point of reference' for the African community as they look for freedom of oppression. Waweru also sees a dichotomy between 'Western thinking of eschatology (in terms of *chronos*) to African thinking of eschatology (*kairos*)'.[41] Chronological or clock time (*chronos*) is quantitative, whereas season (*kairos*) is qualitative, in that it describes a quality of time rather than precisely when it is expected to occur. Kairos saves us from treating Revelation as a timetable and points to the eschatological future that 'transforms the present moment into a particular kind of Kairos.' What I find fascinating is that Waweru has rediscovered the biblical understanding of eschatology in Revelation through his own culture, while ascribing to the passage a view that comes through one western reading, a reading I argued against in chapter 6.

To summarise then, there are three things to take away from this entire discussion of all things new. The first is that all things really does mean all things and it means all things renewed, not all things anew. What I mean is an upgrade, a transformation, not a starting again. Secondly, we need to recognise that some of the things that need making new bear our stamp. This is not to say that only westerners are sinful. However, given that we have exercised the power of empire over the majority of the world for centuries, burnt fossil fuels for longer, and used resources more intensively, we bear a particular blame for the state of the world. Thirdly, we need to continue to challenge our own readings of the bible. When we come to the text of Revelation and look to the message of hope, we need to recognise our need to come out of Babylon. In order to do this, we need to listen to voices from the majority world like those of Humphry Waweru, who shows us how Kikuyu myths tell of a creator God creating a garden to provide for his people. Or listen to Aboriginal Pastor, Ray Minniecon, who applies the message of Deuteronomy 32:8 to the possession of the Land by Aboriginal peoples

---

41 Waweru, *Postcolonial and Contrapuntal reading*: *Part 2*, 157.

When the Most High gave the nations their inheritance, When He separated the sons of man, He set the boundaries of the peoples according to the number of the sons of Israel.[42]

The promise of the garden in the New Jerusalem is a promise to provide land for the needs of all people. In preparation for this, maybe it's time we started giving land back to those we've taken it from?

---

42 Ray Minniecon, "A letter from Pastor Ray Minniecon," *Indigenous Hospitality House Newsletter*, May 2012, accessed 31 May, 2017, http://www.brunswick.unitingchurch.org. au/newspdfs/Indigenous%20Hospitality%20House%20May.pdf.

CHAPTER 9 — RENEWED ECONOMICS

Balancing the books

It is always good to celebrate successes. The modern world exhibits successes worth celebrating, which is exactly what Steven Pinker calls us to do (see chapter 4). As economist, Kate Raworth, points out in her book *Doughnut Economics*, we've made great strides forward since the 1950s in average life expectancy, the number of people living in extreme income poverty (less than $1.90 a day), and access to safe drinking water and toilets. Yet still, one in nine people don't have enough to eat. In 2015, six million children under the age of five died of conditions like diarrhoea and malaria, and two billion live on less than $3 per day.[1] Add to this the breaking or threatened breaking of the nine planetary boundaries, including that of a safe climate, and you get the sense that the world has a long way to go. The reality is that the economic growth that enables economies to develop and can lift people out of poverty can also place people in poverty and destroy the very ecology that our economies rely upon. Note that the prefix eco is the same in both words, ecology and economics, deriving from the Greek word *oikos,* meaning household. We haven't managed our household, or better still, the household of God, very well. That is why our world needs renewing.

A clear model for economics that respects the needs of human flourishing and economic justice, and also respects the planetary boundaries, is Kate Raworth's Doughnut economics. It's one of those 'you must read this' books. So, I begin this chapter by talking about her vision of economics, before turning to look at some theological principles. That said, let's begin with a reminder of why we might need to consider economics.

---

1 Kate Raworth, *Doughnut Economics: Seven Ways to Think Like a 21ˢᵗ-Century Economist* (London: Random House Business Books, 2017), 11.

The promise of Jesus is to make 'all things new' (Rev 21:5). That's a program of the renewal of all things. It's also a program for the present, not some far-off future, although it will eventually find its fulfilment and closure. And then there's this:

> For all the nations have drunk of the wine of the wrath of her fornication, and the kings of the earth have committed fornication with her, and the merchants of the earth have grown rich from the power of her luxury. (Rev 18:3)

It's to economics we must go.

The Cuckoo of Growth

The doughnut is an attempt to provide economics with a new icon. We all like icons: simple to understand images that articulate in an easy-to-see manner some deep-seated aspect of our culture and worldview.[2] What does the doughnut encapsulate? Think of what a doughnut looks like. It has a hole in the middle and has an inner and outer edge. In the case of doughnut economics, the inner edge represents the social foundation of society. It affirms the role of an economic system to serve the needs of human flourishing, not the other way around. Of course, what is missing from Raworth's analysis is a foundation for this. For the Christian, it is that humans are not simply *homo economicus*, an economic being, and an invention of philosopher, John Stuart Mill, who said that the political economy treats humans simply as those who 'desire to possess wealth.'[3] Neither are we merely *homo sapiens;* wise beings separated from other creatures by superior intellect and tool making ability. We are the *imago Dei* or image of God. The respect for human flourishing is part of what it means to love your neighbour as yourself because you love the God in whose image they are made. Our economic systems must do the same.

I'm a big fan of wildlife documentaries, especially by the BBC, and particularly when they are narrated by David Attenborough. I really loved his *Life of Birds* documentary series and have been a twitcher (birdwatcher) for a number of years. One of the birds I struggle with, and

---

2 Raworth, *Doughnut Economics*, 22.
3 Raworth, *Doughnut Economics*, 97.

it reminds me of the largely amoral nature of the non-human creation, is the cuckoo. It is a parasitic bird that removes one egg from the nest of another species, replacing it with one of its own. The cuckoo's oversized chick then ejects the rest of its adopted siblings from the nest and monopolises the attention of its adopted parents, making them work overtime to feed it. Raworth describes GDP and the obsession with growth as the cuckoo in our economic systems. Growth is promoted for its own sake, without any regard to the cost for the poor, or the finite nature of the earth system in which it occurs. Donella Meadows, who was an author on the 1972 *Limits to Growth* report, describes the growth obsession as 'one of the stupidest purposes ever invented for any culture.'[4] What kind of assumptions about human beings and the world is encapsulated by an exponentially growing curve? How can such a thing be made green, sustainable, or smart? In the 1860s, social thinker, John Ruskin, declared that

> There is no wealth but life ... That country is the richest which nourishes the greatest number of noble and happy human beings.[5]

That word again, nourishing. Noble and happy. Images of true humanity. This is the goal of a regenerative and distributive economy (ideas we'll examine theologically later) captured by the Sustainable Development Goals.

The obsession with GDP and human beings as rational, wealth gathering beings, turns us into automata. Raworth cites research on university students studying economics. After three years of study, Israeli students rated altruism much less important than they had before they started. Likewise, US students who studied economic game theory became more selfish. If you assume the worst of humans, you become so.[6] Some Christians will cite the doctrine of 'total depravity,' saying 'of course people are selfish'. But the image of God insists that people are not always thoroughgoing evil creatures, just as experience demonstrates. Even Adam Smith, the father of modern economics, knew

---

4 Raworth, *Doughnut Economics*, 40.
5 Raworth, *Doughnut Economics*, 42.
6 Raworth, *Doughnut Economics*, 100.

this.[7] This is a case of *you are what you worship* and the market isn't a pleasant god. It's also true we're not very rational. We are prone to following the crowd and possessing various cognitive biases that affect our decision-making.[8] So, economics should nurture human nature and endeavour to play on the best, not the worst of it. We might say, don't play on the fallenness of human nature (though have protections in place to account for and limit it) but instead appeal to the image of God.

One of the interesting things about Raworth's book is the focus on systems.[9] For too long, economics ran on very simple assumptions about linear systems. But the real world is not like that. Real systems exhibit chaos, they are dynamic. This is how the climate works, how nature works. Understanding that both human and natural systems are complex is the first step in understanding that they are interrelated. In other words, to live within the doughnut is to understand that it's about the *oikos*, *eco*nomics and *eco*logy, or more broadly, earth systems science. Raworth notes that simple-minded ideas of equilibrium in economic systems need to be expanded to think about feedbacks, dynamic systems, and the possibilities of instability and crashes, like that of the Global Financial Crisis of 2008 (considered the worst financial crisis since the Great Depression of the 1930s). She considers that four planetary boundaries broken, many still in extreme poverty, and one per cent owning fifty per cent of the world's financial wealth, is a system headed towards collapse. It is hard to argue with that, although I'm sure the Steven Pinkers of the world might try.

Redistribution

Raworth also says that the doughnut economy must be distributive. She counters the myth that inequality needs to grow in a society before it gets better. Rising inequality has been observed in many western economies without a significant closing of the gap. Meanwhile, the East Asian 'miracle' of the mid-1960s to 1990s saw rapid growth with low inequality and falling poverty rates. Capitalism in general tends to grow inequality, which in turn is self-sustaining (think lobbying by

---

7 Raworth, *Doughnut Economics*, 103–104.
8 Raworth, *Doughnut Economics*, 109f.
9 Raworth, *Doughnut Economics*, 129f.

the wealthy) and unsustainable.[10] The more uneven a society is, the more likely they are to have teen pregnancy, mental illness, drug use, lower life expectancy, and a whole raft of other issues. Concentration of wealth in the hands of the few also occurred leading up to both the 2008 crash and the great depression of 1929.

Redistribution takes many forms. Of course, taxing the rich, the very rich, and multinationals, is an obvious thing to do. Recent promised tax cuts in Australia favour the rich.[11] Meanwhile trickle-down economics is a joke as tax cuts in the US have not delivered anything other than dividends for shareholders.[12] But what else might work?

One way is to redistribute land ownership. Landsea is an organisation that works to secure land rights for millions of the world's poor, mostly rural. As their website observes,

Three-quarters of the world's poorest people live in rural areas where land is a key asset. Of those people, more than a billion lack legal rights over the land they use to survive, causing entrenched poverty cycles to persist over generations.[13]

This should ring bells for a familiar biblical concept we will examine shortly. Landsea works with governments and other organisations with low-cost land purchase schemes. Take, for example, the story of Babil Roy. Her father died before she was born, her mother when she was two and a half. Now fourteen, she tends a small garden in the home of her uncle who supports her. Landsea trains young girls like Babil in kitchen gardening, and helps them to better understand their rights to land and access government programs and resources. Babil has also accessed funds from the government to help keep her in school and support her

---

10 Raworth, *Doughnut Economics*, 169.
11 Gareth Hutchens and Katharine Murphy, "Australia's high earners will benefit most from tax reforms, says thinktank," *The Guardian*, 10 May, 2018, accessed 28 May, 2018, https://www.theguardian.com/australia-news/2018/may/10/australias-high-earners-will-benefit-most-from-tax-reforms-says-thinktank.
12 Stephen Grenville, "Why Trump-style company tax cuts won't achieve the same results in Australia," *ABC News,* 8 May 2018, accessed 28 May, 2018, http://www.abc.net.au/news/2018-05-08/donald-trump-corporate-tax-cuts-australia-malcolm-turnbull/9733854.
13 Landsea Rural Development Institute, accessed 28 May, 2018, https://www.landesa.org/who-we-are/.

garden. Her harvest will feed her family, with some given to neighbours and even sold to market if there is a surplus.

Another method of redistribution people are turning to is monetary redesign. Grassroots Economics is

> a non-profit foundation that seeks to empower marginalized communities to take charge of their own livelihoods and economic future. We focus on community development through economic empowerment and community currency programs.[14]

These programs involve the introduction of vouchers to be used within communities. It was first introduced in a slum in Mombasa, Kenya, in 2013. The Bangla Pesa is used among a community of over two hundred traders, mostly women, and provides currency stability and liquidity. People who buy into the scheme must be endorsed by four others before they can start using the vouchers. The currency is used alongside the Kenyan shilling, which pays for things like electricity.[15] A local official believes the scheme is unnecessary and backwards, saying that 'It is just barter trade and it should be discouraged. We are in the 21st century. How can people still engage in what was done centuries ago? It is inappropriate.'[16] Yet locals praise it. As barber, John Wacharia, stated during a three day power outage, it was the Bangla Pesa that 'allowed me to provide for my family, eat, and survive when I could no longer work.'

The above schemes demonstrate how little it can take to make the most of social capital, the energy, enthusiasm, hard work, and innovation of those who would otherwise be written off as helpless and hopeless. This doesn't get the rich West out of its promise to contribute, such as the promised but not delivered 0.7 per cent of income to overseas development assistance. Such funds, Raworth suggests, could be given directly to the global poor as a universal basic income supplied by mobile phone. One such scheme is already under way in Kenya by the

---

14 Grassroots Economics, "About Us," accessed 28 May, 2018, https://www.grassrootseconomics.org/about.

15 Raworth, *Doughnut Economics*, 186.

16 Winnie Atieno, "Mombasa County commissioner opposes use of community currency," *Daily Nation*, 11 May, 2017, accessed 28 May, 2018, https://www.nation.co.ke/news/Mombasa-county-discredits-use-of-Bangla-Pesa/1056-3923174-445i0bz/index.html.

US based organisation GiveDirectly.[17] This is in addition to free-at-the-point-of-use services such as education and health care.

The redistribution of wealth can also be achieved by redistributing knowledge. What if the internet was available to provide open-source design and a global knowledge commons? In 2002, William Kamkwamba was the fourteen year old son of Malawian farmers. He had to drop out of school because his family could no longer afford the fees. But this, along with his naysayers, could not stop him from borrowing a book on energy from the local library and making a sixteen-foot windmill out of scrap items, with which he was able to power four light bulbs and two radios at home.[18] William tells his own story in a Ted talk about the impact of drought, school fees on the poor, and the value of books and education. He simply wants to encourage others to believe and not give up.[19]

From Caterpillar to Butterfly

Another myth that Raworth skewers is that just as inequality must rise before it can fall, so environmental impacts must do the same. We can and must 'create to regenerate'.[20] Ecological degradation is not something that can wait until a country becomes rich enough to be able to afford to give it proper attention; the global aggregate is the breaking of planetary boundaries and the coming climate apocalypse. Such thinking merely pushes the burden onto future generations. Even when a country's apparent footprint goes down, that merely hides the fact that manufacturing has been pushed overseas, and manufactured goods are shipped back, adding to the climate footprint. For Raworth, the solution is to move from a caterpillar to a butterfly.

The caterpillar is the linear economy, which features in the Story of Stuff video.[21] In Raworth's scheme, it is depicted by a horizontal line of

---

17 GiveDirectly, accessed 28 May, 2018, https://www.givedirectly.org/.
18 Raworth, *Doughnut Economics*, 202.
19 William Kwakamba, "How I Harness the Wind." Filmed July 2009 in Oxford, England. TED video, 5:48. https://www.ted.com/talks/william_kamkwamba_how_i_harnessed_the_wind.
20 Raworth, *Doughnut Economics*, 206.
21 The story of Stuff Project, accessed 29 May, 2018, https://storyofstuff.org/.

take → make → use → lose. From the environment we take energy that produces greenhouse gases, and resources, often in an unsustainable manner. We make products, sometimes with lax environmental regulations surrounding the products, and often with poor labour conditions. Some of you might remember this being highlighted by Naomi Klein in her book *No Logo*.[22] We then use things, and often only for a short time, dictated by trends, fashion, advertising, attractive renewal contracts (when did you last upgrade a perfectly serviceable mobile phone?) and built-in obsolescence. We might recycle a small amount of this material, but with the recent Chinese ban on imported recycling materials, we can see this system is broken and in need of urgent repair.[23]

We can, and we should, tax resources fairly. For example, a carbon price or tax is needed to help reduce carbon pollution. Or we should price water fairly to allow people ready access to basic human needs and we should charge more for any excess (and not give it away for next to nothing to mining companies or water bottlers). But Raworth recognises that this is not enough. The caterpillar needs to become a butterfly. This relies upon the idea that business should not be allowed to do nothing, or simply do what pays, like greenwashing to entice the ecologically minded middle class. Instead, business should be generous, that is, regenerative, by design. This means giving back to the living system of which we are a part by mimicking its circular nature. This cycling forms the wings of the butterfly.[24]

Think about the way nature works: nutrients are consumed (food), made into body parts, which in turn can be consumed. Organic material (dead bodies, poo, dead leaves, etc.) are recycled at various stages. Think about gardening where you might use blood and bone, or compost from the kitchen. In a circular economy, recycling is a last resort and simply discarding material into landfill is avoided. Instead: repair, reuse, refurbish. Coffee beans can be used to grow mushrooms, which in turn feed animals, whose manure can fertilise the ground.

---

[22] Naomi Klein, *No Logo: 10th Anniversary Edition* (Glasgow: 4th Estate, 2010).

[23] Ivana Kottasová, "China trash ban is a global recycling wake up call," *CNN Money*, 20 April, 2018, accessed 29 May, 2018, http://money.cnn.com/2018/04/20/news/china-trash-recycling-environment/index.html.

[24] Raworth, *Doughnut Economics*, 220.

Phones can be refurbished with new screens. In 2010, an estimated eighty-five per cent of used mobile phones in the EU were not being reused or recycled. As big business seems loath to do it, Raworth thinks that best hope for the circular economy is open-source, where anyone is able to reuse a product's materials.[25] In Togo, e-waste, much of which is shipped illegally from the EU, China, and US, has been used to develop a 3-D printer. Founded back in 2012 by Togolese architect, Sénamé Agboginou, WoeLab promotes urban renewal by sourcing locally and creating sustainable technology.[26] The company began as a crowdsourced venture for about $4000. It is now developing a 'multifunction agricultural robot' and putting 3D printers into schools. Such 3D printing technology can be used to repair medical equipment that would otherwise not be usable for two months while waiting for replacement parts from overseas.

Raworth's last big idea in her challenge to traditional economics is to be sceptical about growth. Returning to where she started, Raworth points out that the strong economic growth of the past two hundred years has been due to a cheap source of energy, fossil fuels, with a single gallon of oil containing the same amount of energy as forty-seven days of hard human labour.[27] That makes the idea of peak oil rather frightening. You can see why, in our oil addicted state as traditional supplies begin to decline, countries like Canada are turning to their tar sands. Quite apart from the continued greenhouse gas emissions that result when the oil is burned, there are other environmental concerns. The process of mining tar sands produces a toxic sludge of waste products that is left in unlined ponds currently covering two hundred and twenty square kilometres, an area of land equivalent to seventy-three New York Central Parks, 4.2 million Wembley football pitches, or nearly twelve and a half thousand MCGs. Mining this stuff

produces over 3,600 tonnes of CO_2 emissions per hectare, consumes freshwater at a rate that rivals the daily water use of several major

25 Raworth, *Doughnut Economics*, 230.
26 Tyler Koslow, "West African WoeLab is Creating 3D Printers and Robots From E-Waste," 3Dprint.com, 2 May, 2016, accessed 29 May, 2018, https://3dprint.com/132350/woelab-ewaste-printer/.
27 Raworth, *Doughnut Economics*, 263.

Canadian cities combined, and has destroyed a New York City-sized chunk of boreal forest and muskeg habitat.[28]

Growth is costly, it seems, more costly than we have realised. So, what does Raworth see as the mechanisms for getting off growth?[29] Ideas include fixed rather than profit-based returns on investments, and money that loses value if it doesn't keep moving. Talk about tax justice instead of tax relief and talk about investment rather than spending. Close loopholes for the world's richest people and corporations and tax accumulated wealth rather than income streams. Seek greater employment by having a shorter working week. And most importantly, give people something to aspire to other than economic growth, like emotional, rather than material, abundance. Here, surely, is where the gospel comes into its own.

The Restorative Economy
– completing our unfinished millennium jubilee

Jo Knight, National Advocacy Coordinator, TEAR Australia.

The Restorative Economy is an exciting think piece written by Christian development agency Tearfund and arrives at similar conclusions to Raworth and Klein, but from the biblical concept of jubilee, which promotes a rhythm of productivity, rest, and community, to counter debt and exploitation. This was the Old Testament command to cancel Israel's debts every fifty years, free any slaves, and return land to its original owners. It was designed to reset the nation's assets, ensuring that inequalities were not passed onto future generations. It's a powerful idea that was used to underpin the Jubilee 2000 debt relief campaign, in which Tearfund played a leading role. "We think that the triple challenges of poverty, environmental sustainability and inequality are the defining issues of our time" says the introduction of *The Restorative Economy*. "Our response to them should guide how

---

28 Tzeporah Berman, "Canada's most shameful environmental secret must not remain hidden," *The Guardian*, 14 November, 2017, accessed 29 May, 2018, https://www.theguardian.com/commentisfree/2017/nov/14/canadas-shameful-environmental-secret-tar-sands-tailings-ponds.

29 Raworth, *Doughnut Economics*, 272f.

we live, how we vote, what we buy and how we pray." Paul Cook, Tearfund's Advocacy Director, said:

We've come a long way. Globally, levels of poverty have halved in the last twenty-five years alone. Life expectancy, health and education indicators are better than ever before, and technology has helped save millions of lives and improve productivity, especially for smallholder farmers in poor countries. But if we don't fundamentally change the ways we produce wealth and create prosperity, we will undo all this progress and push millions of people back into poverty.[30]

The report argues that high levels of consumption and carbon emissions have stretched the earth's systems to breaking point, and that the impact – already being felt among some of the world's poorest communities – is most likely to affect people who are currently children, as well as generations to come.

Renew Our World (www.renewourworld.net) is a campaign for the global church that has grown out of *The Restorative Economy*, addressing the overall problem that the predominant economic development model contains a paradox: the more we succeed in economic development, the more we fail on environmental sustainability, with the poorest people impacted first and most. *Renew Our World* is aimed at all of us, not a list of demands for governments. Christians join together in collective responsibility to live within environmental limits, respond to poverty with generosity, and use whatever power we have to press for change. In just over a year since the launch, *Renew Our World* has grown to ten national campaigns in Australia, Brazil, India, Ireland, Netherlands, Nigeria, Peru, UK, USA and Zambia, and the campaign has been taken up by three global networks with immense reach.

Renew Our World, underpinned by *The Restorative Economy*, proposes we can rework our economic systems based on Biblical principles, principles that are just and sustainable. In simple terms, we can make sure all people can make a living and have what they need without wrecking the planet.

Three defining characteristics of this economy:

---

30 Alex Evans, and Richar Gower, *The Restorative Economy: Completing our Unfinished Millennium Jubilee*, (Teddington: TEARFund, 2015).

1. Poverty: Ensure the basic needs of all are met
2. Environment: Keep us within environmental limits
3. Inequality: Keeps inequality within reasonable limits

The *Renew Our World* campaigners know that talking about economics can sometimes seem dry and academic and remind us that, ultimately, we are talking about people. We are talking about ways to reflect God's wisdom, justice and compassion as we go about meeting our material needs, about ways to end suffering and unleash creativity, and about a renewed world in which all people have the chance to thrive.

To get there, the campaign proposes fundamental changes in the three systems that influence behaviour:

Economic system: which determines what we can buy, earn and produce

Legal system: what the law allows in terms of behaviour of people and companies

Socio-cultural system: what society expects, which influences how we live our lives.

Sabbath Economics – Biblical Redistribution

Ched Myers develops a vision for economics based upon the Hebrew Bible idea of Sabbath. He summarises his view in three axioms. Firstly, the world created by God provides enough in abundance for everyone, but this requires that we live within limits. Secondly, disparities in wealth and power are not natural, but are the result of human sinfulness. As a result, this disparity can be mitigated through the practice of redistribution. Thirdly, we have a prophetic mission to call people to this redistribution. He sees this as modelled by the community of faith.[31] This is the 'good news' to the poor and this echoes Jesus' 'Nazareth manifesto' in Luke 4, a definite reference to the jubilee year. Some readers will remember Jubilee 2000, the campaign to cancel third world debt. As Tearfund's *The Restorative Economy* reports, the Jubilee 2000 campaign

---

31 Ched Myers, *The Biblical Vision of Sabbath Economics* (Washington: The Church of the Saviour, 2001), 5.

Achieved extraordinary things, with low-income countries' debt falling from nearly 75 per-cent of their national income in 2000 to just over 25 per cent today. And it showed how the biblical idea of jubilee had the power to bring together Christians, people of different faiths and people of none.[32]

While this captured the imagination of some sections of the church, Myers thinks (quoting Wayne Meeks) that the church has 'long been captive to the market-driven orthodoxies of modern capitalism.'[33] We might describe this as the new Babylonian Captivity of the church. Indeed, William Stringfellow sees in the book of Revelation, a comparison between Babylon and Jerusalem. He observes that

What Babylon means theologically and, hence, existentially for all nations or other principalities in the dimensions of fallenness, doom, and death, Jerusalem means to each nation or power in the terms of holiness, redemption, and life.[34]

Further, he argues that 'The awful ambiguity of Babylon's fallenness is expressed consummately in Babylon's delusion that she is, or is becoming, Jerusalem', and the church is called to come out of Babylon (Rev 18:4–5).[35] The problem for Stringfellow is that the American church 'have been from their origins American cultural productions or Babylonian shrines.'[36] No doubt this includes the market-driven assumptions that Meeks comments on. This can apply to any Western church, and as the so-called prosperity gospel spreads, this Babylonian Captivity threatens to envelop the majority world church as well.

Myers notes that the way economics seems to work is 'trickle up', rather than 'trickle down', noting that CEO's wages have increased in the US while worker's earnings have gone backwards. Politics appears to work to enshrine this inequality and indeed further it, whether the flow upward is domestic or international.

---

32 Tearfund, *The Restorative Economy*.
33 Myers, *Sabbath Economics*, 6.
34 William Stringfellow, *An Ethic for Christians and Other Aliens in a Strange Land* (Waco, TX: Word, Incorporated, 1973), 50.
35 Stringfellow, *An Ethic for Christians*, 55.
36 Stringfellow, *An Ethic for Christians*, 59.

Sabbath is rooted in the first creation narrative. On the seventh day, God ceases from creative activities (*sabat;* Gen 2:2). This Sabbath is associated with divine rest (Ex 20:11 where *sabat* is paired with *nuha*, rest). This divine rest is picked up in the pilgrim Psalm 132, where divine rest is associated with divine rule (vv. 7–8, 14).[37] So, rest for God means ruling the world and providing for our needs. Since we are created to reflect the image of God to the rest of creation, we too are enjoined to rest from our labours. Indeed, the creation story has a double theme for Myers: 'abundance as the divine gift, and self-limitation as the appropriate response'.[38]

Such abundant provision is the lesson taught about the manna in the wilderness (Ex 16). Life is not like it was in Egypt, where the people were subject to conditions under the oppressive Egyptian economy. Myers sees this story as a divine testing to see if Israel was capable of following instructions. He goes so far as to see it as a parable about hunter-gathering, local horticulture, and an egalitarian way of life. There are three instructions in this account. Firstly, every family is to gather just enough for their needs (Ex 16:16–18). Everyone had enough; there was no surplus or shortage. Secondly, the bread was not to be stored up (Ex 16:19–20). The deep irony of the Israelite's labour in Egypt was that they were building store-cities (Ex 1:11). Myers sees instead a concentration of wealth and a circulation of wealth.[39] The third instruction is a Sabbath instruction before the giving of the Sabbath at Sinai. There was to be no gathering on the seventh day (Ex 16:26).

In these instructions, Myers recognises that there is agricultural good sense in letting the land lie fallow. Before the green revolution, it made sense to allow the land to recover. This is a principle that continues today, when we see the effects of agriculture on soil loss and degradation. A 2017 UN study showed that a 'third of the planet's land is severely degraded and fertile soil is being lost at the rate of 24bn tonnes a year'.[40] But more than this, Myers recognises that the concept

---

37 John Walton, *The Lost World of Genesis One: Ancient Cosmology and the Origins Debate* (Downers Grove, IL: IVP, 2009), 71–74.

38 Myers, *Sabbath Economics*, 11.

39 Myers, *Sabbath Economics*, 12.

40 Jonathan Watts, "Third of Earth's soil is acutely degraded due to agriculture," *The*

of Sabbath 'functions to disrupt human attempts to "control" nature and "maximise" the forces of production.'[41] This drive to control goes back to Francis Bacon's understanding of the role of knowledge as power over nature. Michael Northcott argues that a Baconian reading of Genesis 1 has dominated the churches for centuries and has allowed us to manipulate the earth as inert, dead matter.[42] It follows then that there are two correctives. The first is to abandon any concept of control over nature to that of the provision of a good God through creation. This is not to suggest that we 'do nothing', after all, there are commands to gather, grow crops, and so on. This isn't a command to a return to a hunter-gatherer society. Secondly, we need to stop thinking of the non-human world in purely economic terms.

The Sabbath day is extended to a Sabbath year in Exodus 23. The land rests and lies fallow so the poor, and then the wild animals, may eat. We are to make space for the needs of the non-human world. Psalm 104 makes a similar observation for modern irrigating societies when it points out that water is a shared resource for all. In the Sabbath year of Exodus 23, the economically marginalised – the poor and wild animals – are to be provided for. This is a challenge to modern agricultural views where mechanisation is meant to ensure that fields are picked clean and wildlife is forced from the rural to urban areas.[43] We might learn a lesson here from thirteen year old Richard Turere of a Masai community, who invented a simple, solar powered way of deterring lions from taking their livestock.[44]

Guardian, 13 September, 2017, accessed 30 May, 2018, https://www.theguardian.com/environment/2017/sep/12/third-of-earths-soil-acutely-degraded-due-to-agriculture-study.

[41] Myers, *Sabbath Economics*, 13.

[42] Michael S. Northcott, *A Political Theology of Climate Change* (Grand Rapids, MI: Wm. B. Eerdmans Publishing Co, 2013): 102.

[43] For example, foxes in the UK. See Charlie Brinkhurst-Cuff, "Foxes surge into England's towns and cities," *The Guardian*, 17 April, 2017, accessed 30 May, 2018, https://www.theguardian.com/environment/2017/apr/16/urban-foxes-number-one-for-every-300-residents-study-suggests. On wildlife in general see Adam Vaughan, "Urban wildlife: when animals go wild in the city," *The Guardian*, 8 March, 2015, accessed 30 May, 2018,

[44] Richard Turere, "My Invention that Made Peace with Lions." Filmed February 2013. TED Video, 7:20. Posted February 2014, http://www.ted.com/talks/richard_turere_a_peace_treaty_with_the_lions.

One of the key principles that was of interest to the church during the Jubilee 2000 campaign is that of debt release (Deut 15:1–18). This debt release mechanism is an antidote to the tendency of economic systems to concentrate wealth and power into the hands of the few. In India, farming has become more and more difficult. A 2014 study found that of 5,000 farm households across 18 states found that '76 per cent of farmers would prefer to do some work other than farming.' A high percentage of farmers reported repeated losses as a main reason, with '70 per cent of respondents said their crops were destroyed because of unseasonal rains, drought, floods and pest attack.'[45] Debt in the agricultural sector is leading to a wave of suicides. We will return to this in the next chapter.

Wealthy creditors benefit from such a system, leading to Isaiah's denunciation of those who add 'house to house and field to field,' (Is 5:7–8). The idea is that there was not meant to be any poor among the Israelites in the land (Deut 15:4). I've written elsewhere on the continuing relevance of Hebrew Bible justice for the church today, so I won't repeat the arguments here.[46] The point is that there is no reasonable excuse for there being poor among us today either, when there is enough to go around.

This debt release is expressed most fully in the jubilee year, or the 'Sabbath's Sabbath' in Leviticus 25. Socio-economic inequality is dismantled by releasing people from debt (vv. 35–42), returning land to its owners (vv. 13, 25–28), and freeing slaves (vv. 47–55). Everything is reset. People are freed to flourish and provided with the means to flourish. But were people to wait for 50 years? Myers thinks not, seeing strong parallels in the description of the 'Feast of weeks' which was later to become known as Pentecost, and the jubilee, suggesting that Sabbath economics was to be applied at every harvest. Meanwhile, we might insist that it occurs at every government budget!

---

45 Jyotika Sood, "India's deepening farm crisis: 76% farmers want to give up farming, shows study," *The Nature Conservancy*, 11 March, 2014, accessed 30 May, 2018, http://www.downtoearth.org.in/news/indias-deepening-farm-crisis-76-farmers-want-to-give-up-farming-shows-study-43728.

46 See chapter 1 of Mick Pope, *A Climate of Justice: Loving Your Neighbour in a Warming World* (Reservoir: Morningstar Publishing, 2017).

The Hebrew Bible contains a strong prophetic critique against the negation of Sabbath economics. We've already noted the denunciation of Isaiah 5. An infamous story is that of Naboth and King Ahab (1 Ki 21). Naboth's ancestral rights were to trump Ahab's acquisitive desires.[47] It is not above the powerful to murder to get what they want, something we see happening in land grabs in Brazil, for example, as indigenous people are forced to make way for loggers, agriculture, grazing, and dams. The Belo Monte dam was first proposed in 1975 and has since been vigorously opposed by native tribes. The dam will open in 2019 after concessions have been made to reduce the amount of land that will be flooded. The dam company has paid to relocate some members of the various indigenous tribes to housing developments in a nearby city. However, there is little in the way of employment and community, with escalating crime and alcoholism as a result.[48] While dam companies negotiate, others resort to violence. In the Amazonian state of Pará, three people have been assassinated in four weeks, including anti-palm oil campaigner, Nazildo dos Santos Brito. Brito was a leader of a Quilombo Afro-Brazilian community. Quilombola land rights are guaranteed under the Brazilian constitution, but politicians who are closely associated with the agribusiness lobby are challenging land ownership in the courts. [49] The judgement that Elijah brings down upon Ahab is bloody and violent: the collapse of his house. Perhaps in this we hear echoes of what is in Revelation, when the fall of Babylon the Great is the way in which the world is saved (Rev 18). This does not bode well for politicians who collude with unethical corporations.

Economic considerations continue into the New Testament, from the preaching of good news to the poor in the 'Nazareth Manifesto' of Luke 4, to the call to forgive debt in the Lord's Prayer (Mt 6:11f). In the encounter between Jesus and the tax collector, Zacchaeus, we see

---

47 Myers, *Sabbath Economics*, 21.

48 Daniel Stone, "Amazon Tribes Stand Up for Their Survival," *National Geographic*, 23 June, 2017, accessed 30 May, 2018, https://www.nationalgeographic.com/photography/proof/2017/06/amazon-river-dams-displacement-indigenous-elkaim/.

49 Jonathan Watts, "Murdered land activist adds to rising death toll in Brazil's Amazon," *The Guardian*, 18 April, 2018, accessed 30 May, 2018, https://www.theguardian.com/environment/2018/apr/17/murdered-indigenous-land-activist-adds-to-rising-death-toll-in-brazils-amazon.

Luke 4 played out. Zacchaeus understood that he played a key role in the economic oppression of his fellow Israelites. Being a chief tax collector, he made a profit on the taxes that his underlings made. He was in the very centre of the system of Roman economic oppression.[50] We are not told if he abandoned his job, but we know he did make reparations above and beyond what the law required (Lev 6:2–5). All of this was a manifestation of what kingdom or Sabbath economics should look like, for Jesus could then conclude that 'Today, salvation has come to this house, because he, too, is a son of Abraham' (Lk 19:9).

Such Sabbath economics continues into the writings of Paul. Myers believes that Paul understood the 'Christ-event' as a 'cosmic jubilee.'[51] Corinth back in Paul's day was much like many of the rich and cosmopolitan cities of today. The church in Corinth was as much captured by the culture of 'meritocracy, materialism, and elitism' as the church of our day is captured by the Babylon of materialism. Paul attacks this system in a variety of ways. By refusing payment and resisting the patronage system, he challenged the social hierarchy by working with his hands, what Myers calls 'downward mobility.' He challenged the way in which social hierarchy skewed the Lord's Supper. He also demanded that the Corinthian church give to the poor, although appealing to their love (2 Cor 8:8). Myers notes that the basis for all of this is Christ. That God has reconciled the world to God through Christ hides an economic metaphor. The word 'reconciliation' in the Greek is *katallagē,* which originally referred to a payment of debt. In this, Myers sees a straight line between the ministry of reconciliation and economics. It is profoundly anti-imperial, with all of its economic oppression. Ambassadors of Caesar delivered ultimatums to submit to imperial rule. Ambassadors of Christ bring reconciliation at all levels.[52]

Coming out of Babylon

Like Myers and Stringfellow, Ben Witherington calls out the church as being deaf to the 'dominant materialistic paradigm that drives our

---

50 See Pope, *A Climate of Justice,* chapter 6.
51 Myers, *Sabbath Economics,* 52.
52 Myers, *Sabbath Economics,* 56.

culture.'[53] We in the West are wealthy by global standards, even if there is, at times, a profound inequality within western countries. Witherington accuses prosperity teachers of wanting to 'baptize the materialistic orientation of our culture and call it godly and good, call it a blessing from God.' Such materialism is an idol (Mammon), a mechanism for inequality generation and for environmental destruction. In reflecting on Revelation, Witherington notes that there has often been a dualism in our thinking: church and state, faith and business, inner attitudes and outward behaviour.[54] John of Patmos addresses such dualism in chapters 2–3, and 17.

It is said that you are what you eat but theologically you are what you worship. To be part of the Roman Empire meant participation in the Caesar cult. To reject worship of Caesar for worship of the Lamb of God meant social and economic exclusion, if not active persecution. The church in Smyrna was in poverty (Rev 2:9) and Witherington suggests this was due to exclusion from trade guilds. Smyrna was the second city to embrace the imperial cult demanded by Domitian. Witherington reminds us that the poor are under no delusions of the false sense of security that wealth can bring.[55] However, this message of Revelation should also speak to those of us who are rich in our need to rebalance the books, as it were, and stop ourselves from our Caesar worship.

This is picked up in the letter to Laodicea (Rev 3:14–22). We are graphically told that Christ spits them out of his mouth for being neither soothingly hot nor refreshingly cold. Like the cup of coffee left too long, their obsession with wealth and riches hides their spiritual poverty (v. 17). Laodicea was a wealthy town with a medical school, numerous banks, enormous theatres and stadiums. Its wealth came from nearby hot springs.[56] Thankfully, while our wealth can make us spiritually poor, we can yet still buy the things that really matter from Christ: gold refined by fire (by persecution) and white garments, which come through great tribulation (Rev 7:13–14). John is calling the rich church not to be a

---

53 Ben Witherington III, *Jesus and Money: A Guide for Times of Financial Crisis* (Grand Rapids, MI: Brazos Press, 2010), 11.

54 Witherington, *Jesus and Money*, 131.

55 Witherington, *Jesus and Money*, 133.

56 Witherington, *Jesus and Money*, 134.

part of Babylon and prosper financially, but to come out of Babylon and prosper spiritually. For us, it means challenging an economic system that destroys both people and the world around us.

There is no one model for what this coming out of Babylon might look like. The Amish in the US live an agrarian lifestyle without many of the modern comforts of society. Their rejection of much of the world is theologically motivated. However, their agrarian life succeeds, according to financial executive, Dan McLaughlin, due to their embeddedness in a larger society. Simplicity has much to commend it but agrarianism is not necessarily a universal principle.[57] The Franciscans are a fraternity founded by St Francis of Assisi, who practiced obedience, poverty, and chastity. While not everyone wants to entirely forswear the world, monasticism as a principle based on community and economics like a shared purse, is not unusual. The Cornerstone community is a new monastic network that has been in Australia since 1978. The community in Bendigo involves Christians employed in the traditional economy but with a shared purse, community garden, and a life of service.[58]

Back then to Revelation. The contrast then between kingdom and imperial or worldly economics is cast by John as a tale of two women, a radiant bride (Rev 19) and a harlot or prostitute (Rev 17–18). This imagery is potentially problematic, with women being presented in a polarised sense, that is, either passion or purity. There's also the question of glorifying violence in general and against women in particular. The context of the #MeToo movement should make us more sensitive to these things, but we still also need to keep the original context in mind.

The Great Prostitute (Rev 17:1), who is the Mother of all Prostitutes (v. 5), is drunk on the blood of the saints (v. 6). Regardless of which Caesar to sit this under, Rome was no friend of people who maintain that there is only one Lord and God, and who refuse to participate in the Imperial Cult. Empires demand total allegiance. We should be no stranger to this, as aberrant behaviour such as nonviolence, protests

---

57 Dan McLaughlin, "Economic Lessons from the Amish," *Mises Institute*, 21 June, 2007, accessed 26 June, 2018, https://mises.org/library/economic-lessons-amish.

58 For this and other stories about communities see Claire Dawson, and Mick Pope, *A Climate of Hope: Church and Mission in a Warming World* (Dandenong: Urban Neighbours of Hope Publishing, 2014), section 4.

against war, the excesses of capitalism, or the embedded racism in Australia Day or Columbus Day, can quickly get you labelled as 'un-American' or 'un-Australian'. The language of prostitution might be substituted today for terms like sex worker, in order to be more sensitive and pastoral, rather than judgmental and dismissive. But in Revelation 17 we have to deal with the biblical context. Prostitution is used in the Hebrew Bible to depict immorality and idolatry.[59] Israel went from being faithful (to God) to a prostitute (Is 1:21), noting that the result of this is bribery and denying justice to the orphan and the widow.

Returning to our economic concerns, Revelation 17:1–2 starts with a harlot sitting on many waters, a reference to and critique of Roman trade and merchants. Goods were extracted from the four corners of the empire via excessive taxation, slavery, and so on. As Professor of ancient history, Keith Hopkins, has observed, Rome lived in luxury while the rest of the empire lived in relative or actual poverty. He says (and I used this quote in *A Climate of Justice*, but it's just as relevant here):

> the model implies an increased monetization of the Roman economy, the commercialization of exchange, an elongation of the links between producers and consumers, the growth of specialist intermediaries (traders, shippers, bankers), and an unprecedented level of urbanization.[60]

This should remind you of globalisation. From artisans and farmers under heavy taxation, forced to sell to the empire to pay their debts, there is a straight line to the heart of empire via the merchants, who grew wealthy off of Babylon's sensuality (Rev 18:3). John judged this system as idolatrous and not of the character of the people of God. They were to come out of her and have no part in it (Rev 18:4). This is not to say that God is against commerce itself, but against the kind of desire for greed and luxury that Rome exhibited. To say nothing of the fact that its success came off the back of slavery.[61] This use of harlotry to describe Babylon's relationship to merchants also echoes the same language used of Tyre in Isaiah 23 (especially vv. 15–17). Tyre may not have had the wealth of Babylon but did have 'her wealth and her vast

---

59 Grant R. Osborne, *Revelation* (Grand Rapids, MI: Baker Academic, 2002), 608.
60 Hopkins, *Taxes and Trade*, 102.
61 Witherington, *Jesus and Money*, 137.

maritime contacts.'[62] So, there is a clear biblical theme of judgement of nations and merchants, who build wealth because of the idolatry of worshipping created things rather than God, and the injustices that inevitably arise when one amasses wealth at the expense of others.

Now to return to the language of judgement on the harlot. Is it misogynistic sexual murder? Does it normalise sexual violence? Ironically, if Rome is the first empire in mind, then the Caesar and the Senate are all men. The traders would have been predominantly men (though not exclusively, see for example Acts 17). The armies that opened up new territories were all men. In being judged, while the imagery is female, the crimes are first and foremost masculine in nature. Grant Osborne also argues we over read the details if we see the stories of colonised women here, as Tina Pippin has argued. We must see the language of military siege on the one hand rather than individual cases of sexual violence. Likewise, we need to keep the context of Rome in mind specifically, and that of empire in general. Two points follow. We need to confess that violence in general is largely masculine. Mass shootings in the US are perpetrated by men who usually have a history of violence against women. Women disproportionately suffer economic injustice. Climate injustice is disproportionately gendered. Critiques of empire must always bring this out. Secondly, simply because we are presented with certain biblical metaphors, it doesn't mean our messaging needs to be limited to those alone. Empire as seducing rake? As sexual predator? Does our calling out of #MeToo need to be enlarged to encompass empire?

In *An Ethic for Christians and Other Aliens in a Strange Land*, William Stringfellow makes a huge call out of American (and by extension) Western capitalism. He observes that the destruction of Babylon as a nation is associated with the salvation of the world and a sign of divine sovereignty (Rev 19:1, 3, 6).[63] In the first instance, Babylon was Rome, but many writers apply Babylon to present situations as if Babylon stands for empire in every age. Stringfellow, Gorman and others all

---

62 John N. Oswalt, *The Book of Isaiah: Chapters 1-39* (Grand Rapids, MI: Wm. B. Eerdmans Publishing Co., 1986), 427.

63 Stringfellow, *An Ethic for Christians*, 26.

apply the blow torch to the US, one of the world's largest economies and largest polluters, to say nothing of military superpower. So, linking the harlotry of chapter 17 with the money making of the merchants with Babylon in chapter 18, with the celebration and salvation via destruction in chapter 19, we reach a rather uncomfortable conclusion. The salvation of the world is God's ongoing plan to make all things new, which reaches its culmination when Christ returns. Salvation, in the economic and environmental sense, will mean the fall of Babylon today: the Western, capitalist empire. Grant Osborne does observe that one of Babylon's sins was to lead the nations astray.[64] When people in the majority of the world watch Western TV, what kind of lifestyle do they see portrayed and aspire to?

How Babylon falls is, thankfully, up to us, at least in part. Do we go quietly, repentantly, innovatively, following the suggestions of Kate Raworth? Do we bring in a new jubilee, as Ched Myers suggests? Do we come out of Babylon, as Ben Witherington urges us? Or will we fall with Babylon?

---

[64] Osborne, *Revelation*, 608.

Chapter 10 — Renewed Earth

Food Glorious Food

One of the favourite TV shows of my wife, Jo, is *The Great British Bakeoff*. It's quaint, quintessentially British, and lacks all of the hyper-competitiveness and manufactured tension of shows like *MasterChef*. I'm kind of over reality TV as I think it's a dumbing down of an already largely facile medium. A steady diet of reality TV shows is a bit like a steady diet of insert-your-favourite-fast-food-chain-here. But what's with cooking shows anyway? A study conducted in the US found that watching cooking shows was associated with becoming more overweight. It appears as if such shows can normalise cooking with unhealthy ingredients, like lots of butter and other fats.[1] In the UK, cooking shows like those of Jamie Oliver and *The Great British Bakeoff* are at least encouraging people to spend more time in the kitchen.[2] But it has also been suggested, albeit anecdotally, that it's becoming more stressful to host dinner guests due to concerns that our cooking won't be up to TV standard.[3]

Food and diet are important issues. A 2017 report found that about one in five Australian children aged two to four were overweight or obese, and about one in four children aged five to seventeen were overweight or obese.[4] At the same time, a third of Australians aged sixty-five years

---

[1] Roberto A. Ferdman, "The problem with watching too many cooking shows," *The Washington Post*, 18 March, 2015, accessed 11 June, 2018, https://www.washingtonpost.com/news/wonk/wp/2015/03/18/the-unfortunate-side-effect-of-watching-too-many-cooking-shows/?utm_term=.f9c62e74c55f.

[2] James Ramsden, "Do TV cookery programmes really influence the way we cook?" *The Guardian*, 14 July, 2014, accessed 11 June, 2018, https://www.theguardian.com/lifeandstyle/wordofmouth/2014/jul/14/tv-cookery-programmes-influence-jamie-oliver-masterchef.

[3] Zan Romanoff, "Kitchen Anxiety: Handling Home Cooking in the 'Top Chef' Era," *The Atlantic*, 17 November, 2010, accessed 11 June, 2018, https://www.theatlantic.com/health/archive/2010/11/kitchen-anxiety-handling-home-cooking-in-the-top-chef-era/66668/.

[4] Australian Institute of Health and Welfare 2017. *A picture of overweight and obesity in Australia 2017.*

and older who are hospitalised, are overtly malnourished.[5] Malnutrition is also part of the gap between the welfare of Aboriginal Australian and Torres Strait Islander peoples and non-indigenous Australians. A 2016 report found that

Indigenous Australians continue to experience poorer levels of health than non-indigenous Australians and issues such as food insecurity, poor diet, and a disproportionate burden of chronic disease play a key contributing role for malnutrition in indigenous Australians.[6]

Globally, UNICEF notes that

Nearly half of all deaths in children under 5 are attributable to undernutrition, translating into the loss of about 3 million young lives a year. Undernutrition puts children at greater risk of dying from common infections, increases the frequency and severity of such infections, and delays recovery.[7]

Yet, to date there is enough food to go around. One of the problems is rural poverty, according to the World Economic Forum. People can't afford to buy food. Deal with poverty and you deal with malnutrition. But few things are that simple. It is expected that the Sustainable Development Goal of eliminating hunger by 2030 won't be reached without 'well-designed social protection and scaled up pro-poor investments.'[8] Another problem is food waste. In Australia, nearly $10

Cat. no.PHE 216. Canberra: AIHW.

5 Karen Charlton, and Karen Walton, "Starvation in the land of plenty: why Australians are malnourished," *The Conversation*, 4 February, 2015, accessed 11 June, 2018, https://theconversation.com/starvation-in-the-land-of-plenty-why-australians-are-malnourished-27640.

6 Natasha F. Morris, Simon Stewart, Malcolm D. Riley, and Graeme P. Maguire, "The Indigenous Australian Malnutrition Project: the burden and impact of malnutrition in Aboriginal Australian and Torres Strait Islander hospital inpatients, and validation of a malnutrition screening tool for use in hospitals—study rationale and protocol," *Springerplus*. 2016; 5(1): 1296. Published online 2016 Aug 8. doi: 10.1186/s40064-016-2943-5

7 UNICEF, "Malnutrition rates remain alarming: stunting is declining too slowly while wasting still impacts the lives of far too many young children," May 2018, accessed 11 June, 2018, https://data.unicef.org/topic/nutrition/malnutrition/.

8 Jomo Kwame Sundaram, and Hilal Elver, "The world produces enough food to feed everyone. So why do people go hungry?," *World Economic Forum*, 11 July, 2016, accessed 11 June, 2018, https://www.weforum.org/agenda/2016/07/the-world-produces-enough-food-to-feed-everyone-so-why-do-people-go-hungry.

billion in food is wasted each year due to household waste.[9] In the US, a pound per person, per day is wasted.[10] In the UK in 2015, food to the value of 13 billion pounds (i.e. the money, not the weight) was thrown out.[11] The western world throws out more at the consumer stage due to food waste, compared to the majority of the world where, in places like sub-Saharan Africa, it is mostly food loss in the production to retail stage.[12] Efforts of the UN Food and Agriculture Organization have focused on better harvesting and storage methods.[13]

While food waste is a problem, so is its production in parts of the world, due to the way in which the global food system is structured. The situation in India illustrates how western empire brings chaos to the majority world and disrupts otherwise stable socio-economic systems.[14] Farmers have been working the land of southern India for more than ten thousand years. Its soils are fertile and the monsoon has in the past brought abundant seasonal rain. In the 1960s, India joined the *Green Revolution* with increasing use of chemical fertilisers and pesticides, as well as mechanisation. These things bring their own problems as we saw in chapter 2, but what's more, neoliberal economic reforms in the 1990s deregulated Indian markets and opened them up to international trade. Free trade is a good thing, right?

---

9 Luke Cooper, "Australians Throw Away Nearly $10 Billion in Food Waste Each Year," *Huffington Post,* 25 October, 2017, accessed 13 June, 2018, https://www.huffingtonpost.com.au/2017/10/24/australians-throw-away-nearly-10-billion-in-food-waste-each-year_a_23253505/.

10 Oliver Milman, "Americans waste 150,000 tons of food each day – equal to a pound per person," *The Guardian,* 19 April, 2018, accessed 13 June, 2018, https://www.theguardian.com/environment/2018/apr/18/americans-waste-food-fruit-vegetables-study.

11 Rebecca Smithers, "UK throwing away £13bn of food each year, latest figures show," *The Guardian,* 10 January, 2017, accessed 13 June, 2018, https://www.theguardian.com/environment/2017/jan/10/uk-throwing-away-13bn-of-food-each-year-latest-figures-show.

12 Ashley Kirk, and Patrick Scott, "No time for leftovers: The astonishing scale of food waste in the UK and around the world," *The Telegraph,* 2 January, 2018, accessed 13 June, 2018, https://www.telegraph.co.uk/news/2018/01/02/no-time-leftovers-astonishing-scale-food-waste-uk-around-world/.

13 Megan Sheahan, and Christopher B.Barrett, "Review: Food loss and waste in Sub-Saharan Africa," *Food Policy,* 70 (2017): 1-12. https://doi.org/10.1016/j.foodpol.2017.03.012.

14 Janos Chiala, and Vinith Xavier, "India's sugarcane farmers: A cycle of debt and suicide," *Aljazeera,* 3 April, 2017, accessed 11 June, 2018, https://www.aljazeera.com/indepth/features/2017/01/india-sugarcane-farmers-cycle-debt-suicide-170115102045731.html.

In 2015, in the southern state of Karnataka, more than one thousand farmers have taken their own lives. About ninety of them were from the sugarcane-growing region of Mandya. Although there are many factors involved, personal debt is one of several common elements.

Shivanna was a thirty-five year old sugar cane farmer from the village of Sadolalu. He was the sole breadwinner supporting an extended family of seven. In July of 2015, he took his own life by consuming a bottle of alcohol and some pesticide. It was discovered after his death that he had debts of six lakhs (about $9,240): debts that would have taken six good harvests for him to repay. His family faces years of poverty to pay off this debt, including the money that they had to borrow for his funeral. Unfortunately, such stories are all too common.

There are costs at every level of sugar cane agriculture. For a man with no family to help him, Shivanna spent twenty-five thousand rupees ($385) per acre on seedlings and labour hire. NPK (nitrogen, phosphorus and potassium) chemical fertilisers cost tens of thousands of rupees an acre. Mineral fertilisers are part of the Green Revolution but are now problematic. A WWF funded study found that the price of fertilisers has risen faster than that of food. Further, synthetic nitrogen fertilisers 'reduces the humus content and biodiversity in the soil, causes soil acidification and gives rise to emissions of nitrous oxide', which is a greenhouse gas.[15] Harvesting and transporting the crop to the factory also costs more money.

Add to this neoliberal reforms of the global economy. India's opening its markets up to foreign competition has meant that Indian sugar cane growers find themselves competing with large scale industrialised plantations in countries such as Brazil, which is the world's largest sugar producer. It is cheaper to import sugar rather than buy it from local farmers. When subsidies were introduced to prop up exports, the World Trade Organization, the EU, and predictably, Brazil, all complained. Free trade is rarely fair in any meaningful sense. For

---

15 Johannes Kotschi, *A Soiled Reputation: Adverse impacts of mineral fertilizers* (Berlin: Heinrich Böll Stiftung, 2015). https://www.wwf.de/fileadmin/fm-wwf/Publikationen-PDF/WWF-Study_Adverse_impacts_of_mineral_fertilizers_in_tropical_agriculture.pdf.
in tropical agriculture

farmers like Shivanna, this meant that in 2015, the processing factory dropped their price by five hundred rupees per tonne. Factories are often slow to pay farmers, and when Shivanna died, they still owed him money. The system is broken at multiple levels.

Rain, Rain, has Gone Away

For many, the old nursery rhyme has come true, that rain has gone away. In 2014, insufficient rains meant that Shivanna's crops failed. While natural variability in yield and changes in price eat into farmer's small profits, climate change is making it far worse. Droughts are occurring more often and becoming more intense, with resulting losses to the Karnataka agricultural sector over the two years 2014-2016 of more than twelve thousand crores ($1.85bn). Water security is becoming a greater issue in India and many other parts of the world.

As I write this (in the winter of 2018), drought in Australia is currently having an impact on the cattle industry in New South Wales and southern Queensland. The region has had fourteen months of below-average rainfall.[16] Cattle farmer, Margaret Fleck, notes that, as well as a lack of rain, heat is playing a role.

> We can't get over a string of really hot summers. With the sheer consistency of extreme temperatures, the rate of evaporating is so high. We don't have any surface water left on our property.

Rising temperatures are a global phenomenon linked to rising levels of greenhouse gases from the burning of fossil fuels. This doesn't stop politicians past and present from trying to ignore or downplay the connection. Former National Party leader, John Anderson, himself a farmer, warned Australian Prime Minister Malcolm Turnbull against politicising the drought by attributing it to climate change. But since when has it been political to acknowledge peer reviewed, well established science? Rather, it is blatantly political to try and ignore the science, as

---

16 Lisa Cox, "'Australia doesn't realise': worsening drought pushes farmers to the brink," *The Guardian*, 11 June, 2018, accessed 11 June, 2018, https://www.theguardian.com/environment/2018/jun/10/australia-doesnt-realise-worsening-drought-pushes-farmers-to-the-brink?utm_source=esp&utm_medium=Email&utm_campaign=GU+Today+AUS+v1+-+AUS+morning+mail+callout&utm_term=277734&subid=8281893&CMP=ema_632.

so many conservative politicians do. As a former leader of a party that is said to serve farmers, Anderson does a great disservice to them. In times of drought, it is entirely the time to get political and prophetic in our warnings as the church. It will be a lot more than seven thin cows following seven fat cows if we do nothing about climate change. While city people might be tempted to point the finger at farmers for their contributions to climate change, our diets drive what they produce. It's also our role to support those that feed us, and indeed farmers globally, by combating climate change.

Australian farmers are becoming frustrated by the lack of action. Verity Morgan-Schmidt is the CEO of Farmers for Climate Action. She says that comments like those of Nationals leader, Michael McCormack, that 'I'm a believer that the climate is always changing and it's been changing since Moses was a boy' are a 'disservice to many of our farmers who are already facing the reality of climate change.' At the front line of climate change, farmers can see the changes and their impacts. Morgan-Schmidt notes that

> My family has been on properties out in Western Australia for over 100 years. We can say this has well and truly moved beyond natural cyclical patterns. The idea that we could be accused of playing politics by accepting reality is a bitter pill to swallow. The science is clear. Climate change is increasing the severity of extreme weather events that include drought.[17]

Another example worth highlighting is the so-called Arab Spring. A 2013 report found that while the

> Arab Spring would likely have come one way or another, but the context in which it did is not inconsequential. Global warming may not have caused the Arab Spring, but it may have made it come earlier.[18]

---

17 Lisa Cox, "Farmers challenge Nationals' claim drought unrelated to climate change," *The Guardian*, 11 June, 2018, accessed 6 June, 2018, https://www.theguardian.com/environment/2018/jun/06/national-party-comments-on-drought-and-climate-a-disservice-to-farmers.

18 Quoted in Ines Perez, "Climate Change and Rising Food Prices Heightened Arab Spring," *Scientific American*, 4 March, 2013, accessed 4 June, 2018, https://www.scientificamerican.com/article/climate-change-and-rising-food-prices-heightened-arab-spring/.

Sensitivity to food supplies and prices, together with little arable land and water, provides strong factors for social upheaval. The weaker the state, the more prone to collapse it is. I have written at length on the six year long drought in the region and its connection to the Syrian crisis in *A Climate of Justice*.[19] This drought — in an already water parched country — drove 1.5 million people to migrate from rural to urban areas. Cereal crop yields dropped between about fifty and seventy per cent. The climate connection is that warming waters in the Indian Ocean have affected a weather pattern known as the North Atlantic Oscillation. This has resulted in rain-bearing systems being steered away from countries like Syria.

Other researchers focus on factors such as corn to ethanol conversion for biofuel, and associated price speculation.[20] Ethanol conversion, ironically to help combat climate change, raises food prices, and there is a strong connection between food prices and civil unrest. Drought also contributes to increasing food prices via reduced yields, so ethanol and drought push in the same direction. Likewise, price speculation helped drive up prices further, showing how broken our markets are.

These kinds of stories are now happening the world over. You can't eat food if other people can't grow it for you. Other people can't eat if they can't grow their own food. Climate change must be combatted if the world is to be able to continue to feed itself. Famine is that dirty word that we don't want to face but history has shown that it occurs all too often. In order to think theologically about food and famine, let's now turn back to the book of Revelation.

Riders on the Storm

If you do a web search on the term 'riders of the apocalypse' or 'horsemen of the apocalypse' you know you're in for an interesting time. If a reader fails to understand the mythic nature of Revelation and

---

19 Mick Pope, *A Climate of Justice: Loving Your Neighbour in a Warming World* (Reservoir: Morning Star Publishing, 2017), chapter 4.
20 Brian Merchant, "Commodity Traders Helped Spark the War in Syria, Complex Systems Theorists Say," *Motherboard*, 27 October, 2015, accessed 11 June, 2018, https://motherboard.vice.com/en_us/article/wnxe4y/commodities-traders-helped-spark-the-war-in-syria-complex-systems-theorists-say.

wants instead to map every detail onto history, the reconstructions will always reflect their particular interests, or indeed obsessions. However, we must resist the temptation of the fantasists and instead read such passages through the lens of history and literary genre. The results may not be as interesting but they will be more useful, to say nothing of more faithful to John's intent.

The vision of the four riders forms part of the first set of sevens that we find in Revelation, that of the seven seals. Back in Revelation 5 we read that the Lamb is the one worthy to open the seals because he has conquered (v. 5) and because he was slaughtered and ransomed people from every tribe for God (v. 9). The scroll contains the plan of God for salvation, which includes the revealing of his wrath. While the thought of judgement is an unpleasant one, as Joseph Mangina points out, it does involve the setting right of historical evil. Evil cannot go unpunished.[21] In Revelation 6, six of the seven scrolls are opened, before an interlude features the spirits of the martyrs in Revelation 7.

So, who are the four riders? Michael Gorman sees them as representing a chain of events that is all too well known in human history, including military conquest and the breakdown of peace; death, economic injustice, famine and the disease that follows. Not only are these events permitted to happen but are a direct judgement on sin. Gorman stressed that we must not divide human sin and divine punishment: this is a 'false dichotomy and asks for an unnecessary choice.'[22] The Tolkienesque riders are given their authority to carry out their tasks. According to Mangina, the riders represent 'both human and suprahuman agency,' in a way that reflects Walter Wink's understanding of the Powers as the spiritual aspect of fallen human institutions.[23] These powers are more than a mythological way of speaking of alienated human agency, but are powers from without that 'exercise their dominion in and through the

---

21 Joseph L. Mangina, *Revelation* (Grand Rapids, MI: Brazos Press, 2010), 96.

22 Michael Gorman, *Reading Revelation Responsibly: Uncivil Worship and Witness. Following the Lamb Into the New Creation* (Eugene, OR: Cascade Books, 2011), 141.

23 Mangina, *Revelation*, 100. Walter Wink, *Naming the Powers: The Language of Power in the New Testament* (Philadelphia: Fortress Press, 1984), 64-67.

social, political, and technological forces that humans have summoned into being.'[24]

The four riders are: military conquest (Rev 6:2), civil war or strife (v. 4), famine (vv. 5–6), and death (v. 8). The latter three follow on from the first: military conquest leads to internal strife, famine, and death. Death sums up the other three, being the end result of violent bloodshed and famine, and is both God's enemy (finally conquered in Rev 20:14) and servant, as the executor of divine judgement.[25] The third rider bears a set of scales, which demand an economic interpretation. The price for wheat and barley are about twelve times higher than normal, implying famine conditions.[26] Commentators are divided as to the significance of the oil and the wine. Some see these as a luxury, out of the reach of ordinary people.[27] Others recognise them as staple foods and therefore indicate the famine was not severe.[28] Whatever the precise meaning of this, famines are complex phenomena consisting of both natural causes and economic inequalities caused by empire.[29]

This is yet another reason why the message of all things new is important. Making all things new includes our food systems and their closely linked economic systems as we saw in chapter 9. So, let's return to Romans 8 and see what more it can say to us about food and God's plan to renew our world.

A pregnant pause

A critique of empire and its claims is present in Romans 8, even if it is not obvious at first glance.[30] Historically, the groaning of creation in

---

24 Mangina, *Revelation*, 101.

25 Mangina, *Revelation*, 99.

26 Alan F. Johnson, "Revelation," in Frank E. Gaebelian, Ed. *The Expositor's Bible Commentary Volume 12: Hebrews Through* Revelation (Grand Rapids, MI: Zondervan, 1981), 474.

27 Mangina, *Revelation*, 99. Leon Morris, *Revelation: An Introduction and Commentary* (London: The Tyndale Press, 1969), 106.

28 Johnson, *Revelation*, 474.

29 Michael Wilcox, *The Message of Revelation: I Saw Heaven Opened* (Leicester: Inter-Varsity Press, 1975), 71.

30 I discuss this in detail in Mick Pope, "With Heads Craning Forward: The Eschaton and the Nonhuman Creation in Romans 8," in *Ecotheology in the Humanities: An Interdisciplinary Approach to Understanding the Divine and Nature*, ed. Melissa J. Brotton (Lanham:

this passage has been understood to refer to animal suffering, predation and so on, such as found in John Wesley's famous sermon *The Great Deliverance*.[31] In modern scholarship, Romans 8 is sometimes chosen as a mantra for environmental theology and creation care.[32] However, most treatments are largely without regard to the broader context of the passage, which includes a critique of empire. For example, in Romans 1, Paul identifies the good news of Jesus as Son of God and Lord. Tom Wright illustrates how Paul's statement is a statement against empire by quoting an inscription from 9 BC about Augustus, as discussed already in chapter 5. Another example is the inscriptions on Roman coins from the period, which bore the phrase 'Divi filius', or son of God.

The title Lord is used to translate the divine name YHWH in the LXX, the Greek translation of the Hebrew Bible.[33] Caesar is identified as saviour, bringer of peace, god, and the world's true lord. In contrast, Jesus is the Son of God, shown to be Lord by his resurrection from the dead (Rom 1:1–4). Jesus is the one who brings peace with God on the cross (Rom 5:1) rather than the Pax Romana, which was bought by the sword.

While empire sits in the background of Romans 1, and possibly chapter 5, what about Romans 8? Robert Jewett observes that the personification of nature such as we find in this passage is also observed in Greco-Roman literature, where it can groan under winter's dormancy or can express joy at its deliverance under the emperor.[34] A return to agricultural productivity was of central importance to the Roman civic cult. People who are fed and entertained are unlikely to revolt: bread and circuses. These claims of empire stand in stark contrast to Paul's claim that creation cries out in birth pains (Rom 8:22) and looks forward

---

Lexington Books, 2016).

[31] John Wesley, *The Great Deliverance*. Accessed 30 May 2015. http://wesley.nnu.edu/john-wesley/the-sermons-of-john-wesley-1872-edition/sermon-60-the-general-deliverance/.

[32] R.J. Berry (ed), *The Care of Creation* (Nottingham: Inter-Varsity Press, 2000): 18-22. Cheryl Hunt, David G. Horrell and Christopher Southgate, "An Environmental Mantra? Ecological Interest in Romans 8:19-23 and a Modest Proposal for its Interpretation," *Journal of Theological Studies* (2008) NS.

[33] Wright, *What Saint Paul Really Said*, 71.

[34] Robert Jewett, *Romans: A Commentary* (Minneapolis: Fortress Press, 2007), Jewett, *Romans*, 516-517.

to the resurrection of the church (v. 19). The earth can be considered our resurrection womb.[35]

The groaning was manifested in a number of ways. Rome was responsible for significant deforestation as the result of timber harvesting for construction and metal smelting.[36] This led to flooding of the Tiber, river mouth silting, and soil erosion. It also led to the spread of malaria, which was thought to be due to bad air (what the term 'malaria' literally means) rather than mosquitoes.[37] Erosion, as well as microclimate change, was widespread in ancient Rome and Greece, leading to a decline in agricultural production. Malaria is believed to have played a role in the fall of Rome.[38] The bones of forty-seven babies from a 5th century cemetery outside of Rome show signs of anaemia, a condition associated with malaria. There is cultural evidence of witchcraft, designed to keep away the evil spirits, which were thought to cause disease.[39] The air quality in Rome itself was also poor and hazardous for human health, as the Roman Senator, Seneca, could observe. So bad was it, with the air being filled with 'clouds of ashes, all the poisonous fumes they've accumulated', that he apparently fled Rome and could feel an improvement in his health immediately.[40] So, while an understanding of the connection between forest clearing, mosquitoes and malaria would have been lost on the Romans, they could see other things for themselves. The bondage to decay is therefore relational, reflecting humanity's misrule, which included an impact on agriculture.

---

35 Douglas Moo, *The Epistle to the Romans: New International Commentary on the New Testament* (Grand Rapids: Wm. B Eeerdmans Publishing Company, 1996), 513. Hunt et al., *Environmental Mantra*, 22.

36 Lara O'Sullivan, et al., "Deforestation, Mosquitoes, and Ancient Rome: Lessons for Today," *Bioscience* 58 (2008): 756-760.

37 O'Sullivan et al., *Deforestation*, 757.

38 J. Donald Hughes and J. V. Thirgood, "Deforestation, Erosion, and Forest Management in Ancient Greece and Rome," *Journal of Forest History* 26 (1982): 60-75.

39 Alison Abbott, "Earliest malaria DNA found in Roman baby graveyard," *Nature* 412 (2001), 847.

40 Stephen Mosley, "Environmental History of Air Pollution and Protection," in *The Basic Environmental History* edited by Mauro Agnoletti, and Simone Neri Serneri, 145 (Heidelberg: Springer, 2014).

So, given that Paul could see how we upset God's order, and that creation looks forward to being released from its bondage to decay (v. 21), this must inform our mission. Too often we focus on our own fate (quite naturally) or that of our family and friends, but forget that 'God saves us *with* and not *from* creation.'[41] So, does this shape our understanding of all things new and God's plan to renew our world? It is true that we do not save the world: Christ does this upon his return. However, we live proleptically, which is to live in hope. The creation has been subjected to our misrule in hope of a future redemption that is tied to our resurrection. But since the creation will be renewed, as will our relationship to it, and this message is part of the gospel we preach, we should practice what we preach!

The kingdom of God is one of peace and justice for the human and non-human creation. We need to limit our impact on the rest of creation, and undo some of the damage that we have done. This means managing our food systems so that both humans and non-humans can flourish. It is to this challenge that we now turn.

Food Justice

Apart from dealing with climate change, both mitigating the worst of its impacts by cutting our fossil fuel addiction and adapting to the change we can't avoid, we need to deal with food justice. Dr Vandana Shiva and Ruchi Shroff write about seed slavery in India in *Seed Satyagraha: Civil Disobedience To End Seed Slavery.*[42] Satyagraha means the force of truth and was a principle that Gandhi used in his non-violent resistance. The main point of their work is to protect food diversity from seed companies who are using intellectual property rights in an apparently manipulative manner. Seed laws seek to enforce uniformity and licensing and registration of seeds used, criminalising

---

41 Mick Pope, *Preaching to the Birds? The Mission of the Church to the Creation* (Eastwood: Morling Press, 2013), accessed May 12, 2015, http://www.morlingcollege.com/sites/default/files/files/2013%20Annual%20Lecture%20Booklet.pdf. Also published as Mick Pope, "Preaching to the Birds? The Mission of the Church to the Creation," in *Speaking of Mission: Volume 2*, edited by Michael Frost, 107-120. (Eastwood: Morling Press, 2013).

42 Dr. Vandana Shiva & Ruchi Shroff, *Seed Satyagraha: Civil Disobedience To End Seed Slavery* (New Delhi: Navdanya, 2015). Accessed 4 June, 2018, http://seedfreedom.info/wp-content/uploads/2015/09/Seed-Satyagraha-Booklet-1.pdf.

biodiversity, according to Shiva and Shroff. Tamara Wattnem claims that these seed laws threaten seed sovereignty, defined as

> people's right to save, replant, breed and share seeds, and their right to participate in decision-making processes regarding rules and laws that regulate their access and use.[43]

Wattnem distinguishes between formal seed systems, which are 'heavily regulated systems made up of public institutions and private industries engaged in scientific plant breeding', and informal seed systems, which are 'completely unregulated and dependent on farmers' knowledge.' These informal systems use native seeds and those not patented by large companies. Their use is not controlled by these companies, including seed exchange networks. Such networks are still the preferred sources for seeds, especially for small scale growers.

In other words, given that most people in the majority of the world get their food from small farms, it is the informal network that feeds them, and this is the system that Shiva and Shroff are fighting to protect. And it is quite a fight. Ten companies account for about two-thirds of all seed varieties, which are subject to intellectual property law. In order to expand the market for these large companies, the informal seed systems need to be made illegal by seed laws. This means farmers are forced to buy into a system where the seeds sold are non-renewable, under patents, and they ensure 'an absolute monopoly and an end to our diversity.'[44]

This is little more than an agri-empire. While Wattnem notes that seed uniformity was an 'essential element of the Green Revolution and of industrial agriculture more broadly', she also acknowledges that seed laws 'generate path dependence and rigidify production regimes, making it difficult to discard them and/or to reimagine them.' Shiva and Shroff are more blunter in calling it 'monopolistic control.' A seed Babel, if you will.

---

43 Tamara Wattnem, "Seed laws, certification and standardization: outlawing informal seed systems in the Global South," *The Journal of Peasant Studies*, 2016. DOI:10.1080/03066 150.2015.1130702.
44 Shiva and Shroff, *Seed Satyagraha*, 5.

So, if all things new means freedom from all empires that use coercive power, then Christian organisations should be involved in protecting seed sovereignty. In particular, EFICOR in India has developed a seed bank.

> Farmers in the villages are highly dependent on agriculture as their only source of income. Therefore, there is a need for seed procurement during the growing season. Due to poverty, it is a huge economic burden for farmers to purchase the seeds every time from the market. Often farmers are forced to borrow money from money lenders, at 50% interest.

> In order to address this problem, EFICOR forms farmers group in villages, and provides one certified seeds to the farmers group. Farmers are taught how to treat and store the seeds. After cultivation, farmers return seeds back to the seed bank, which are stored and reused in the following agriculture season. Since the seeds are certified seeds, farmers are able to use them for 3 to 4 years. Farmers group manages the seed bank and all the records. Though it is a small initiative, it has a significant financial impact in a farmer's life. It is evident that after the initiation of the seed bank, farmers stopped needing to seek loans from money lenders. This has saved them from being exploited economically and psychologically.

Apart from becoming involved in food justice, can the church become involved in shaping the way farming is done? This is the idea behind *Farming God's Way*.

Farming God's Way

Farming God's Way is

> a well-balanced biblical, management and technological solution for the agricultural domain, to come out of poverty with what God has put in their hands, and to reveal the fullness of His promised abundant life.[45]

Biblically, it includes acknowledging God and God alone, which fits well with our themes of rejecting empire. This also involves understanding God's all-sufficiency, which is counter to the common theme of scarcity in economics. Bringing tithes and offerings to God

---

45 Farming God's Way, "Overview," accessed 11 June, 2018, http://www.farming-gods-way.org/overview.htm.

echoes the Law and the continuing practice of providing for others in the New Testament.

Management skills focus on how to teach the poor to make a sustainable profit to help lift themselves out of poverty, producing food on time, to a high quality and with minimum wastage. The technical aspects are based on 'the laws that God has put in place in creation for the most productive ecosystems in the world', which includes no ploughing, one hundred per cent mulch cover (what they call God's blanket) and crop rotation. The website carries a training manual and they run regular training events.

Take, as an example, the case of Dickson Shuwali:

Dickson lives in a rural poverty stricken area called the Lower Shire in Malawi. Food aid streams into the area every year and the plight of the poor just gets worse. Dickson's father used to get an average of just three 50kg bags from the acre he handed on to Dickson as his inheritance. In his first year of doing Farming God's Way they had a severe drought, but still managed to harvest 5 bags, where 4 of those came from a small area where he had put God's blanket down. His neighbours all around him harvested very little and some nothing at all. In his 2nd year he got 45 bags; 3rd year 54 bags & 4th year 69 bags. That is a 23 fold yield increase!!!

Dickson is walking in God's promises where God said 'we would have life more abundantly.'[46]

Of course, the problem of climate change will make Dickson's life harder, as it will for all farmers, but the future of small farms needs to look a lot more like this.

Fighting Climate Change at the Dinner Table

In order to deal with climate change, and associated issues such as soil degradation, fertiliser run-off, and the loss of more and more of our remaining forests to agriculture, we need to realise that it is time to seriously reconsider our diets. TEAR Australia/Renew Our World's

---

[46] Farming God's Way, "Testimonies," accessed 11 June, 2018, http://www.farming-gods-way.org/testimonies.htm. See also Bountiful Grains Trust. "Farming God's Way Testimony Dickson Shuwali Malawi". YouTube video, 0:40. Posted [August 2011]. https://www.youtube.com/watch?v=OhD5ydYHoHE.

The Future of Food Report calls for us to consider a plant-rich diet.[47] Some Christians embrace vegetarianism or veganism for reasons relating to the way in which animals are treated as inputs into a system, as opposed to individual creatures. While we can argue about human need or lack thereof for animal protein, and the rights or wrongs of consuming other creatures, the food system is certainly often cruel. A shocking recent example of this was the death of two thousand four hundred Australian sheep being exported to the Middle East. The sheep died from overcrowding, heat exhaustion and lack of food and water.[48]

Other Christians see the elimination of animal protein from their diets as a direct application of texts like Isaiah 65:17–25. Here we get a description of the new heavens and earth written well before Revelation 21. We read that 'The wolf and the lamb shall feed together, the lion shall eat straw like the ox; but the serpent—its food shall be dust!' (v. 25). The kingdom of God is one of peace and nonviolence, so we might extend that to our relationship with non-humans and our diets. This leaves open the question of non-human carnivory in the eschaton, even though this is not the primary focus of texts like Romans 8. But for humans, at least, we have choices in our diet, and if reasons of animal welfare don't sway your dietary choices, action on climate change should.

A recent study has shown that a vegan diet

is probably the single biggest way to reduce your impact on planet Earth, not just greenhouse gases, but global acidification, eutrophication, land use and water use.[49]

Let's take land use for example:

without meat and dairy consumption, global farmland use could be reduced by more than 75% – an area equivalent to the US, China, European Union and Australia combined.

---

47 Matthew Maury, *The Future of Food*, (Blackburn: TEAR Australia, 2018).

48 Marty McCarthy, "Australian farmers question the future of live sheep exports," *ABC News*, 25 April, 2018, accessed 13 June, 2018, http://www.abc.net.au/news/2018-04-25/live-sheep-exports-australian-farmers-call-for-ban/9696748.

49 Damian Carrington, "Avoiding meat and dairy is 'single biggest way' to reduce your impact on Earth," *The Guardian*, 1 June, 2018, accessed 11 June, 2018, https://www.theguardian.com/environment/2018/may/31/avoiding-meat-and-dairy-is-single-biggest-way-to-reduce-your-impact-on-earth#img-1.

That means land for natural forests, for wildlife, carbon storage in plant matter and soils, and water filtration, among other things. In terms of greenhouse gases, red meat is the biggest culprit, with up to one hundred and five kilograms of the stuff emitted for every one hundred grams of meat. For the dedicated carnivore, there are a lot of much friendlier options. The lead scientist on the study, Joseph Poore, notes that the large variability in environmental impact from different farms and farming methods does mean that there are many opportunities to reduce environmental harms, and the global population doesn't necessarily need to become vegan. That said, most westerners eat way too much meat, and cutting out red meat will have a large impact. It might be a missed steak to cut down on red meat, but it won't be a mistake!

For those not ready to take the vegan plunge, at least try reducing your meat and dairy intake. Have a meat free day, limit the amount of meat in the meals you have, or have meat only in one meal per day. I have friends in the Orthodox tradition who fast during Lent, and only eat vegetables or fish. Climate change doesn't give us the choice between modifying, or not modifying our diets, but given something so central as eating, it needs to be one of the many places we make a choice for renewing our world.

Other suggestions from *The Future of Food* include buying fair trade foods, seasonal foods (to reduce energy used in greenhouses or air transport), reducing food waste (composting, eating food before it goes off), and cutting down on food packaging.

Food as mission

I want to finish on a positive note about food. Firstly, Jesus' eating of food post-resurrection (Lk 24:42–43) points to the ongoing centrality of eating to our humanity. We are fundamentally physical, with physical needs and physical limitations. The fact that Jesus could eat in his resurrection body suggests that we will too. That side of our nature is valued by God because it will also be taken up into the resurrection life. So, we'd better get this food thing right, and eat proleptically, prophetically, and missionally.

The New Testament presents us with the idea of an eschatological banquet. That's a fancy way of saying that when Christ comes back, there will be a party. There will be food. Christianity is fundamentally a faith of celebration and food is characteristic of celebration because of its sheer sensual nature. While food can become an idol — when was the last time you heard a sermon on gluttony, I wonder? — it is also a precious gift from God. That's both food as nourishment *and* food as enjoyment. In Luke 14:15–24, this eschatological banquet includes the poor, the crippled, the blind, and the lame. The religious establishment who rejected Jesus won't be included. This is the model for how we are to treat the poor now: to feed those who can't repay us (Lk 14:14). Food is to be shared with those who need it, graciously and freely, for such is the character of God and the nature of his kingdom.

This great feast is pre-figured in the Passover meal (Lk 22:15–16) and carried on in the Lord's Supper. Indeed, if you read 1 Corinthians 11:17–22, you see that the Lord's Supper was originally part of a real, substantial meal. What stopped that? You guessed it, the marginalisation of the poor. People were feasting and getting drunk, while slaves would arrive late with little to eat. Instead of an opportunity to share food (Acts 2:46), it was a way of humiliating or bringing shame on those already shamed by their society. We need to recapture that sense of being able to eat together in a way that doesn't shame those who bring little or can't bring anything, let alone bring the MasterChef perfect meal. But we still need to eat together and include others from outside into our feasting. That inclusion can be a literal eating with others or thinking about global food inequality and working to ensure others can eat better.

It's also worth pondering Jesus' 'preferential care for the poor.' Jesus ate with the marginalised to be sure, including prostitutes and sinners of various sorts. But Jesus also ate with tax collectors, who grew wealthy off the backs of their fellow Israelites and collaborated with the Romans. Eating isn't just with those excluded because they are poor but also those who are rich. Further, Jesus ate with prostitutes and tax collectors at the same time, since Roman-style banquets usually included prostitutes for the after-dinner entertainment.[50] Jesus also ate with Pharisees because he loved them too (e.g. Lk 7:36–50 in Simon the Pharisee's house).

Our feasting should be inclusive. It is community based, so eating with those with whom you worship is a declaration to the world that God's kingdom has been and is being established in the church (which is not to confuse the church with the kingdom of God, but that's an idea for another time). Having frozen meals that are both ethical and available for those in need is a practical way of embodying community. Being inclusive enough to include the needy in our community is also deeply missional.

Another way of making food profoundly missional, practical, and restorative is the idea of church or community gardens. Being tied back to soil, to others, reusing our compost, learning the rhythm of the seasons, eating meals that have fewer carbon miles, and sharing meals where the labour has been shared.[51] Coming back to the idea of reduced meat intake, if you witness in an area with Muslims, Hindus, or the growing proportions of vegans, are you prepared to abandon or at least subsidise the sausage sizzle with something designed for the non-carnivores, or those who won't eat beef or pork? While Paul wrote about not eating food sacrificed to idols, the idea of not making others stumble is a very broad missional principle, as is becoming all things to all people in order to save some.

What is important to remember in all of this is that we don't — in our desire to get food right — fall into the trap of inventing new purity laws. Jonathan Cornford reminds us that the goal isn't simply to be seen to be doing the ethical thing for its own sake, or for dividing those who are 'in' from those who are 'out.'[52] To be honest, I've seen vegans be every bit as self-righteous as Christian fundamentalists. Such an approach has never converted anyone to anything. Instead, as Cornford reminds us,

---

50 David Instone Brewer, "Bible Scandals: Prostitutes," 2012, accessed 11 June, 2018, https://www.bethinking.org/bible/bible-scandals/4-prostitutes.

51 Miriam Pepper, "Church-based community gardening: Where mission meets ecology in local contexts," *Australian Journal of Mission Studies*, 6, no 2 (2012): 54-59.

52 Jonathan Cornford, *Coming Back to Earth: Essays on the Church, Climate Change, Cities, Agriculture, and Eating* (Reservoir: Morning Star Publishing, 2016), 100.

Paul's instructions on eating are all about the relational implications — be it our relationships with friends from church, the global poor, future generations, or even non-humans — and that 'For the kingdom of God is not food and drink but righteousness and peace and joy in the Holy Spirit' (Rom 14:17).

All of this anticipates the making of all things new and celebrates that 'Blessed are those who are invited to the marriage supper of the Lamb' (Rev 19:9). It reminds us that making all things new begins in our kitchens as a prophetic witness to the world.

CHAPTER 11 — RENEWED IMAGINATIONS

Imagine

I'm a bit of a Beatles fan but discovered them well after they broke up in 1970, as I was only one at the time. I grew up listening to them on vinyl. I was never a huge fan of John Lennon's solo career, but I was shocked like many when he was gunned down in 1980 by a self-confessed attention seeking sociopath.[1] Mark David Chapman shot Lennon four times in the back in his doorway, right after Lennon had signed an album cover for him. It was a waste of two lives, and a tragedy in the life of a third, Yoko Ono, Lennon's widow.

Lennon wrote the song *Imagine*, which is now embedded in the popular imagination. We are asked to imagine a world where there is no ideology that gets in the way of a unified humanity: no religion with its belief in heaven and hell, where all things are in common, and where we live in peace. It is a wonderful dream we are invited into, a utopia, a heaven on earth. It is so easy to be sceptical, cynical even. Much music these days celebrates misogyny, violence, and sex. Lennon's vision seems quite naïve, and yet people, since time immemorial, have dreamed about utopia. And this too is the vision of Revelation 21; a world where heaven becomes united with earth, all things are made new, and God 'will wipe every tear from their eyes. Death will be no more; mourning and crying and pain will be no more' (Rev 21:4). This is when God makes all things new.

We've spent much time looking at key passages, challenging long held myths and doctrines. But doctrine is not enough, indeed the book of Revelation is evidence of that. Think about another incident in the bible. At the end of Luke's gospel, we learn that Jesus tells his disciples that they are to begin proclaiming the gospel in Jerusalem, but they

---

1 Harriet Alexander," John Lennon's killer revealed details of shooting as he was denied parole for the ninth time," *The Telegraph*, 16 September, 2016, accessed 21 April, 2018, https://www.telegraph.co.uk/news/2016/09/16/john-lennons-killer-revealed-details-of-shooting-as-he-was-denie/.

were also to go to the Gentiles (Lk 24:47). In his second volume, Luke records that Jesus tells them to be his witnesses to the ends of the Earth (Acts 1:8). So, what did it take to get Peter, impetuous, loud mouthed, quick to speak but slow to think Peter, to go to the Gentiles? In the first instance, it was a vision (Acts 10:9–16). Sometimes more doctrine is not what we need. Instead, we need an expanded imagination.

The imagination can be a powerful thing; it can lead people astray. The second commandment tells us we are not to make idols and yet Christians have done so in the name of Christianity for centuries. In *The Screwtape Letters*, Lewis reminds us that we can make images of God and pray to them instead:

> I have known cases where what the patient called his "God" was actually located-up and to the left at the corner of the bedroom ceiling, or inside his own head, or in a crucifix on the wall.[2]

Imagery can inspire the imagination in the wrong direction. Hence, we see at times during the Reformation a strong trend of iconoclasm. Iconoclasm is the attacking and sometimes destruction of cherished beliefs or institutions. In the Reformation, this included the destruction of religious images. Steve Ozment claims that much medieval religious art had it coming, given the role it played in picture catechisms. Lurid imagery of people in purgatory or hell, or the depictions of the seven deadly sins as animals, were designed to frighten or shame people into repentance, and became impediments, rather than spurs, to spiritual growth.[3] The resulting popular iconoclasm represented both the feeling of betrayal and the desire for reform.[4]

The reactions to art during the Reformation were mixed. Luther admired art so long as it wasn't put to idolatrous use, and he opposed the destruction of stained glass and religious statues, whereas the Anabaptists had no time for such things.[5] Calvin favoured simplicity in art and was not interested in a purely aesthetic appreciation of it,

---

2 C. S. Lewis, *The Screwtape Letters* (Glasgow: Harper Collins, 2001), chapter 4.

3 Steven E. Ozment, *The Reformation in the Cities* (New Haven: Yale University Press, 1975): 26–27.

4 Ozment, *The Reformation in the Cities*, 44.

5 Lewis W. Spitz, *The Renaissance and Reformation Movements Volume II: The Reformation* (St Louis: Concordia Publishing House, 1971): 573.

according to Leslie Spelman.[6] He claims that the early church only began to use images once it was in decline, but that since art was a gift of God, it should be used for pure and legitimate (religious) purposes only. While Luther embraced music and wrote hymns of his own, Calvin strictly stuck to the Psalter. His focus on simplicity and the words themselves is reflected in his admonition that 'the ears be not more attentive to the modulation of the notes, than the mind to the spiritual import of the words.'[7] This included rejecting four-part harmony. Accordingly, Spelman accuses Calvin of placing cold logic over all else. Apart from music, Spelman concludes that Calvin both freed art from church control and forced artists to find other subjects. Spelman also believes Calvin's attitude produced a 'Puritanic ethic against art.' This included the general idea that art was sinful because it was both immoral and a waste of time.

While it might be hard to find such an obvious critique today, there are elements of it in Alain de Botton's TV series *The Perfect Home*. In episode three, he considers church architecture.[8] He believes that the goal of medieval Catholic churches was to reorient our souls and 'turn us into different and hopefully better people.' Visiting a monastery restored by Cistercian monks, de Botton observes that they carefully reconstructed the original architecture because they believe that where you are can influence what you can believe in. Buildings can inscribe values, and beauty in a building can be a lesson.

Meanwhile, Protestantism doesn't fare so well in de Botton's analysis. He understands the worldview of Protestantism to be that the state of the soul has nothing to do with where you live or worship. It is not topocentric or place-centred, but logocentric, or focused on the Word. And while we can know and experience Jesus anywhere, has it led to an aridity in our faith? Interviewing a member of a Protestant church that meets in a rather dull building, he learns from her that what matters is what's inside. For de Botton, much of the world is now

---

6 Leslie P. Spelman, "Calvin and the Arts," *The Journal of Aesthetics and Art Criticism*, 6:3 (March 1948): 246–252.

7 Spelman, *Calvin and the Arts*, 248–250.

8 *The Perfect Home*. Episode 3. Directed by Neil Crombie. Written by Alain de Botton. Channel 4. May 2006.

Protestant in its view of architecture, where beauty is well down the order of importance.

By now you'd be familiar with the weird things in Revelation. It's full of mythical creatures, of symbolic use of numbers, of beautiful gems, huge architecture, and impossible realities like the end of death. The book of Revelation contains: fantastic elements used to describe a deeper reality. While this book has been largely cognitive, the book of Revelation, and the mission it calls us to, have expanded imaginations through things both beautiful and downright disturbing. Sometimes a solid piece of prose won't be enough but a word picture like a bride, a garden, or a fearsome beast will do it. Maybe a song that moves us, or a piece of poetry. Maybe a painting? The book of Revelation is liturgy, song, drama. We need the theopoetics of Revelation to expand our imaginations, to be able to think about what the new heavens and earth will be like. We also need it to expand our ethical imaginations to live hopefully and to act and speak prophetically as we point others to this present and future reality.

New songs for a new heavens and earth

As Michael Gorman observes, Revelation is full of song. This is particularly clear from Revelation 4–5 that we considered earlier.[9] The vision we are given of the praise of God and the Lamb as reigning now is meant to challenge, embolden, and give us hope. And if there is one thing that Christians often like to do, it is sing. Tom Wright often says that 'Heaven is important, but it's not the end of the world.' He means that the resurrection and heaven come to earth is our future. No cartoons of sitting on clouds and playing harps, no making the scenes of Revelation 5 our eternal future. As Wright also argues in *Surprised by Hope*, the bible is not simply interested in 'life after death', although we could argue endlessly about what happens when we die. The so-called 'intermediate state' is a topic of much discussion. A literal reading of Revelation would suggest we praise God in heaven until the

---

9 Michael J. Gorman, *Reading Revelation Responsibly: Uncivil Worship and Witness. Following the Lamb Into the New Creation* (Eugene, Or: Cascade, 2011), 112–114.

resurrection. But this is an intermediate state. The point is not 'life after death' but 'life after, life after death.' [10]

And so, with this in mind, we should see that our hymnody is horrible. It gets heaven so wrong. I don't mean to criticise well-meaning Christian song writers down through the ages. Well, actually yes, I do. It's so important. The songs we sing shape our theology as much as, if not more than, the sermons we hear. If we want to imagine a world where God is making all things new, we need to sing about it. This means singing about peace, justice, and creation care. And getting heaven right. I want to help you understand how unhelpful it is. But to avoid any hassles, I will use public domain hymns, and then leave it to you to go 'heaven heresy hunting' with modern songs. So here goes.

Home, written by Charles E. Orr in 1900 based on Revelation 3:21 says

Oh, home of my soul
In that far away goal,
Each day brings me nearer to thee;
The great throne so white,
And my crown shining bright,
Mine eyes ever longing to see.

I've never sung this but it's a nice example of what not to sing. Note that we get closer to heaven, rather than it getting closer to us? Note also how it makes death our goal and seems to pass over life; its joys, beauties, and duties to love and serve our neighbour. It's incredibly dualistic in talking about the soul, despite the fact that the Hebrew word, *nephesh,* is a holistic term meaning the whole self. This verse is a nice dose of Plato and not John of the Apocalypse.

Away in a Manger is, for me, one of the more cringe worthy carols. Sorry, it just is. There is the clanger of 'But little Lord Jesus, no crying he makes.' Why? What baby doesn't cry? Are you telling me Jesus didn't cry? Is crying sinful? Augustine believed even infants showed sinful behaviour. But apart from identifying simple reactionary behaviour in babies as sin, we get the following

---

10 Tom Wright, *Surprised by Hope* (London: SPCK, 2007).

Be near me, Lord Jesus; I ask thee to stay
Close by me forever, and love me I pray.
Bless all the dear children in thy tender care,
And take us to heaven to live with thee there.

I suppose this is comfort in an age where children can die young. The idea that we live with Jesus in heaven is not wrong if one holds to an 'intermediate state' as Revelation suggests. But this isn't to be our final resting place. I guess you can't get too detailed in a kid's Christmas carol but I do think we can do better than this.

Another song that muddles things nicely is Horatio Spafford's *It is well with my soul.*

But Lord, 'tis for Thee, for Thy coming we wait,
The sky, not the grave, is our goal;
Oh, trump of the angel! Oh, voice of the Lord!
Blessed hope, blessed rest of my soul.
And Lord, haste the day when my faith shall be sight,
The clouds be rolled back as a scroll;
The trump shall resound, and the Lord shall descend,
A song in the night, oh my soul.

Here we have the rapture. The Lord descends (check) so we might leave the grave (check) but our home is the sky? Also note that rest is for our soul, not for our whole selves, resurrection body included.

So what passes muster? Handel's Messiah takes Revelation 5:12–14 and just sings it. In a sense, this is what we should be doing, acknowledging that the Lamb is worthy and give blessing, honour, glory and power to the one who sits on the throne and the Lamb. God is in charge now. This isn't all we should be singing, but it begins with the fundamental reality of God and Jesus as worthy of all praise: one as creator, the other as redeemer (in John's language, both are both). Christians can't be the serving community unless they are first the worshipping community but our worship needs to get heaven right.

My challenge to song writers is to have a go at capturing both a solid new heavens and earth theology, a biblical resurrection theology, together with our need to come out of Babylon. Counter-cultural music. Peace and justice oriented music. Songs and new hymns that speak of a revolution of peace, love, and hope. Songs that praise God as creator of this wonderful world, Jesus as the one who makes all things new, and our calling to be part of this mission to both preach and embody the gospel of all things made new.

Protest Songs for a World Being Made New

And so, it is to music and the poetic I now turn. Luke Vassella is a wedding singer (who else thinks of the movie?)[11] Indeed, he is much more than that. He has also written many songs for Gasfield Free Northern Rivers.[12] This campaign is opposed to coal seam gas or CSG. Not only does CSG continue our fossil fuel addiction, but it threatens the 'biodiversity, water resources, agricultural lands and sustainable industries of the Northern Rivers.' In 2016, submissions were sought to the 'Select Committee on Unconventional Gas Mining.'[13] Luke's submission was a series of songs.[14] The song *No Future (On a Dead Earth)* describes the impacts of CSG, imagining a world that needs to be made new. Then there's *The Loyal Man*, which describes sympathetically the plight of police in the middle of protests

If policy fails the public, and puppeteers pull the strings I'm just part of the machinery, what can I do about these things?[15]

Luke was part of a discussion at the Inspiracy 2 festival in Newcastle, 2018, where I also spoke.[16] The discussion asked, *Can art change anything?* I asked Luke how he thought his music could be part of making all things new.

I witnessed how music served the momentum of a gentle revolution leading up to and during the Bentley Blockade in 2014. It helped

---

11 http://mail.lukevassella.com/Home.html, accessed 21 June, 2018.

12 Gasfield Free Northern Rivers, accessed 21 June, 2018, http://csgfreenorthernrivers.org/.

13 Parliament of Australia, "Select Committee on Unconventional Gas Mining," accessed 21 June, 2018.

14 For the play list see https://www.youtube.com/playlist?list=PL_AJRDmz8qY5vrpqJkusi 35xJye09yhm7, accessed 21 June, 2018.

15 Lyrics used by permission from Luke.

16 "Inspiracy 2: A Climate for Change Sustainability Festival," accessed 21 June, 2018, https://www.inspiracy.org.au/.

define the purpose, affirm the commitment and maintain the resolve, particularly during trying times. For example, when over 800 NSW police were expected to remove us by force. My personal mantra walking up the hill at 4:45am to the main blockade gate A was the 'Prayer of St Francis', "make me a channel of your peace". A song heard in the church of my youth and many churches since. I witnessed a communal sense of altruism and what seemed like something of a glimpse of the kingdom of God during the Bentley Blockade. It was unprecedented, being described as the Eureka stockade of our era. Our wildly diverse community was unified to stop the formidable gas industry from getting a foothold in the Northern Rivers, and music was a vital ingredient in that powerful, non-violent movement.

Poetry for a World Being Made New

Joel McKerrow is an impressive figure.[17] At well over six feet, with long dreadlocks, the only thing more impressive than his stature is the power of his spoken word poetry. He is the Artist Ambassador for TEAR Australia and has produced albums, books, and written for various Christian publications and blogs. According to his website, Joel speaks internationally 'on the intersection of spiritual formation, social justice, creativity and identity.' One piece pertinent to the themes of this book was written for the *For Tomorrow* campaign.[18] He declares that

For tomorrow, our hope,

shall be a louder voice

than our apathy.

Our apathy shall finally take a step forward, and our steps forward
  shall lead us somewhere mean,

something hold,

meaning like friends hold each other,

crying,

I am,

crying for this world to change.

---

17 https://www.joelmckerrow.com/, accessed 21 June, 2018.
18 Joel McKerrow, "Joel McKerrow's 'Hope For Tomorrow'," accessed 21 June, 2018, https://www.fortomorrow.org.au/stories/story/joel-mckerrows-hope-for-tomorrow.

Tears of empathy,

sometimes apathy,

I cry today,

for tomorrow even these tears

shall be wiped from our faces.[19]

I asked Joel, what role he thought his work plays in helping us imaging this tomorrow he speaks of so passionately.

As a poet I tell stories.

But I am not the only one.

We live in a world that tells stories. Our society sells us a certain reading of reality. An economic script to shape our lives around. We are told, in no uncertain terms, what it means to be a productive member of our civilisation. Namely, that we give ourselves to the Western Dream, regardless of the cost to others or to the earth. We are promised so much and sent on the wild goose chase of reaching this horizon of happy bliss. Yet, when we look at the wake of such lifestyles, we can see the fractured and broken reality that is strewn behind us. Environmental decay. Anxiety. Depression. Family breakdown. The growing gap between the haves and the have-nots. The growing FEAR that sits within the gap. Fear demands a certain understanding of the other. It forces anything unfamiliar to be named as dangerous. To take a stranger and paint them. To take a culture and blame them. And isn't this world thick with the dripping paint of our prejudice.

And all of these realities stem out of the societal stories that we have believed for so long. That we have grown up within. A fish in a bowl doesn't know that it is wet. Until the bowl cracks.

We need a better story.

Enter the poet. Enter the writer. Enter the movie maker. Enter the artist. Enter the story-teller.

When I write my poetry, I feel as though I am doing two things: I am naming what is and I am calling people to what may be. I am critiquing one story and offering another. It is subversive in this sense. It takes the version of reality being sold to us and seeks to name a sub-version. An

---

19 Words used by permission from Joel.

ulterior. A new way of being human together.

This is exactly the same device that I, as an artist, see being used in Revelation. The naming of the current reality and a calling to a new reality. A new creation. It is a script of defiance and dreaming. The writer uses hyperbole, imagery, metaphor, simile, all the tools in my own toolkit, and in yours too, to speak of this newness. To be a realist of a larger reality. A painter outside the margins. This is who we are. This is who I desire to be.

May imagination set us free from the constraints of our bigotry and our bias. May we see things that are not yet and name them as present. The deeper stuff that sits beneath the fear. Our imagination is our hope and our hope denies the current ordering. To look at the world with Kaleidoscope eyes, to see the things we have forgotten, to remember freedom.

One of my favourite quotes about poetry is this: 'Don't sit the poem like a test, enter it like a garden, enter it like a forest and just see it as it is, and be who you are in response' (Mark Thedinnick). I wonder if we should do the same with the dreams of a new reality we see in the scriptures. Poetry is about evoking a response in its audience. A movement. A dissatisfaction that shall lead to change. I wonder if you have ever let yourself be moved by poetry. I wonder if you have ever let yourself be moved by the imagery in scripture of this new creation where the old has gone and the new has come and the wars cease and the babies are born healthy and the tears are wiped away. The oppressor sits down with the oppressed and he is forgiven right there and then and I sit down with the oppressed and I am forgiven right there and then... and friend...you are too. Invited, too. We all get to join in this day when the earth is restored and the Great Barrier Reef once again glistens and the old growth forests are not cut down and Bangladesh is not covered in water and its people are not forced into labour. We get to join in the great day when Israel and Palestine sit at the same table. We get to sit down at the same table. God sits down at the same table.

This is the world I dream of.

And I believe poetry, this imagery, this imagining, it takes us there before we are even there.

It reminds us of the world that is to come.

Singing to Renew Our World

The *Renew Our World* campaign has been co-creating with artists, poets and musicians across the world. In the lead up to the UN Climate talks in 2017, young people in Nigeria wrote a creative set of poems on climate and clean energy and performed them on the radio. Animated video versions of the poems were also used in Germany, where the UN Climate talks were taking place for the global campaign's worship night, have featured in poetry performances promoting the cause in Australia, and are being used in the Scottish Parliament for the campaign on climate change. I have included one at random from the collection, with permission from the Renew Our World campaign, titled *Wondering.*

I once wondered...
If the earth had nostrils,
But no lip to verbalise.
Choking within,
From polluted air, now internalised.

This earth we live in,
For resources to be harnessed,
We must change our sights and wear new views,
Every possibility simply can be hinged on a SWITCH!
Not a docket to a wall,
But a set of values imbibed,
A paradigm shift for the next level.
A healthier earth with a fresh breath.

So Let's switch!
From coal to solar,
Vast is the worth of clean energy to fossil fuels.
Coal is dug and bought.
Sunlight free and limitless to tap.
A country without power failure is a country unhindered.
Let's switch!

Let the wondering cease.
Let's switch!
Let innovation and possibilities kiss.
Oh yes! Let's switch!
Clean energy is all we preach.

The *Renew Our World* campaign takes seriously the idea that we need to sing from a new song sheet if we are to imagine a world where God is making all things new. South African author, musician and television company CEO, Dawn Faith, has been tasked with writing such a song.[20] The lyrics, as they were available at the time of writing this book, are reproduced here.

Verse 1

the forests are groaning in need of resurrection
the waters are rising up crying for attention
creation is calling, reaching for redemption
we need you now…
Lord hear our prayer…

Chorus

give us your love
give us your touch
to meet this world in need
to be your hands and feet
give us your heart
give us your eyes
to serve in love and truth
to see the world renewed
renew our world

---

20 https://www.dawnfaith.com/, accessed 21 June, 2018.

Verse 2

you hear the prayers of the hungry and the thirsty,
your sons and your daughters seeking sanctuary.
the Oppressed and Oppressor in need of your salvation
we need you now...
Lord hear our prayer...

Chorus

give us your love
give us your touch
to meet this world in need

to be your hands and feet
open our eyes
open our minds
to serve in love and truth
to see the world renewed
renew our world

Bridge

the earth is restored by the sound of your voice
creation encountering your love through us
the kingdom of heaven revealed by your church
we're building your kingdom as we care for earth
(the) mountains and hills are now bursting in song
(the) trees lift their hands as they're singing along
the kingdom of heaven revealed by your church
we're building your kingdom as we care for earth

Everyone is an artist

I don't mean to belittle the efforts of the experts, the poets, musicians, painters, sculptors, dancers, actors: you know, all those creative types. But everyone can be an artist. If the world that God made was very good, then the one that is coming — this world made new — will be amazing. And we all have a role in this evolving beauty. Every act of kindness, act of justice, every word that gives life, every healing touch, every act of faith and of hope. These things are beautiful, they are art. They are acts of creation and not destruction, acts of love and not apathy. It is our love letter to the world.

God and the Lamb are making all things new. Will you join all of the other artists in this great work? We need you.

Glossary

Amillennialism – the belief that the 1000 years mentioned in Revelation 20:4 refers to the present era of the church.

Anthropocene – an era of Earth history where humanity is the dominant geological force.

Apocalypse – the Greek word for Revelation. The revealing or unveiling of something.

Armageddon – the great battle associated with the return of Christ in Revelation 16:16.

Atmospheric aerosols – pollutants from industry, burning of solid fuels for cooking and heating, etc. that reduce air quality and damage human health.

Baal – the Canaanite storm god.

Biogeochemical flows – flows of chemicals in the Earth System. Includes nitrogen and phosphorous, which has greatly increased due to fertiliser use.

Biosphere integrity – the stability of the living world, including biodiversity.

Carbon Direct Removal (CDR) – a method of reducing global warming by removing carbon dioxide from the air.

CFCs – Chlorofluorocarbons. Gases used as refrigerants, propellants (aerosol sprays), and solvents. Responsible for stratospheric ozone depletion.

Climate change – the total response of the climate system due to global warming, which includes sea level rise, changes in wind patterns, ocean currents, etc.

Dispensationalism – the view that history is split into distinct epochs, where God's will is progressively revealed.

Doughnut economics – a model of economics developed by Kate Raworth that respects both planetary boundaries and the need for human flourishing.

DDT – Dichlorodiphenyltrichloroethane. An environmentally damaging insecticide.

Earth System – the five spheres of the planetary system: geosphere (solid earth), atmosphere (air), hydrosphere (oceans, fresh water, rain), cryosphere (ice sheets and glaciers), and biosphere (life).

Eschatology – a branch of theology that studies the end times or last things.

Farming God's Way – a well-balanced biblical, management and technological solution for the agricultural domain.

Geoengineering – the intentional manipulation of planetary systems at a global scale.

GDP – Gross Domestic Product.

Global warming – a rise in global temperatures due to greenhouse gases released by burning fossil fuels, land use changes, and the manufacture of cement.

Great Acceleration – the increase in economic activity and subsequent impacts on the Earth System beginning in the second half of the 20th century.

Greenhouse gas – a gas that absorbs heat, warming the planet. Includes methane, nitrous oxide, and carbon dioxide.

Heaven – where God dwells and rules. Heaven is also where the dead in Christ dwell until the resurrection.

Imperialism – the extending of power by a country or corporation that involves colonisation, use of military force or economic policies.

Lyme disease – a tick carried disease, spreading in countries like the USA due to climate change.

Microplastics – small pieces of plastic less than 5 mm long.

Millennium – the 1000 year reign mentioned in Revelation 20:4.

Novel entities – long-lived human made pollutants such as plastics.

Ocean acidification – the increase in the acidity of the oceans due to the release of carbon dioxide.

Parts per million (PPM) – a measure of the concentration of carbon dioxide in the atmosphere.

Planetary boundary – a measure of the health of the Earth System.

Post-colonialism – a theoretical approach in theology that is concerned with the lasting impact of colonisation in former colonies.

Postmillennialsm – the view that the 1000 year reign of Revelation 20:4 occurs after the return of Christ and a period known as the Tribulation.

Premillennialism – the view that the 1000 year reign of Revelation 20:4 occurs before the return of Christ.

Preppers – people preparing to survive the end of civilisation.

Prolepsis – anticipation of future events. To live proleptically is to live hopefully and expectantly in the present.

Rapture – the purported removal of believers from the Earth before the Tribulation at the return of Christ in 1 Thessalonians 4:17.

Sabbath Economics – a model of economics championed by Ched Myers that focuses on biblical principles of wealth redistribution.

Sea level rise – the rise in the height of the oceans due to warming water and melting ice sheets.

September 11 (9/11) – the hijacking of four commercial airplanes and their subsequent crashing into the World Trade Centre in New York, the Pentagon in Washington, and into the ground near Shanksville, Pennsylvania.

Solar Radiation Management (SRM) – methods cool the planet by reflecting sunlight back into space.

Stratospheric ozone – a gas high in the atmosphere that absorbs harmful ultraviolet radiation. The amount of this gas has decreased due to the restrictions on the use of CFCs in industry.

Taxonomy – the branch of science concerned with the classification of living organisms.

Tiamat – the Babylonian sea goddess. Demythologised as 'the deep' in Genesis 1.

Tribulation – a period of time of great suffering before the reign of Christ, prominent in millennial views.

STUDY GUIDE

This guide is written for both individual and group use. The chapters are not of even length, and neither is every chapter explicitly biblical in content, so you may merge weeks, or swap material around, depending on the time available.

1. Houston, We Have A Problem

1. Where were you on 9/11? Or is there an event, either a human caused tragedy – public or personal – or a natural disaster that was significant to you? How did you react to it at the time? What kind of questions did it force you to ask about good and evil, and God's plan for the world?

2. Read Matthew 5:1–11 and Isaiah 6. The church often can project the idea that 'we have got it right.' How do these texts affect the way in which you think the church should address issues of evil and injustice in the world, especially given the various scandals the church has been involved in?

3. Are you optimistic or pessimistic about the future? Why?

4. The number of 400 ppm (parts per million) may seem very abstract. Why do you think scientists are having a hard time reaching the church with its message? How do stories like those of Tonga and other Pacific nations help make climate change more real? Spend some time researching the impact of climate change on the people of the Pacific and praying for them. How might you or your church help them in practical ways?

Prayer: Lord God, in the midst of all the evil and suffering in the world, keep us mindful of the fact that evil divides every human heart. We turn from our sins, the world, and the devil. Purify us as your church to go out into the world to proclaim the good news. Amen.

2. Apocalypse Now

1. There is a lot of scientific detail in this chapter. Was there anything in particular that struck you as significant, or to which you could respond personally? What kind of emotions did it produce? Do you know of specific examples of friends or people you know suffering as a result of one of these boundaries being broken?

2. Does the future concern you at all? What makes you concerned/not concerned about the planet?

3. Read Psalm 104. What do you learn about the value of the world around us to us and to God? Is there anything you find helpful like going on bushwalks, gardening, or watching documentaries to help you appreciate the world around you? Your group might like to organise an event like a bushwalk with readings of scripture and prayers.

4. Read and reflect upon Lamentations 1. In particular, think about how human actions and driving humanity into exile from the Earth. What emotions does this provoke? Do we lament enough over the state of the planet? Spend some time in prayer lamenting the state of the world, human and other than human.

Prayer: Lord we lament over the state of your good creation and how we have abused it. As we face exile from our home, we repent and pray for your mercy and forgiveness. Amen.

3. East Of Eden

1. What did you learn from the chapter about what it means to be made in the image of God and how we have failed to live up to this? Was this understanding of sin new to you? What kind of ways have you understood sin in the past?

2. How would you share the gospel with someone over a meal by using this understanding of sin and the image of God? How different would that look to more traditional approaches?

3. Why do you think that Christians often reflect more on individual sins and their impacts on our lives, rather than how they can release a larger-scale chaos?

4. How would you respond — given what you have read in the chapter — to someone who said that a weather disaster that can be associated as being more likely due to climate change, was an act of judgement by God on some specific issue?

5. How does identifying a spiritual power behind human institutions help us deal with justice issues and reconcile it with more traditional understanding of the gospel and the mission of the church? Can you see any dangers with 'demonising' institutions? What might it mean to exorcise an institution that was contributing to injustices in some way? Can you think of any institutions that need this?

Prayer: Lord God, you are a God of order, not disorder, and yet we have released disorder into your world by our actions. We pray for ourselves, our institutions, and our society, that they might be reconciled to you. We pray for the creation, that order might be restored. Amen.

4. Beam Me Up, Goddy

1. How much is technology a part of your life? Do you take it for granted? Does it add or take away from your quality of life? Think, for example, of your screen time.

2. To what extent do you agree with the idea that technology is a form of 'heavenism' and a secular religion? What signs do you see of this?

3. Read 1 Kings 18. How much do you think we turn to technology as a saviour for the problems that it has helped create? Can you think of any examples other than geoengineering?

4. If a global disaster of some sort (plague, climate change, global conflict) were to occur, how different to the 'doomsday preppers' should the approach of the church be? Do you think this is how large sections of the church would react or would they resemble the broader culture? You can find episodes of the show on YouTube.

Prayer: God of Abraham, Isaac, Jacob, and the Lord Jesus Christ. Help us to worship you alone and not our technological idols. We pray for wisdom as we adapt to a changing world. Amen.

5. It's Not The End Of The World

1. The book of Revelation is just plain weird to some. Have you ever discussed apocalyptic literature with friends outside of the church? How does the church add to their confusion? How can you explain how the book can be understood in a way that advances the gospel and work for justice?

2. Read through a few chapters out loud as a group and identify the kinds of symbols and figures you identify? Can you relate them to Hebrew Bible (Old Testament) passages or the gospels? Use a cross-reference bible if you need to.

3. Are there sections that you find problematic because of their violence or imagery?

4. How does identifying the social and political setting help our reading the text of Revelation? Does it become more or less revolutionary a book? If the church is to become a 'Revelation church,' what would it look like?

Prayer: Lord of history, we do not long for the end of the world, we do not want to live in fear, and we do not want to waste time trying to work out when you will return. Until you do, keep us faithful. Amen.

6. Who's The Boss?

1. Why do Western Christians feel like they're persecuted? Find some stories of the persecuted church from Open Doors or Voice of the Martyrs. Why is the message of Revelation such comfort to persecuted Christians? Looking again at Revelation 2–3, what kind of warning do you think Revelation has for comfortable Christians who think they are being persecuted?

2. Read Revelation 4–5. What do you learn about the rule of God and the Lamb? Why is it encouraging to you to know they are in charge now? How does this compare with your lived experience?

3. Compare the scene of Revelation 4 with Isaiah 6. How does this shape the prophetic calling of the church? Can you think of prophetic actions you could be involved in to witness to the empires of this world?

4. What difference does our view of the millennium make to caring about climate change and other justice issues?

Prayer: Lord of History, we thank you that you reign now, despite appearances to the contrary. Keep us grateful for our blessings, mindful of those who truly suffer for the gospel, and prophetic in our witness. Amen.

7. Beam Me Up, Goddy — Part 2

1. Why do you think Christians focus on heaven so much? How has this influenced how those outside of the church understand Christianity? Can you think of examples from movies or TV?

2. Do you believe in 'the rapture' as it has often been understood? If so, how have you reconciled that with the idea that the church should be involved in justice issues? Was the chapter helpful in understanding an alternative to this view? How would you discuss it with someone who thought differently?

3. What is the 'rapture in reverse'? How is this different to the traditional rapture? How does it help us with understanding a justice oriented mission of the church? How would this understanding affect how you would speak to a Christian from Kiribati about sea level rise?

4. Read Revelation 21–22. What images and ideas stand out to you? How do you react emotionally to these images? In particular, how does the theme of temple join up throughout the bible, and how does that affect your view of the church's responsibility towards issues like climate change?

Prayer: Lord of Heaven and Earth, we long for your rapture in reverse. Knowing the world has a future, help us to care for it in the present. Amen.

8. All Things New

1. The traditional way the gospel has been preached has been solely concerned for saving people's souls? Discuss.

2. How does understanding 2 Peter 3 as speaking of purification

rather than destruction change the way we understand how we live our lives? Think both about personal piety and justice issues. How would you explain this to someone who thinks the world will literally be burnt up?

3. How does Colossians 1 inform what 'all things new' means in Revelation 21:4? What difference does that make to your 'hope for heaven'? Discuss some examples of things that need to be made new. What might these things look like when made new? How does that shape how they look now?

4. What does Romans 8 tell us about the importance of the non-human creation and our relationship to it? How do you relate to the broader creation from day to day? Are you ever distressed by the way we mistreat our non-human neighbours?

5. What does 'Babel in reverse' mean for justice in general and climate justice in particular in a post-colonial world? Have you ever thought about the impacts of colonialism and the complicity of the church in colonisation and racism? Are there aspects of your thinking that are unconsciously racist?

Prayer: Lord of all things, as your people on earth, help us to be responsible in the way in which we relate to the rest of creation. Give us ears to hear from our sisters and brothers from other parts of the world, knowing that we alone do not own the truth, and are ourselves in need of repentance. Amen.

9. Renewed Economics

1. Is the phrase 'the love of money is the root of all evil, not money itself' a cop-out or the truth? How much of our thinking about money is embedded in modern assumptions about things like growth and wealth?

2. What kind of wealth redistribution systems can you think of? What have you been involved in? In what sorts of things could you or your church become involved? Think both in terms of money like microloan services (Kiva), aid and development (both personal and raising government spending to 0.7% of GDP) and goods and services like op shops and the like.

3. How can we more broadly apply the idea of Sabbath Economics at an individual and corporate level — thinking both in terms of the church and the sorts of things to lobby governments to do? You might like to re-read Leviticus 25.

4. If you were looking for up-to-date metaphors for empire to best describe our broken economic systems, what would you use? Why is it important to consider moving beyond the harlot imagery?

Prayer: Our Lord and provider, give us generous hearts and open hands to share the resources of the earth with justice. Make us forgivers of debts and not given to greed. Amen.

10. Renewed Earth

1. How have you seen or understood creation to be groaning? What difference does it make to your understanding to appreciate the context of empire behind Romans? How does that help apply Romans 8 to food production today?

2. Have you given thought to eating less or no meat? What sorts of things do you think stop people from changing their diets for the sake of others, human and other than human? Do you think texts like Romans 8 or Isaiah 65 point to a vegan future, or are there other good reasons for Christians to cut down on animal products?

3. In what kind of food based ministry can you and your church become involved? Think about community gardens, food banks, shared meals, and so on. What biblical principles do such ideas involve and how do they address climate, justice, and evangelism?

4. Bring some food items from your pantry to the study. Where does the food come from? Can you identify how it was sourced, for example, is it sustainable palm oil? Is it fair trade? Rainforest friendly?

5. How radical is saying grace in our modern age of plenty?

Prayer: Our Father in heaven, give us today our daily bread, and help us not to take more than we need. Keep us thankful in an age of both plenty and want, and willing to eat in a way that is kinder towards others. Amen.

11. Renewed Imaginations

1. Read through Revelation 4–5. What difference does it make that we understand these passages as hymns or songs for how we read and apply the text?

2. Sit down with some of your favourite songs and examine what they say about heaven and our destiny. How would you re-write them in light of the ideas presented in this book?

3. What role does art play in imagining a world where all things are made new? Do you have any music, poem/spoken word, theatre, movie or similar that inspires you?

4. Reflect on the Dawn's song lyrics and the poem from the start of the book. What emotions do they provoke? Do they inspire you to care more for the planet? Is there something you feel inspired to write, paint, draw, or some other form of artistic expression to give voice to your fears, laments, hopes, or desire for change?

Prayer: Creator of all, your Spirit gives creative talents to your church. With these gifts, help us to imagine a world made new, and to live and work imaginatively towards this world. Amen.